In Bed

MY YEAR OF FOOLIN' AROUND

In Bed

MY YEAR OF
FOOLIN' AROUND

BRENT L. KENDRICK, PH.D.

LUMINARE PRESS
WWW.LUMINAREPRESS.COM

In Bed: My Year of Foolin' Around
Copyright © 2023 by Brent L. Kendrick, Ph.D.

All rights reserved. This book or any portion thereof may not be reproduced or used in any manner whatsoever without the express written permission of the publisher, except for the use of brief quotations in a book review.

Printed in the United States of America
Cover art by Mike Caplanis—acclaimed artist, illustrator, and caricaturist—based on the essay "In Bed with Famous (and Not-So-Famous) Writers" (249–53).

Luminare Press
442 Charnelton St.
Eugene, OR 97401
www.luminarepress.com

LCCN: 2023903257
ISBN: 979-8-88679-246-1

*Dedicated to
Audrey,*

*my oldest sister, who listened patiently,
eagerly, joyfully, and lovingly
each Sunday night
as I read these essays to her over the telephone
one-by-one, week-by-week.*

In
Memory
of
My Partner

Patrick Allen Duff
(17 March 1960–28 January 2021)

LIST OF BED LINENS

A Special Sheet for My Faithful Blog Readers 1
An Invitation to Join the Author In Bed 5

Touching Lives through Giving 13
A Cursive New Year's Resolution 20
The Power of Consistency and Persistence 23
The Final Drive 26
Call and Response 29
Honoring an Angel 35
What a Way to Live! 39
Running Reference 42
I'm a Spring Teaser 45
My Imaginary Guests 51
Spaces and Habits of Famous (and Not-So-Famous) Writers 56
Two Ways of Looking at the World 61
Baking Up My Past 65
Heading Out 71
Get Behind Me, Satan! 74
In Praise of Bridge Builders 78
Get Behind Me, Satan—REVISITED 85
Glimpses of My Father's Hands 90

Fit as a Fiddle: The Inefficient Way	94
Take Two | Fit as a Fiddle: The Intentional Way	100
The Joy of Weeding	103
Oh, No! Sourdough!	109
Directions to the Magical Land of Ideas	116
In Praise of Work	120
The Circle Is Unbroken	126
OHIO on My Mind	129
The Final Drive: The Chilling Backstory	135
Wrapping My Head Around Age	140
Living with a Writer	146
Take Two: Living with a Writer—More Frostian Moments	155
Take Three. Living with a Writer: Owning Up to My Own Eccentricities	161
Take Four. Living with A Writer: Modern Applications of Ancient Writing Artifacts	170
Gr!t 'R Done!	182
The Story of Angel Falls	189
Ten Guaranteed Tips to Increase Blog Traffic | Top-Rated and 100% Unproven!	197
Why an Education Matters: The Softer Side	207
Piecing Together the Pieces of a Tale	212
Less Is Not Always More Until It Is	223
Writers: Our Forever-Friends	231

Foolin' Around with Time	239
Two, Together	244
In Bed with Famous (and Not-So-Famous) Writers	249
A Wardrobe of My Own	254
It's Not a Corset. Don't Force It.	259
My Gardening Attire	264
A Halloween Obsession	270
The Other Side	280
Celebrating the Gateway to Who I Am	287
Hor(r)o(r)scopic Contemplations	292
The Joy of Baking	298
My Literary Fruitcakes	303
Turning Towards	312
Growing Up More than Once	316
Fruitcake Magic	323
Finding Far More than My Fitbit	326
About the Author	332

A Special Sheet for My Faithful Blog Readers

"If a tree falls in the forest and no one is around to hear it, does it make a sound?"

We have all grappled with the age-old question, "If a tree falls in the forest and no one is around to hear it, does it make a sound?"

No doubt, a physicist would answer with a resounding, "Yes. The existence of sound is objective and does not depend on its being heard."

On the other hand, some philosophers might take a contrary view, arguing that sound is subjective, existing only in our minds.

I often think about that brain teaser late at night when I should be sleeping. Instead of sleeping, however, I look at the statistics for my blog—*The Wired Researcher*. That's where these essays first appeared during 2021–2022. Even at my age, I still need validation!

I ended up with a confirmation. "You're reading my blog! Therefore, it is! Therefore, I am!"

In fact, a lot of you are reading my blog: 6,625 from 59 countries all around the world. I am in awe:

- Australia
- Austria
- Bangladesh
- Belize
- Bhutan
- Bosnia & Herzegovina
- Brazil
- Bulgaria
- Canada
- China
- Czech Republic
- Denmark
- Ecuador
- Egypt
- France
- Germany
- Greece
- Guatemala
- Hong Kong SAR China
- Hungary
- India
- Indonesia
- Ireland
- Italy
- Japan
- Kenya
- Lithuania
- Luxembourg
- Malaysia
- Mexico
- Morocco
- Nepal
- Netherlands
- Nigeria
- Norway
- Pakistan
- Philippines
- Poland
- Portugal
- Qatar
- Romania
- Russia
- Saudi Arabia
- Serbia
- Singapore
- Slovenia
- South Africa
- South Korea
- Spain
- Sri Lanka
- Swaziland
- Sweden
- Switzerland
- Turkey
- Turkmenistan
- Ukraine
- United Kingdom
- United States
- Vietnam
- Ukraine
- United Kingdom
- United States
- Vietnam

I have no idea how you found your way into my life but knowing that you were out there reading my posts strengthened me and uplifted me during a year when I needed to be strengthened and uplifted.

Thank you from the bottom of my heart.

An Invitation *to* Join the Author *In Bed*

Take my word for it. I never—absolutely never—intended to fool around in bed, certainly not every day, seven days a week, for an entire year.

Ironically, it wasn't until I couldn't fool around in bed that I actually started foolin' around. Keep reading, and I'll explain.

It is a truth—universally acknowledged—that all couples have their own daily rituals that are as established and as given as the sun coming up, the sun going down, or the hands of a clock moving clockwise. So it was with the many rituals that my late partner and I enjoyed for the twenty years that we were together. One of our favorites was one that we did in bed. (Relax. This book is rated safe for anyone of any reading age.)

We had the habit of going to bed each night precisely at 8 o'clock. I would gently massage Allen's head and scalp until he dozed off to sleep. Sometimes, I am certain that I dozed off first. But, if I did, I was unawares, and Allen never mentioned it. Maybe I kept right on rubbing after I fell asleep. Who knows.

And in keeping with the rules of our Habitualist Order, we awoke without alarm the next morning at 4 o'clock. Well, I caused my students great alarm, sometimes, when I responded to their emails at that time of day—some did not even know that time of day existed—while I waited for the coffee to brew and while I readied up for my daily indoor 20-mile bike ride. Biking was one of my rules of our Habitualist Order. Allen had some rules of his own that only he followed, such as reading *The New York Times*, *The Washington Post*, and *The Wall Street Journal* after the coffee had brewed and he could start enjoying a cup.

But the 4 o'clock morning ritual is only related tangentially to the backstory of this book. It's the 8 o'clock nightly ritual that matters.

Allen died unexpectedly on January 28, 2021, after a short, three-month battle with lung cancer.

After his death, I continued going to bed and getting up at the same ritualized times. What else could I do? He and I had done it that way for twenty years. Yet without Allen, the ritual lost its meaning. Without Allen, the ritual was empty.

But I kept at it anyway. Looking back, that was probably a good thing. It gave structure and a semblance of normalcy to the early days of the COVID-19 Pandemic when the entire world longed for a semblance of structure and normalcy.

More important, perhaps, it gave rest during a time when I needed rest as I grieved a grief that knew no rest. It gave rest as I threw myself more and more into my teaching and my research. It gave rest as I planned an elaborate celebration of Allen's life and legacy to be held at our mountaintop home later in the year.

Establishing the Patrick Allen Duff Endowed Memorial Scholarship at Laurel Ridge Community College (formerly Lord Fairfax Community College) was the easy part of planning the ceremony. Allen was an educator and a certified surgical technologist at Valley Health's Shenandoah Memorial Hospital. I set up the scholarship to support students enrolled in the health sciences, with preference given to those enrolled in the surgical technologist program.

The harder tasks of getting ready for the celebration consumed my every waking hour during the months ahead.

Giving the house a deep cleaning kept me busy during the cold, icy, snowy winter months.

Readying our specimen gardens on a 20-acre mountaintop, largely in the woods, took all of Spring. Even when Allen was alive and we gardened together, as we always did, it was always a challenge. Doing it by myself seemed beyond doing, yet I had no choice but to do it because we both took great pride in our gardens. How could I have a celebration of Allen's life without having the gardens at their best. Most of our gardens were well-established and needed little more than Spring cleanup and fresh mulch.

But since we always enjoyed a tropical touch in the gardens as well as on our decks, cleanup was followed by mass plantings of Elephant Ears, Hibiscus, and SunPatiens.

Spring turned into one of our hottest and driest summers ever. I had to water the new plantings daily. Day after day, I dragged water hoses from one garden bed to the next. I watered deck plants early in the day, but I had to do it again sometimes after dinner.

Everything was shaping up beautifully except for the last garden bed that Allen and I had begun but did not get to finish. We had planted some hardy bananas at the lower end, but we hadn't done much else. That area still required major cleanup, design, and landscaping.

I grappled fiercely with that challenge, especially since June was upon me, and I had no plan. I was at a loss.

It was during that period of grappling that Allen spoke to me in a dream, and his voice is as clear to me now as it was then, as it ever was and as it ever will be:

"Build my garden."

When I awakened the next morning, it was as if Allen's dream command brought with it a perfect design in more ways than one. I knew that what Allen told me to do wasn't as much about his garden as it was about my doing something that would bring me a sense of healing, that would give me a renewed sense of purpose.

I walked down to our unfinished last garden and, in an instant, I could see the shape of a heart. I paced it off, and a 25-foot-wide heart started to become a reality. As I walked back and forth, up and down, Allen's "Build my garden" echoed through my mind. Step by step, I knew that a heart-shape would be the focal point of our last garden. I knew that the heart would be a Zen Garden. I knew that I would scatter Allen's ashes within that heart garden, just as one day mine will be scattered there joining his. Scattering our ashes in the gardens had been an agreed-upon plan (with legal documentation to support our wishes) going all the way back to the early years of our partnership. Since I was older, though, I always thought that Allen would be the one honoring my final wishes.

But here I was preparing the garden to honor Allen's wishes. Building the garden took me all of June and the first two weeks of July. I framed the heart in flexible bronze metal. Inside, I framed three circles, one centered in each lobe at the top of the heart and one centered near the tip of the heart. In the upper circles, I planted Angelina Sedum—Allen was, after all, my angel—and in the lower circle I planted a Southern Magnolia that his colleagues at Shenandoah Memorial Hospital gave me in his honor.

I filled the rest of the heart with three tons of white pea gravel that I brought home in fifty-pound bags and spread, bag by bag, with tears and love.

Obviously, a garden's not a garden without flowers. I surrounded the heart with alternating red and white SunPatiens. And since it was a Zen Garden, I had a Zen rake custom made. It leans against the stone bench that my two oldest sisters and I bought in Allen's memory. It's on the west side of the garden, looking deep into the heart.

After six months, I had everything ready for "Celebrating the Life and Legacy of Patrick Allen Duff" on July 24, 2021.

Early that morning, Allen's mother and brother and I scattered his ashes in the heart garden. Using the Zen rake, we softened them into the pebbles, creating concentric heart shapes within the master heart.

Later that afternoon, neighbors and friends (who knew us both) along with Allen's hospital colleagues—all dressed in their surgical scrubs to honor him as a Surgical Technologist—joined us at home to enjoy some of Allen's favorite foods and drinks and to pay tribute to his lasting love and lasting legacy.

I have not a doubt in the world: Allen was there, through it all, looking down, smiling his twinkly smile, whispering in his gentle voice, "Well done, my Love."

From then and continuing through fall, I stood by Allen's heart daily, communing with him and with that which is bigger than him, bigger than me, bigger than you, and bigger than all of us. Some days—warmer ones—I walked the gravel barefoot as I Zen raked, so that I might be more mindful of death's sting and God's love.

In early November, I replaced the SunPatiens surrounding the heart with Dwarf Boxwoods. Immortality. Over time, they will grow together and create a hedge. Protection.

By December, my outdoor labors had ended. I found myself indoors again. Indoors with me. Indoors with Ruby, our dog. Indoors with all the memories. Indoors with all the rituals, including going to bed each night at 8 o'clock. Indoors. Indoors. Indoors. Again and again and again.

One night as I lay in bed, doing my best to fall asleep but finding that doing my best was not good enough, I realized that the old ritual could never exist anymore. How could it? Allen was gone. I realized that I needed to create a new ritual, one that would be meaningful to me.

In a flash, it occurred to me that I could continue to go to bed at 8 o'clock, but instead of lying there trying to go to sleep, I could lie there and fool around with words and ideas until sleep found me. I could lie there in bed and write. I could lie there in bed and ... blog. I could resurrect my *The Wired Researcher* blog going all the way back to 2012. I could breathe new life into it, simply by writing every night while lying in bed, right on the smartphone that Allen had given me.

And that's just what I did. From that night forward, writing in bed at night on my Smartphone became my new ritual. Some nights, I write until 9:30. Some nights, 10:30. On occasion, 11:30. Am I a wild party animal or what!

I love my new ritual in ways that I never expected.

For starters, it's almost like meditation, and, if it's not like meditation, then it's certainly like mindfulness. Nothing exists except my Smartphone, my fingers, and my ideas. During my nightly writing time, I have no past. I have no future. I have only the silky soft luxuriousness of the present, as I fool around with words and ideas for as long as I want until the words and ideas and the foolin' around cradle me into soft and peaceful slumber.

Another thing that I like about foolin' around in bed is that, for the first time in my life, I am giving myself permission to write light-hearted personal essays. My decades of prior writing had been research-oriented and scholarly. Now it seemed that the time had come for me to enjoy a new way to fool around with ideas and words. Even on my days of heaviest heart, I found myself eager to go to bed at night because I knew that my draft blog post would be waiting for me.

Equally important, foolin' around in bed made me walk the talk that I had talked to my Creative Writing students for decades:

So, you want to write? What's stopping you?
Write. Just write.
Write one page a day. Just one page a day.
After a year, you'll have 365 pages.

I wanted to write. I wanted to write every night. I wanted to publish my blog post every Monday. I did just that for an entire year. Lo! I ended up with the book that you're reading.

I never had any intention of publishing this book, of giving life everlasting to my year of foolin' around in bed. All that I set out to do was come up with a meaningful bedtime ritual.

But here we are. You and I. Together. Hopefully, you're reading this book in bed, under the sheets. That's exactly how I wrote this book. In bed. Under the sheets. I am so glad that you bought the book. I'm so glad that you let me share with you the book's backstory.

What will make me even more joyous, however, is if you find at least one essay in this collection that speaks to you, that resonates with you, that comforts you.

As you read, I hope that you are comforted in knowing that:

- Our sorrows are shared sorrows.
- Our sufferings are shared sufferings.
- Our joys are shared joys.
- Our triumphs are shared triumphs.
- Our lives are shared lives.

We are not alone.

DECEMBER 28, 2021

Touching Lives through Giving

"We make a living by what we get, but we make a life by what we give."

— Sir Winston Churchill
(1874-1965; British statesman, soldier, writer, and Prime Minister of the United Kingdom.)

As a student and as a professor, I have learned some of my best life-lessons through classroom repartee—those lively, light-hearted and spontaneous exchanges that give way to intellectual magic.

As this season of celebrating and gifting winds down and as the year 2021 that gave us all fantods comes to a thankful end, I am reminded of one those magically powerful exchanges from long, long ago. However, its initial significance has been outdistanced by its long-range influence: perpetual mind food (more accurately, soul food) given freely (perhaps, unknowingly). It matters little or not at all whether it was intended for mind or soul. It matters little or not at all whether it was given deliberately or unknowingly. I have savored it and relished it down through the years.

I was a 25-year-old graduate student in an American Literature class at the University of South Carolina. One of the short stories that the late Professor Joel Myerson gave us to read was "Life Everlastin'" by Mary E. Wilkins Freeman.

I knew that I had better know all the intricacies of the story before going to class. It was, after all, a graduate class. Equally important, the class was so small that we met in a small conference room and sat around a small oval conference table, with Professor Myerson charismatically leading us. Youthful (only several years older than I and the rest of the class), energetic, and intellectually stimulating, he inspired us to come to class prepared to engage in stimulating conversations, demonstrating our abilities to analyze literary works. Professor Myerson was a Formalist and a Textual Bibliographer. Nothing mattered but the literary work itself. Nothing mattered but the text. Without doubt, I needed to give that story my best.

I had been introduced to Freeman the semester before when another professor gave us some of her stories to read, and I had fallen in love with her fiction. Having to read her "Life Everlastin'" was a joy for me.

I read the story initially, and I gave it a second reading, and I am confident that I gave it yet a third reading. Professor Myerson loved giving literary works a close reading. So did I.

I wondered what take he would give the story.

Would he give it a close reading based on the story's accurate depiction of New England village life?

Would he give it a close reading focusing on the sharp character delineations of the two diametrically opposite sisters? Maybe Mrs. Ansel who is totally preoccupied with being fitted for a new bonnet: "She was always pleased and satisfied with anything that was her own, and possession was to her the law of beauty."

Maybe her spinster, non-churchgoing sister, Luella Norcross, who was always giving to others, who was always going "somewheres after life-everlastin' blossoms. ... If she was not in full orthodox favor among the respectable part of the town, her fame was bright among the poor and maybe lawless element, whom she befriended."

Would he take the conversation up a notch or three by pitting seemingly shallow churchgoers (e. g. Mrs. Ansel) against those of seemingly deeper convictions (e. g. Luella Norcross) who stayed home and foraged the fields in search of life everlasting blossoms to give away, much in the same spirit of Emily Dickinson's "Some keep the Sabbath going to Church"? Or would he perhaps compare Mrs. Ansel's apparent lack of religious depth to E. E. Cummings' poem "the Cambridge ladies who live in furnished souls"?

Or might he go even deeper and explore the story as a subtle indictment of religion similar to the charge that Mark Twain gave organized religion in his "Jumping Frog of Calaveras County." Who does not recall the fact that Dan'l, the frog, was so full of quail-shot that he when he went to hop, "he couldn't budge: he was planted as solid as a church and he couldn't no more stir than if he was anchored out."

And, without doubt, Professor Myerson had to give the backbone of the story lots of attention: Luella's discovery of two murdered neighbors; her discovery that the alleged murderer (John Gleason) was holed up in a vacant house next to her home; her realization that she had to give him up to the law; and her dramatic decision that she had to give in to her faith: *"I don't see any other way out of it for John Gleason!"*

I went to class fully prepared to give my own two cents worth on any or all of those angles.

Indeed, we gave all of them lively pursuits, all that is save one. We did **not** discuss what seemed to me to be the very essence of the story: life everlasting.

I was stunned. No. I was surprised. I suspected that it was with deliberate intent that Professor Myerson did not take the conversation in the direction of the story's obvious eschatological meaning: the destiny of the soul and of humankind after death. I knew that he wanted us to think about—and talk about—that aspect of the story independently without giving us any coaching.

Silence fell over the class.

There I sat, feeling that we had an obligation to move toward the eschatological and that he had an obligation to take us there. I gave a question that broke the silence.

"So, Professor Myerson, what exactly **is** life everlasting?" I was hoping that the question I gave him would make him squirm.

But he had the upper hand and knew precisely how to make me squirm. An expert in the Socratic method, he gave the question right back to me. "What do **you** think it is, Brent?"

Aha! The chance for repartee had arrived! I gave in to the moment. I seized it.

I looked him square in the eye, with an ever-so-innocent look, as I gave him nothing more than the straight botanical definition—a flowering plant in the mint family, noted for its healing, medicinal properties. Then I rambled on about Luella's inclusion of life-everlasting in the pillows that she made and gave to help neighbors, especially those who were asthmatic.

I could tell that Professor Myerson was on to me. I was known for this sort of academic maneuvering, and he was not amused. He gave me his over-the-glasses look that he was so skilled in giving.

I waited to see what he would say—he always said something whenever he gave that look—but we both had to give up for the time being. Class ended.

But Professor Myerson always had a way of getting his way, in one way or another. This time would be no exception. A few days later he stopped me in the hall. With a twinkle in his eyes, he gave me an offprint of one of his articles that had been published in a scholarly magazine. On the front, he had written:

> *Brent,*
> *This is life everlasting.*
> *Joel Myerson*

"What does **that** mean?" I pondered, as I walked away. I confess, however, to no small degree of jealousy. At that point in my life, I was unpublished. Nothing had appeared in print under my name. But here was Professor Myerson—already a well-known, published scholar, albeit a young one—giving me an inscribed, offprint of his most recent scholarly article.

I had to give this gift more thought.

Did he realize the full impact of his gift?

Or was he a young professor giving me the selfsame banter that I had given him in class?

Or was his gift more serious? Was he giving me another way to look at life everlasting—perhaps different from the traditional eschatological view? Was he suggesting that we live on forever through what we share with others, especially ideas that are immortalized in print? Maybe so. After all, some cultures believe that we live as long as our name is spoken. If that was his intent, he succeeded. Here I am blogging about him, nearly fifty years later. Here I am placing his name in public view, albeit this time under my own name. Whoever reads this blog post will speak his name, even if silently. They may even share my story with others. **Professor Myerson continues to live.**

His inscribed offprint had an immediate impact. It gave me some extra encouragement not only to finish my doctoral degree in American Literature but also to publish my own scholarly articles and books. I wanted to give my ideas away to others through the printed word. When that happened for the first time, I was thrilled, and the high that I experience now through being published is as high as it was then.

But here's the greater truth. His gift touched my soul perhaps more than it touched my mind. It kept me mindful that as human beings we all have needs—immediate and long-range.

It kept me mindful that the needs are great, always and in all ways. In fact, during these pandemic years, the needs are daunting. No. They are staggering.

Fortunately, for us and for others, the ways that we can touch lives through giving— whatever it is that we have within ourselves to give—are countless.

We can give our *ideas.*
We can give our *talents.*
We can give our *time.*
We can give our *purse.*
We can give our *love.*

We can give ***ourselves—mind, body, and soul.***

Our gifts need not be large. Our gifts need not be given with any expectation of ever knowing how much they touch others' lives or of how much they impact others' lives. This much, though, we do know about giving. It connects us to one another. It binds us to one another. It makes us aware of our relatedness to one another.

Who knows? Maybe, just maybe, when we touch others' lives by giving freely of ourselves—without any expectation of receiving anything in return—we might be edging our way, even if unawares, closer and closer and closer toward the very essence of life everlasting.

DECEMBER 31, 2021

A Cursive New Year's Resolution

"We spend January 1 walking through our lives, room by room, drawing up a lot of work to be done, cracks to be patched. Maybe this year, to balance this list, we ought to walk through the rooms of our lives ... not looking for flaws, but for potential."

— ELLEN GOODMAN
(b. 1941; American journalist and syndicated columnist.)

I have never been a big believer in New Year's resolutions. In fact, I have never ushered in a new year with any firm resolution to do—or not to do—something. This year, however, I may make an exception. This year, I may make one, single solitary resolution.

Here's why.

Last week I sat down to write some personal notes to a few alumni of Lord Fairfax Community College where I am a professor of English. It seemed to me that the personal touch would be the right touch.

Armed with my blue-ink, roller ball pen—and just barely into my second note—I realized that something was wrong. My fingers felt cramped. My upper arm muscles felt atrophied. My relaxed and cursive grace of yesteryear was gone.

I was "drawing" my letters. They were tight and cramped like my unused writing muscles.

Once upon a time, I knew how to use those muscles, and they were robust and firm.

Once upon a time, I knew how to write naturally and smoothly and uniformly.

But that was long ago when I wrote letters in cursive—in longhand—with my special pen, on my special paper.

Suddenly, I realized that I had not written in longhand for a long, long time. For nearly four decades, I have word processed nearly everything. I just don't "do" longhand anymore, beyond the mechanical "Enjoy the holidays" or "Feel better soon" or "I love you" scrawls. How strange, especially considering that I love reading published volumes of letters and, in fact, I spent ten years locating, deciphering, and editing the letters of New England writer Mary E. Wilkins Freeman, and I am now working on a revised, updated, two-volume edition.

Suddenly, I realized that I have not received many personal longhand letters and notes in a long time either. Over time, the volume has decreased steadily, and I no longer need trunks and file cabinets to store those personal artifacts, treasured *objets d'art*. Handwritten notes from friends and family have been hardly better than the scribbles I have sent their way. *Touché*.

Paradoxically, I receive far more communiqués these days. My smartphone goes with me everywhere because I want to stay connected and be accessible. My email inbox has nearly reached its maximum storage capacity. Truthfully, those messages are far more frequent, far more detailed, and far more extensive than the longhand letters of yesteryear.

I store these electronic messages in virtual folders, where, hopefully, they will remain, virtually forever. But I doubt it. Maybe I should start printing those messages. Maybe I should start putting them away somewhere for safekeeping.

I'm thankful that I sat down to write personal notes to some former students. Writing them has given me a wake-up call. I realize that some traditions can be preserved alongside all the marvelous advances that propel us magically forward.

Ironically, here I sit at my computer on New Year's Day, pecking away at the keyboard, wondering: What else in my life is cramped? Atrophied? What else should I re-train? Re-learn? Preserve? Potentialize?

For now, I'll resolve to make one—just one—New Year's resolution for this year and this year only. I'll strive to renew my old tradition of reaching out to folks from time to time with longhand letters—my hand, my pen, my ink, my paper, my postage stamp. My arm, my hand, my mind, my heart, my soul—retrained to a cursive tradition that is natural and social and graceful.

JANUARY 10, 2022

The Power of Consistency and Persistence

"'Tis true there is much to be done [...] but stick to it steadily, and you will see great Effects, for constant Dropping wears away Stones, and by Diligence and Patience the Mouse ate in two the Cable; and little Strokes fell great Oaks, as Poor Richard says in his Almanack, the Year I cannot just now remember."

— BENJAMIN FRANKLIN
(1706-1790; American statesman, author, publisher, scientist, inventor, and diplomat; *Poor Richard Improved*, 1758.)

A few years ago, I bought a new indoor bike. I had to. The axle on my old bike snapped, just like that. I wasn't surprised: I had biked 20 to 30 miles on it every day—seven days a week—for the previous eight years.

I was surprised, however, by the total mileage: 73,000. Actually, I was stunned. If I had biked from West Quoddy Head (Maine) to Point Arena (California)—the two most distant points within the mainland United States—it would have been 2,892 miles. Round trip: 5,784 miles. I had biked from sea to shining sea and all the way back again, the equivalent of 13 times.

Incredible. Impossible. Yet, I did it, even though I had never intended to do so. All that I had set out to do was to bike regularly—no, faithfully, every day, seven days a week.

I've been thinking about other things that I have done regularly.

Like the $25 Series E Savings Bonds that I started purchasing bi-weekly in the 1960s when I was in college and kept purchasing for decades. When the time came to buy my first home, I was surprised by my investment. Actually, I was stunned. I had a down payment for a row house in the shadow of the United States Capitol. My own piece of the American Dream.

Incredible. Impossible. Yet, I did it, even though I had never intended to do so. All that I had set out to do was to save regularly—no, faithfully, every other week.

Or what about the pocket change I started saving daily when my niece/goddaughter was born? That first year, pennies. The next, pennies and nickels. Then, pennies, nickels, and dimes. Pennies, nickels, dimes, and quarters followed. Finally, all of my pocket change. I saved it regularly—no, faithfully, every day, seven days a week. Seventeen years later, when it came time for Minnie to go to college, it was time for me to take all of my coffee cans—chock-full of daily pocket change—to the bank. I was surprised. Actually, I was stunned. The total? Nearly $10,000, not nearly enough for even one year's tuition, but certainly more than enough for textbooks, computers, cell phones, and even a $500 Series EE Savings Bond. A future as bright as a shiny new penny.

I shared these examples and my essay-in-progress with my students. One emailed me later, "I think your essay would be marvelous. Your three examples are kind of unbelievable, but, of course, anyone could bike 13 times round trip across America or save up a down payment for a house or start a college fund if they tackled those goals a little bit at a time, fairly regularly."

Yes, Bonnie: that's my point, precisely. Anyone can achieve any goal—regardless of how impossible or how incredible it may seem—simply by tackling it a little bit at a time regularly and faithfully.

Anyone can.

Anyone.

JANUARY 17, 2022

The Final Drive

"Knocking? No. Pinging? No. Tapping? Yes. Tapping. A rhytnmic tapping, tapping, tapping, growing louder and louder and louder as I climbed my mountain, homeward. Neighbors stared. Dogs ran. This was a palpable noise that required reckoning."

My two-door Jeep Wrangler was a substantial investment. I took good care of it, hoping that it would last forever. I felt that it deserved the longevity that I desired, so I came up with a fool-proof, sure-fire plan.

I read the owner's manual carefully and repeatedly.

I vowed: never skip scheduled service appointments.

I pledged: always review the maintenance and service checklists, always review the safety checklists, and always review the fluids checklist.

Easy promises for something worth so much. Right?

I swore to review faithfully all the other checklists. Tires—pressure, tread, spare, jack/tools. Lights—headlights, hazard lights, park lights, and fog lights.

I even swore that I would check all the general things that need periodic checking: hoses, filters, batteries, and belts.

My fool-proof plan worked well.

My Wrangler aged over the years, but gracefully so.

Fading headlights didn't matter much since I don't drive a lot at night anyway.

Failing sound systems mattered more. Silence is golden for some, but not for me. I figured out with great speed how to jerry-rig my iPod to a Bluetooth speaker. Voila! I had perfect surround-sound gospel music wherever I went.

The miles crept up and up and up. I couldn't turn back the odometer, but I couldn't stand to look at it either. So I opted to use just the trip-odometer to track single, solitary journeys. Those lower numbers comforted. But, in the back of my head, I was mindful that the real engine mileage was getting higher and higher.

And then came the day when I forgot to recharge my jerry-rigged sound system. Alas! No music.

For once, I heard internal sounds, and they were not what I expected. I had never heard such reverberations before.

Knocking? No. Pinging? No. Tapping? Yes. Tapping. A rhythmic tapping, tapping, tapping, growing louder and louder and louder as I climbed my mountain, homeward. Neighbors stared. Dogs ran. This was a palpable noise that required reckoning.

My local mechanic figured that heavier oil with an additive would reduce the friction and lower the noise. His concoction became a new part of my old plan to keep the Wrangler going.

Sadly, the remedy didn't last long. The tapping grew louder and louder, even after I recharged my sound system and regained my soul music. I knew that it was time for my Wrangler to go back to the dealership, back to the manufacturer.

Off I drove.

It only took an hour for the diagnosis: faulty hydraulic lifters. My heart sank.

It rose again, though, when I heard the recommended fix: replace the lifters. We all believed the old Wrangler still had lots of miles ahead.

It took hours to get the job done. One led to two; two led to three; three led to four; and four led to saddened faces.

Yes. The lifters had been replaced, but the repair hadn't worked. The problem was deeper. The whole engine had aged, had given away.

That was it. Finis!

Little did I know—when I drove my Wrangler back to the dealership, back to the maker—that I would not drive it again.

I emailed a friend about my dilemma.

"Does this mean your poor Wrangler is in the shop getting that rattle fixed? Or worse …???" she probed.

"Worse," I answered. "It looks like the engine is shot."

"Awww, I'm sorry. Wranglers are sort of human, aren't they?"

"Yes," I mused. "Both are wrangling for the final drive."

JANUARY 21, 2022

Call and Response

"We seize the unrealistic question—the call—as an opportunity to formulate a response. Maybe my 'call' and our 'responses'—yours; mine; my students'—might be just enough to anchor us, to ground us, to keep us steady, and to keep us connected to what matters most."

A few months before Daniel Boorstin retired in 1987 as the 12th Librarian of Congress, I had the honor to interview him. It was a rare opportunity. Armed with pencils and pad, I was readied with more than an ample number of questions, the answers to which I hoped might reveal new insights into the man whose prolific, prize-winning books included the trilogy: *The Americans: The Colonial Experience* (1958); *The Americans: The National Experience* (1965); and *The Americans: The Democratic Experience* (1973).

I still remember one of those questions.

I wanted to know, as preposterous as I knew the question to be, what book in the Library of Congress he would keep if he had to throw every book away save one.

I still remember Dr. Boorstin's response. It stings as much now as it did then.

"Oh, I can't answer a question like that. It's not realistic."

Of course, he couldn't. After all, the Library of Congress is the largest library in the world with more than 25 million cataloged books.

Nonetheless, he proceeded to respond to my unrealistic question.

"I might say the *Oxford English Dictionary* (*OED*). When dictators burn books—let me say the first books to keep are the books that would be burned by a dictator. I'm saddened that people in parts of the world ... can't read what they want. We should weep for our fellow human beings who can't read whatever they want."

You would think that I would have learned a lesson about asking unrealistic questions.

And I did.

But if you're thinking that I learned not to ask unrealistic questions, you're wrong.

What I learned is this: ask the questions even if they might be perceived as unrealistic.

And that is exactly what I have always done. And that is exactly what I will keep on doing.

It should come as no surprise, then, when I tell you that I love asking my students questions, even unrealistic ones.

Just last week, smackdab at the beginning of the semester, I tossed one to my Creative Writing students:

"*'What important lesson have you learned during the COVID-19 Pandemic?' Write a 500-600-word essay responding to the question.*"

I had no sooner given the assignment than Dr. Boorstin's comment started reverberating in my memory. "I can't answer a question like that."

But after the echo quieted, I remembered that Dr. Boorstin

responded to my question anyway, unrealistic as he considered it to have been.

And I remember so vividly that his response joyed me, thrilled me—not so much for the content (though I think that his selection of *OED* was a stellar choice)—but more because he graciously went right ahead and responded to a question that he had just stingingly characterized as unrealistic!

Truth be told, it wasn't until just now—this very moment, actually—that I realized how successful I was with that interview. I went into the interview simply hoping that I might gain at least one new, unique insight into this acclaimed historian. And I did! By asking my unrealistic question, I gained a priceless response: Dr. Boorstin's statement that the *OED* might be the one book from the millions of books in the Library of Congress that he would save.

Search and explore, if you will, all the published interviews with Dr. Boorstin, and I daresay that you will not find this little nugget anywhere other than in the September/October 1987 issue of *Insights: The Library of Congress Professional Association Newsletter* that published the full interview.

But I digress, as I am so inclined to do, as I so love to do when I'm foolin' around with ideas and words.

Let's get back to my students, wherever it was that I left them before my digression caused my moment of forgetfulness! Ah, there they are: I found them again. I usually do! It seems that they might be talking about how preposterous the topic is that I asked them to explore, how unrealistic it is.

If they feel that way, I get it. I feel that way, too. No doubt, you do, too. No doubt, we all feel that way because we have all gone through so much during a pandemic that has lasted for two years and that threatens to dog us into the future. Globally. Nationally. Personally.

How do we cope with the challenging times ahead, whatever they might be?

Maybe, just maybe, we make it through the same way that my students will make it through as they write about what they have learned.

Maybe, just maybe, we take a moment to pause.

Maybe, just maybe, we take a moment or three or more from all the busy-ness that so often preempts the genuinely important things in our lives.

We let our minds wander. We pause in wonder. We think about what we have learned. We reflect.

We seize the unrealistic question—the call—as an opportunity to formulate a response. Maybe my "call" and our "responses"—yours; mine; my students'—might be just enough to anchor us, to ground us, to keep us steady, and to keep us connected to what matters most.

I have no idea how my students will respond to the call—absolutely no idea. I am writing this blog days before I will have seen their submissions. But I am confident that they will respond. And it won't be because of a grade. It will be because they have an opportunity to sort through it all.

It will be an opportunity for them to explore a question that, perhaps, no one has asked them to explore before, especially with the requirement that they chronicle their explorations in writing.

As they sort through it all and share what they have learned, I reserve to them the right to preface their lessons learned with the same caveat that Dr. Boorstin used to preface his response: "I *might* say [...]."

Tomorrow, my students **might** change their minds and explore another lesson learned. Actually, I hope that they do!

Whatever it is they might say, I will value, honor, and

respect their responses. For they will have done what I hope each of us will do as we grapple with a pandemic that baffles science and scientists and that requires daily changes to the game plan.

Respond. Write. Distill.

Since my students have to grapple with and respond to my unrealistic question, it seems to me that I should have to do the same. It seems to me that I should have to sort through my own pandemic experiences and arrive at a lesson that I have learned.

And that's exactly what I'm doing in this post.

What I have learned (re-discovered, if you will) is how much I love fooling around with ideas and words. It brings me great delight. It always has. As a child, I fooled around with ideas and words in the dictionary, letting one definition lead me to the next and that one to the next and so on, just as my mother ran reference in her Biblical commentary books. It was so easy to get lost running after ideas and words. Sometimes I even lost myself.

More important, though, sometimes while fooling around with ideas and words, I landed upon moments when a great calm washed over me and comforted me and made me believe that everything might be all right after all.

It's akin to what Robert Frost observed about poetry and about love: "[Poetry] begins in delight and ends in wisdom. The figure is the same as for love. No one can really hold that the ecstasy should be static and stand still in one place. It begins in delight, it inclines to the impulse, it assumes direction with the first line laid down, it runs a course of lucky events, and ends in a clarification of life-not necessarily a great clarification, such as sects and cults are founded on, but in a momentary stay against confusion [...] Like a piece of ice on a hot stove the poem must ride on its own melting" ("The Figure a Poem Make," *Collected Poems, 1939*).

I'd like to claim that thinking about today's post began in delight. It did not. My initial thoughts were a mishmash of all that I have missed out on—lost, if you will—during the last two years. I won't even begin to list my woes and heartaches and tragedies here because you know them all, already, all too well. I'm betting that yours have weighed as heavily on your spirit as they have weighed on mine.

I had to reign myself instanter. I had to shift my focus from lost to found. From lost to learned.

Ideas and words have always anchored me and held me fast during the raging storms of life, even before the pandemic, and they will continue to do the same long afterwards.

As soon as I made that much-needed attitude adjustment, my essay-in-progress—this post—started giving me delight! Then, I allowed impulse to take over, and I went with the flow as the essay rode along on its own melting.

And, by the time that it ended—as it is about to do—I had a moment of clarity—perhaps even a moment of wisdom.

I am delighted that I called on my students to tackle my unrealistic question.

I am even more delighted that I tackled it myself because in sorting through my own lessons—in creating my own "call and response"—my essay ran a course of lucky events, and I achieved my own Frostian stay against confusion, momentary though it might be!

JANUARY 27, 2022

Honoring an Angel

"May there always be an angel by your side."

— BLESSING

My belief in angels goes all the way back to my childhood in the coalfields of Southern West Virginia.

I'm not too surprised. My mother was a Pilgrim Holiness minister, and she had read both the Old Testament and the New Testament more than thirty times. She was well versed in the text and the context surrounding the 273 references to angels in the King James Bible.

She anchored me squarely and securely to my belief in angels, and it has lingered with me and has fascinated me throughout my life.

Angels are acknowledged, of course, in many of the world's major religions, aside from Christianity. They figure prominently in Judaism, Islam, Hinduism, Buddhism, as well as in belief systems such as New Age Spirituality.

I am not alone in my belief. Some polls show that nearly 80% of Americans believe that angels are real, year-round, ethereal beings. Among Americans who attend weekly religious services, the belief jumps to 94%, and among Evangelical Christians, it edges up to 95%.

Angels are messengers who comfort, protect, provide unconditional love, and serve others. Some are earth angels. Sensitive souls, lending the helping hand even before the cry for help can be heard. Seeing the good in those who might not see it in themselves. Feeling pain when others hurt. Possessing an aura that makes others confide and trust. Encouraging the discouraged. Turning to nature for quiet, for renewal.

My belief in angels is strengthened by personal experience. My life was blessed by an Earth Angel for twenty years, all the way up until his death a year ago today.

I knew that Allen was an angel from the moment that he won my heart, from the moment that I won his. We knew that we had each met our soulmate, that we had each found our way home.

I told him so on the spot, right then, right there. He smiled with an angelic smile that only he could smile: coy and twinkly-eyed, all angel like.

As we came to know one another better, I was even more convinced, so much so that I promised to one day write an essay about him as the angel in my life. "I hope that you will," he beamed, giving me what was by then the angelic, twinkly-eyed smile that was his signature smile that I so adored.

Ironically, when Allen died, I had never gotten around to writing that promised angel essay.

To be certain, it was not because of any waning conviction that an earth angel had entered my life with perfect timing, as angels always do.

Looking back, I think that it was simply because, rather than write the essay, we chose to live it jointly in every dimension of our earthly life together, side by side. Partners. Lovers. Friends. Hikers. Cyclists. Chefs. Gardeners. Educators.

Obviously, we lived it separately as well. Allen was an incredible human being, accepting whatever life offered. No moans. No groans. No complaints. He knew the power of surrender. He knew the power of acceptance.

Like all Earth Angels, Allen loved serving others, helping others, and healing others. As a Surgical Technologist, he was a passionate practitioner not only in multiple hospital settings where he distinguished himself but also at the colleges whose Surgical Technology Programs he directed.

Like all Earth Angels, his aura inspired—in patients, in students, and in others—confidence and trust.

At our end-of-day, before-dinner cocktail conversations, Allen was always at his angelic best as he talked about his challenging surgeries or about his precepting experiences. Always at those moments, I could count on seeing his angelic, twinkly-eyed smile.

Like all Earth Angels, Allen gave unconditional love, and his unconditional love met with the same from me. During our life together, we learned the value of affirming our mutual love. Whenever we went our separate ways throughout the day and always at bedtime, we made a point of saying, "I love you." Without fail. "I love you." We wanted those three words to be the last thing that we heard. And indeed, "I love you" was the last thing that each of us said to the other, just minutes before Allen died.

Like all Earth Angels, Allen turned to nature—to gardening—for quiet renewal. He helped turn a mountaintop wilderness into a coveted botanical oasis for the two of us. Always true to himself and his beliefs, he took greatest joy in watching small, undernourished—and sometimes unwanted—plants thrive and flourish under his care, against all odds, against all wishes. Perhaps even greater was the perpetual joy that he derived from the ever-so-constant, ever-so-required, and ever-so-faithful maintenance of our gardens, spending hours and hours and hours on end—with great satisfaction—pulling weed after weed after weed, fervently and constantly, up by the roots, one by one by one.

Little wonder that when I started to write Allen's obituary a year ago, it was as if angel wings brushed across the page, just as magically as Allen had brushed across and touched our lives together.

Immediately, I knew that I would anchor his obituary to angels. It began with: "A kind, gentle, and angelic soul—ever so quiet and ever so reserved but ever so full of life and light and ever so much loved by all who knew him personally and professionally is with us no more."

Little wonder that I ended his obituary with: "Now, Allen gardens forever and forever and forever with angels."

But obituaries are not the final word.

And death is not the end.

Twenty-one years after my promise, I'm actually writing the essay honoring my angel—Patrick Allen Duff.

And as I honor him, he's right here by my side, always, giving me back his coy, twinkly-eyed, angelic smile, once more and forever.

JANUARY 31, 2022

What a Way to Live!

"As I get older and older and older, my determination is getting stronger and stronger and stronger, especially when it comes to using things up."

I am a Baby Boomer with an incredibly strong work ethic and a fierce willingness to roll up my sleeves and get the job done. But like the Silent Generation before me, I am frugal. Whatever I have, I'm going to use it, and I'm going to use it up.

As I get older and older and older, my determination is getting stronger and stronger and stronger, especially when it comes to using things up. Like certain toiletry items. My toothpaste. My hairspray. My shaving lather.

I can't see inside my toothpaste tube. But what I have found is this: just when I think there's nothing left inside, I can always get more. All that I have to do is press from the bottom up. Sometimes it's enough to last another week. That's amazing, especially since I was ready to toss the tube aside as empty and of no more worth. Here's what's even more amazing. After that week is up, if I start rolling the tube from the bottom up—rolling really tightly—I'll get enough toothpaste for a few more days. The manufacturer would be surprised.

The trick? Keep pressing. Keep rolling. Always with full belief and full determination.

The same thing happens with my aerosol hair spray and my aerosol shaving lather.

I can't see inside those cans, either.

They, too, seem to be empty long before they are. If I set them on the shelf and wait a little longer, perhaps an entire day, and then shake a little harder, out comes enough lather to give me a clean shave and out comes enough spray to hold my silver strands in place. This might go on for days before they are really used up. Manufacturer surprise, again.

The trick? Keep shaking. Always with full belief and full determination.

It takes patience. It takes work. Actually, it takes quite a bit of both. Needless to say, the toothpaste doesn't squirt forth with full gusto, falling off the brush as it sometimes did when the tube was full. And needless to say, the shaving lather never goes flying off the palm of my hand as it sometimes did when the can was full. And the hairspray doesn't rearrange my strands into an upswing as it sometimes did when the can was first sprayed. Simply put, the outcomes are by no means as spectacular as they were before the tubes and cans were nearly used up.

Even so, I always celebrate the fact that I found enough remaining inside to get the job done just as well as when the tubes were fully plump and the cans were fully pressurized.

That's how I want my own life to be. When I'm feeling empty—when it seems that I have little left, perhaps nothing—I hope that my Maker surprises me with enough resolve to keep working my hands, my heart, my mind, and my soul—fiercely determined to keep on keeping on until every bit of me is used up.

What a way to live! What a way to celebrate life!

FEBRUARY 6, 2022

Running Reference

"When I was a boy of fourteen, my father was so ignorant I could hardly stand to have the old man around. But when I got to be twenty-one, I was astonished at how much the old man had learned in seven years."

— Attributed to Mark Twain
(1835-1910; American writer, humorist, entrepreneur, publisher, and lecturer.)

We're all probably familiar with Mark Twain's observation that the older he got the smarter his father became.

Ironically, no evidence exists that Twain actually authored the words credited to him far and wide, over and over.

Doubtful authorship, however, does not diminish the truth: we grow wiser with age. In our twenties, we see our parents differently than we did in our teens. Life experiences and hindsight heighten our perspectives.

Looking back on my teens, I never considered either my father or my mother to be ignorant.

But in my mid-twenties, as a graduate student, I had an epiphany not too unlike Twain's.

Mine, however, was not about my father. It was about my mother. Let me share what I learned.

As a Pilgrim Holiness minister, my mother was well versed in the Bible, forwards and backwards. She loved discussing the Bible and the nuances of Scripture with anyone and everyone.

Sometimes, as a child, I was a silent listener as she talked with members of her own congregation, and sometimes with people from other denominations and faiths. Either way, everyone went their separate ways with a clear and deeper understanding through my mother's insights.

Sometimes the Scriptural explorations would intensify, and the circle of friends would expect my mother to provide an interpretation of Scripture, right then and there on the spot. She was, after all, the minister.

But my mother would not be beguiled into answering what she did not know.

Her response in such situations lingers still, as I hear her saying in her characteristic, soft-spoken voice, "Let me go home and run reference."

"Let me go home and run reference."

And that's exactly what she did, though, at the time—as a youngster—I had no idea what she was doing, exactly.

I never saw her do it. I suppose she did it privately in the few quiet moments that she would have claimed as her own throughout the day and night as a minister, wife, and mother of six.

After running reference, she always continued the Scriptural inquiry with her parishioners and neighbors the next day, and, sometimes, for days thereafter. That which had been confusing became coherent and intelligible.

What she had been doing became abundantly clear to me when I started graduate school.

My mother had been doing scholarly research. When she ran reference, she was consulting multiple Biblical commentaries, especially her treasured *Matthew Henry Commentary on the Whole Bible*, originally written in 1706. Her research brought informed clarity to her interpretations.

When she ran reference, she was—in her unpretentious way—conducting Biblical research right there in our Southern West Virginia coal camp. It was every bit as sophisticated as the doctoral research in American Literature that I would later chase up and down and all around the ivory halls of academe, at a major four-year university.

When I had that epiphany in my twenties, I can't begin to tell you how proud I was of my mother for the scholarship that she had been doing all down through the years. I am grateful that I told her so.

I chalk up my love of research to my mother's influence. Whenever I'm working on my own scholarly projects, I am always mindful of my mother.

And, to this day, I can still hear my mother saying, "I have to go home now and run reference."

FEBRUARY 14, 2022

I'm a Spring Teaser

*"Everybody talks about the weather,
but nobody does anything about it."*

— CHARLES DUDLEY WARNER
(1829-1900; American essayist, novelist. The witticism is
often attributed erroneously to his friend Mark Twain.)

I have been forecasting the weather forever.
One of my favorite "meteorological barometers" is the sky! I stare at it. I swear by it.

I especially swear by "Red sails at night, sailors delight. Red sails at morning, sailors take warning."

Who would have thought that variations of that weather adage go all the way back to Shakespeare ("Venus and Adonis" [lines 453-46]) and to the Bible (Matthew XVI: 2-3)?

Be that as it may, it gives me lots of traction, especially when it comes to forecasting fierce thunderstorms and fierce snowstorms.

And that's exactly how I like my storms and my forecasts. Fierce. "Fierce" may not be a crowd pleaser, but it's a sure-fire attention getter.

Without doubt, forecasting the weather predates my modest efforts. It also predates Biblical weather forecasting by Lord knows how long.

Well, we do know that it goes at least as far back as 650 B.C., when the Babylonians predicted weather based on clouds and haloes.

Then around 340 B.C., Aristotle wrote his *Meteorologica*, a treatise about rain, clouds, hail, wind, thunder, lightning, and hurricanes. It remained the weather standard until the 17th century.

Fast forward from then until now. The advances are far too many for me to mention even briefly. Lucky me. Luckier you.

But there is one fancy scientific gadget for forecasting weather that stands heads and shoulders above the rest.

I mention it only because I own one. It's a Fitzroy Storm Glass. A group of my Creative Writing students gave it to me years ago.

I wish that you could see it. I keep it in my kitchen on top of a fabulous antique corn sheller. About all that I can say for it—the Fitzroy, not the corn sheller—is that it's a wonderful *objet d'art*, and it always draws attention to the corn sheller. (Other folks, it seems, are no more interested in a scientific approach to weather forecasting than I am.)

Nonetheless, I have a pretty good track record when it comes to predicting storms, particularly snowstorms.

If you want proof, ask around. Neighbors. Students. Colleagues.

Better still, ask my former and present college presidents. I always give a heads up when a snowstorm is headed our way. I want to make sure that the "college-closed announcements" go out early—preferably the night before—so that I can sleep in the next day. Ah! The exquisite luxury of getting up at five instead of four!

And if those folks won't give me credit for my Snow-Casting accuracy, let me just say this in self-defense. What I lack in accuracy I make up for in hype. I'm a snow-hype maximizer. Local grocery store chains love it when I get folks all cooked up over a storm headed our way. I'm the one who spurs on all the frenzied shopping that leaves all the shelves empty.

That's what I've been told at any rate. I hope that's true, because then I won't feel too bad when my forecasts are from time to time hundreds of miles or so off track or a few weeks behind or a few weeks ahead of schedule. They're still good for the local economy.

If you're wondering how I established my track record for weather forecasting and my reputation for weather hype, let me explain.

It's as simple as I am. I use one of the oldest methods ever: patterning. I observe what's happening in the natural world around me. Trust me: I've been around long enough to put two and two together and come up with lots of observations and patterns. Sometimes they're about the weather.

Patterns are helpful—really helpful—in predicting the arrival of spring (Vernal Equinox) as I am about to do right here for 2022, soon and very soon.

However, before sharing those patterns and my prediction for spring's arrival, there's something that I simply must get off my chest.

I know that Punxsutawney Phil saw his shadow on February 2, ran back inside, warning us all of six more weeks of winter, thereby putting his official arrival of spring pretty close to what it would be officially this year anyway: March 20.

But based on what I'm seeing in my local mountain patterns, I'm convinced that the famed Pennsylvania groundhog (*Marmota monax*) is wrong.

Actually, I'm so convinced that I have every intention of getting my own groundhog. Her full name will be one that regular folks can pronounce from one year to the next without having to consult *HowtoPronounce*. Hmmm. Edinburg Eve might be perfect.

Then I'll set up my own groundhog club right here on my mountain, right in my own backyard! It would be locally significant, and it would draw world-wide media attention. (**Note to myself:** This is, without doubt, a perfect *GoFundMe* dream opportunity. Be careful not to share this idea with others. Someone will steal it for sure. **This is hot. Really hot.**)

Here's how I know that Phil is wrong, based on six patterns showing up around here.

No. 1. When my **witch hazel** (*Hamamelis Virginiana*) blooms. I can always count on a bouquet by the end of February. This year, though, I gifted a neighbor with some blooming branches in early January. That's a healthy month earlier than usual. It probably, perhaps, doesn't mean a thing.

No. 2. When local **striped skunks** (*Mephitis mephitis*) mate. Around these parts, they mate in mid-February, no doubt because of Valentine's Day. This year, they've been at it since late December. They get so carried away by their amorous pursuits that I see them all the time, all on and all along the highways. Dead. That's even more than a month early. It probably, perhaps, doesn't mean a thing either, other than stinky dead skunks.

No. 3. When my **mourning doves** (*Zenaida macroura*) start courting. Charlie and Alabaster took up here years ago, and they normally start their courting rituals in late February. But as I live and breathe, when I looked out onto my deck last week, there they were, feathers puffed and ruffled, cooing and wooing and strutting all around with no shame whatsoever. That's the third early spring harbinger that I am witnessing. It has to mean something.

No. 4. When **robins** (*Turdus migratorius*) return to the area. Although I have not seen a single, solitary robin yet, I have heard from my faithful weather correspondent in Strasburg (Virginia, not Austria) that robins appeared in her yard last week, a full month earlier than usual.

No. 5. When my **tree peonies** (*Paeonia suffruticosa*) start budding. They never bud until late March, sometimes early April. Guess what? They have swollen buds right now. One more piece of evidence. One more pattern.

No. 6. I saved the best for last. When the **faerie ring** (*Crocus fatum*) blooms. The same well-informed and faithful Strasburg informant just a few days ago informed me that her faerie ring is blooming. As proof that it was blooming on time, she shared a copy of the email that she sent me last year on February 9 announcing her blooming faerie. Oh, dear. Now that I'm re-reading her emails more carefully, it seems that her point was nothing more than the fact that her faerie ring is blooming right on time. Still, this piece of evidence could have been so strong and so convincing that I don't have the heart to take it out.

Taken singly, the evidence probably, perhaps, might not mean anything. Yet I am mindful of the power of one.

Taken collectively, the evidence probably, perhaps, might mean everything. I am mindful of the power of many.

Before I make my declaration about spring's arrival (which I am about to do), let me say succinctly, as is my custom to which you can attest, that my declaration is based on the full reckoning of all the scientific evidence, weather lore, and mountain patterns at my disposal, offset and adjusted as necessary to advance my own whims based on how the winds blow.

We are, as I have shown clearly and convincingly, one full month ahead of schedule in terms of the arrival of spring weather.

Yes: more snows will probably, perhaps, fall.

Yes: the innumerable meteorologists who are probably, perhaps, reading this post right now, hoping to strengthen their own forecasts and give themselves greater credibility (albeit stolen), are scratching their proverbial heads trying to make sense of it all. I wish them well.

But pay neither the snow nor the meteorologists no mind whatsoever.

What Mother Nature knows, she knows.

And has she not brought forth into full and plain view, for everyone to see and now to understand, evidence from a wide assortment of her best witnesses? She has.

Witch hazel. Skunks. Robins. Tree peonies. Faerie rings.

As you share this spring teaser with social media far and wide—and I hope that you will—remember not only to consider but also to credit the source.

You heard it first, right here. An early spring awaits us. I tease you not.

FEBRUARY 21, 2022

My Imaginary Guests

"I have a funny mental framework when I do physics. I create an imaginary audience in my head to explain things to—it is part of the way I think. For me, teaching and explaining, even to my imaginary audience, is part of the process."

— LEONARD SUSSKIND
(b. 1940; American physicist and founding director of the Stanford Institute for Theoretical Physics.)

It seems to me that if a noted physicist like Leonard Susskind can admit to having a funny mental framework and imaginary audiences, a simple English professor like me can, too.

My funny mental framework is an occupational requirement when I do literature. I spend a lot of time exploring literary white spaces, I spend even more time reading between the literary lines, and I spend the most time helping my students develop their own funny mental frameworks.

My imaginary audiences are simply a carryover from childhood. Truth be told, my imagination is probably the only part of me that's still intact and in shape after all these years. I guess it's a prime example of "use it or lose it." Believe me: I've used it.

Indeed, I've had to use it more than ever since COVID's arrival a little more than two years ago, especially when it comes to house cleaning.

I had just as well tell you up front. I love a clean home, but I hate house cleaning.

It's tedious. It's odious. It's repetitive. And worst of all, it's never done. Just when I think that I have finished, I discover that I have to start all over again. Where on earth does all that dust come from? And who put all those streaks on my windows right after I cleaned them with streak free window cleaner?

It's a good thing that my late partner, Allen, felt the same way about house cleaning. We both preferred cooking. (The heady perfume of Thai spices always out fragranced lemony Pledge.) Or gardening. (The wishful anticipation of spring flowers always out did our untidy offices.) Or hiking. (The quiet time with nature always out maneuvered the roar of the vacuum cleaner.) Or cycling (The revving up of heart and lungs always out powered mopping the kitchen floor.)

Yet we knew fully well that house cleaning was a necessary evil. So we faced it head on. Occasionally. But no more often than necessary.

We developed a foolproof strategy for keeping our home clean. Invite guests!

If the house didn't need much cleaning, we'd have dinner guests.

If the house needed a little more attention, we would have overnight guests.

And if the house needed lots of cleaning because we had simply frittered away our spare time with silly things like cooking, gardening, hiking, and cycling, we would have weekend guests.

Never, absolutely never, did we ever let the house get to the point of needing so much cleaning that we had to invite guests to stay longer than a weekend. We took Benjamin Franklin at his word: "Guests, like fish, begin to smell after three days."

Whether our guests were with us for the weekend, for an overnight, or just for dinner, we knew that we would have a truly joyful time.

Equally important, or maybe even more, we selfishly knew that we would enjoy the spic-and-span home that preparing for company always brings, almost as magically as a self-cleaning oven—well, at least in my wired imagination.

But all of that was before COVID-19.

Since COVID-19, we've all had to change the way we live. But I'll tell you one thing: COVID-19 has not changed the way that I see house cleaning. It's still tedious, odious, repetitive, and never-ending.

Actually, it's even more so because since COVID-19 I don't entertain a lot, especially since winter has kicked in and since Omicron has kicked our butts even harder.

These are the times when I find myself summoning up my imaginary guests.

They're helping me keep my home clean, the way that I like it to be.

I have lots of real cleaning strategies that I really do use when I conjure up my imaginary guests.

Sometimes my strategy focuses on who my imaginary guests are. If they're family or friends or neighbors, I rationalize that they've seen my home clean at least once before so their memory of that memorable degree of cleanliness will no doubt equal my imaginative degree of imagination. In that situation, the cleaning doesn't make me break out into a sweat.

But if my imaginary guests are my colleagues, I shift my strategy. They may or may not have seen my home before. And it really doesn't matter because I know that they are as skilled in exploring white space and reading between the lines as I am. They'll be exploring everywhere and looking under everything. In that situation, the cleaning makes me break out into a big time sweat.

Either way, just imagine the cleaning that I get done for guests who never come. That's fine by me. My home still gets cleaned.

Another strategy focuses on what parts of my home my imaginary guests might visit.

Dinner guests: Kitchen. Dining room. Living room. Guest bathroom. I can get those rooms readied up right fast. Done in an hour.

Overnight guests: Same as for dinner guests plus guest bedroom. No big deal since the guest bedroom is not used that often. Done. Add an extra thirty minutes.

Weekend guests: Same as overnight guests plus the entire rest of the house because they want to see it all. These imagined guests require me to roll up my sleeves and do some deep cleaning. Done, in just one day, but begrudgingly so.

Another strategy that I use to house clean for imaginary guests who never show up is perhaps my favorite though most feared

How soon will they arrive?

Tomorrow? Today? This afternoon? In an hour? They're in the driveway? No way! OMG! The nerve!

Trust me. Panic can clean a house faster than any other strategy!

I can't begin to tell you how much I treasure all of my imaginary guests—whoever they are, wherever they are, and whenever it is that they will never arrive. I bless each and every one of them for all that they're doing to help me with my tedious, odious, repetitive, and never-ending house cleaning.

One day, though, they really might arrive. Oh, how I long for that day to come. Real guests in my clean home. For dinner. For overnight. For a weekend. (For longer? Never.)

When that time comes, I'll be so proud to show off my spic-and-span home that my imaginary guests and I have maintained, waiting for my real, honored guests to arrive.

FEBRUARY 27, 2022

Spaces and Habits of Famous (and Not-So-Famous) Writers

"I started working on something, and it was really bad. It was crummy. But I was really so happy just to be working on a little crummy thing. I would get home, and I would think, 'It's waiting for me. My crummy thing.'"

— Louise Glück
(b. 1943; American Poet and Winner of the 2020 Nobel Prize in Literature; "The Poet's View," 2014.)

Writers' lives have always fascinated me. Their writing spaces and their writing habits have fascinated me perhaps even more.

Some writers' spaces make me feel right at home. I'm thinking of Albert Camus, Arthur Miller, Dylan Thomas, Jack London, Ray Bradbury, Wallace Stegner, William F. Buckley, Jr., and Carl Sandburg. Their writing spaces are filled with stacks of papers and books just like one part of my office. They seem to thrive on chaos as much as I do.

In stark contrast are the well-organized and sparsely furnished writing spaces of E. B. White, Edith Wharton,

Edward Albee, F. Scott Fitzgerald, George Bernard Shaw, H. L. Mencken, and Hunter S. Thompson. Their writing spaces are aesthetically beautiful, with everything positioned perfectly, but those spaces would be far too still—far too quiet—for me.

Interestingly enough, Maya Angelou doesn't have her own writing space. She rents a hotel room in the towns where she lives. She goes there to write every day.

Angelou's method would not work for me either. I couldn't afford that kind of luxury.

Aside from writing spaces, writers have preferences about how they're poised when they write. It might surprise you to know that not all writers write while sitting down.

Some stand. Ernest Hemingway, Thomas Wolfe, and Philip Roth are a few examples.

Some lie down on their beds, notably Maya Angelou, Truman Capote, and Edith Wharton.

At least one writer dons his gravity boots and hangs from an exercise frame to think things out: Dan Brown.

What time of day do famous writers work?

Some are early birds. Toni Morrison (4am), Benjamin Franklin (5am), and Ernest Hemingway (6am).

Others, night owls: Franz Kafka and Charles Bukowski.

And what about daily writing quotas?

James Joyce prided himself on a well-written sentence. A good writing day for him? Three sentences.

Ernest Hemingway, 500 words. John Steinbeck, 1 page. Stephen King, 6-10 pages.

Ray Bradbury, a lot. One short story a week.

Henry Miller worked on one thing at a time until it was finished.

Mary E. Wilkins Freeman worked on three stories at a time, on three different typewriters.

You've guessed it already. Famous writers are downright quirky.

But what about writers who are not famous? Are they quirky?

I can only answer for myself. I'm definitely not famous, but I definitely have one or four quirks.

Let me share a few of mine. I am doing so only because I casually shared one of my quirks in an email to a friend. Here's what she wrote in response:

"I was interested in your note the other night about how you are now writing in bed! I have lots of questions! None of my business! But I'm still interested!

"On a laptop? Cup of tea by your side? Wine? Cocktail? Pencil and paper? Do you rewrite as you go along or wait until the end?

"How do you label your docs?"

Before tossing my reply out into the world for all to read, let me put things into context.

My home is on a mountain top. My office is downstairs where I have sweeping views of the valley below and the mountain range beyond. Nearest the expansive window looking out onto my stone patio and my gardens below is my sparse desk with an HP All-in-One Computer and a lamp. This is where I do my professorial academic work.

To the back of my office is an old Shenandoah Valley farm table (bookcases on the side walls) with an HP Elite-Book and a lamp. That's the research end of my office where I'm currently working on a two-volume book tentatively titled *Dolly: Life and Letters of Mary E. Wilkins Freeman*. That part of my office is cluttered chaos, but I know what's where.

Obviously, I need one dedicated space for my academics and another one for my research.

What I had not realized, however, until my friend asked about my blog-writing habits, is that I need a third area for working on my blog!

Here's where and how I work on my blog. It's what I shared first with my friend and now with you, my readers.

"What I am about to share will shatter your image!

"I am literally in bed, usually around 7:45pm, and I try to write until 9:30pm or so. This new routine—started just before Christmas—seems to give me a better night's sleep, though I am now sleeping in until 5:30am.

"Yes, I have a cocktail: a Bunnahabhain Scotch, neat, waiting for me on the night table. No laptop. I'm doing the thinking, writing, revising, and editing right on my smartphone, while lying all comfy in bed.

"No docs. I'm doing it all as drafts in WordPress.

"I find that having four or five different posts going at once lets me focus on what my mood requires.

"I've never written in this manner before, but I like it a lot. Actually, I love it. It makes me feel very much like a writer must feel. When I write now, I am done with the busyness of the day. It's quiet, and my mind just settles in peacefully on ideas and fooling around with words!

"So there! You heard it first right here! And what you're reading here might well find its way into a future post. I just had an idea!"

Indeed, "the idea that I just had" is exactly what you're reading now: a blog post sharing glimpses of the spaces and habits of famous writers and one not-so-famous writer: me.

What I didn't share with my friend is this. The multiple posts that I work on—each in various draft stages—start out as little more than ideas, sometimes bad ones. To paraphrase Louise Glück, I say to myself as each day winds down and I get ready for bed: "They're there. My crummy draft posts are waiting for me."

Who on earth would have dreamt that writing could become such a comforting, lay-me-down-to-sleep bedfellow?

MARCH 6, 2022

Two Ways of Looking at the World

"Though we see the same world, we see it through different eyes."

— VIRGINIA WOOLF
(1881-1941; English writer, considered one of the most important modernist 20th-century authors and a pioneer in the use of stream of consciousness. *Three Guineas*, 1938.)

I live a quiet life. My days tend to have the same shape, with my activities anchored to specific times, so much so that at any appointed hour, I spring automatically into action. It's similar, in many ways, to the meticulous scheme that Benjamin Franklin followed so faithfully and immortalized in his *Autobiography*.

A daily routine works for me as well as it did for Franklin. I swear by mine. Actually, I live by it.

Unlike Franklin, though, who got up at 5:00am, I tease myself (and sometimes others) claiming that I am a little more industrious because I get out of bed at 4:00am.

And, again, unlike Franklin, I start my day with robust

physical activity rather than with passive—though well-intentioned—reflections about what good I shall do for the day, as Franklin did.

What Franklin did, of course, is all fine and well. But I prefer to engage in those reflections as I start my days—each and every one of them, seven days a week—by biking indoors for 20 miles.

As I bike, I listen to music. Not just any music. Generally, it has to be soul-filled Black Gospel music. But some White Gospel music slays me in the spirit of their singing, too, so those songs are on my biking playlist.

While biking recently, two songs by White Gospel groups caught my attention. In fact, those two songs got me to thinking about the importance of attitude in our lives.

Those two songs are at the heart of what you're reading right now.

Both deal with the Biblical event recorded in the Gospel of John 11:1-44.

It's the story of Lazarus. When he fell ill, his two sisters—Mary and Martha—sent for Jesus. But when He received word, He did not hurry to the side of His three friends. He remained where He was.

When Jesus finally arrived in Bethany, Lazarus had been dead for four days. Jesus ordered that the gravestone be rolled away, and then He raised Lazarus from the dead.

Even though both songs celebrate the same miracle, each sees it through different eyes.

The first Gospel song is by The McKameys. They wrote the lyrics to "Right on Time."

Their lyrics are consistent with the Biblical account. Having been sent for, Jesus tarried, Lazarus died, and they laid him in the tomb. And as they said their last goodbyes, they looked: coming down the road was Jesus, right on time.

"Right on Time," the song's title, is repeated five times in the lyrics.

"Right on time." Five times.

There is in the McKamey's version a celebration of the belief that the Miracle Worker knows our needs—whatever they might be—and that He will arrive to meet those needs right on time. His time.

It is a comforting way to look at the world.

The other song, it seems to me, sees the same Biblical event from a slightly different perspective. It's a song by Karen Peck and New River: "Four Days Late."

In their version, when Christ arrives, Martha runs out to Him, telling Him that He could have healed Lazarus if He had gotten there sooner.

And then the Miracle Worker gets an upbraiding: "But you're four days late and all hope is gone."

Imagine that! He who had performed twenty-eight miracles previous to raising Lazarus from the dead was now charged with being four days late for His twenty ninth!

"Four days late" is repeated six times in the song.

"Four days late." Six times.

In fairness to Karen Peck and New River, they use the "four days late" refrain to remind us that whatever we're going through we should be mindful that the Miracle Worker will always be on time for us, even in those times when we think He's late.

Nonetheless, "Four Days Late" seems more like a lamentation than a celebration.

Same Biblical event. Seen somewhat differently through different lyrics.

What it comes down to is attitude. On time? Late?

And isn't that true with all of us? What's our attitude as we look at the events in our lives? Right on time? Four days late? Either way, the outcome is the same.

Why not look at each day as a rich, multifaceted, unpredictable, right-on-time miracle?

MARCH 14, 2022

Baking Up My Past

"If baking is any labor at all, it's a labor of love. A love that gets passed down from generation to generation."

— REGINA BRETT
(b. 1956; American author, inspirational speaker,
podcaster and newspaper columnist.)

Make no mistake: I love to bake! My earliest baking triumph was a total disaster. I was four years old. My mother turned me loose in the kitchen to bake a cake all by myself, as she pretended to busy herself in the adjoining room, ready to rescue.

Rescue? What on earth could possibly go wrong? After all, I had been hanging out in the kitchen since forever, watching my mom bake one delicious cake after another, one sweet, tasty day after another into oblivion.

But something went terribly wrong. I measured the baking powder incorrectly. Neither I nor my mother knew until batter oozed out the door of our South Bend, wood burning cook stove, onto the kitchen floor.

Then my mother helped me understand the companion joy of baking: cleaning up the mess.

More, she made me bold enough to give a botched bake another try! I have no doubt that my second attempt—that same day, of course—was a resounding success. Ironically, though, what lingers is the initial memory of cake batter oozing out onto the floor like lava spewing out of Mt. Vesuvius.

That first bake—catastrophic though it was—got me hooked on baking, and through baking, I discovered that cake is the way to everyone's heart. It can also be a mirror into the past.

For example, my mother's favorite cake was a twelve-layer strawberry stack cake, make (preferably) with wild strawberries. Her mother always baked it for mom's birthday. Later in life, when I baked that cake on mom's birthday, she insisted that mine was every bit as good as any that her mother ever made (even if my strawberries never quite measured up to the wildness of the ones that her mother picked each May).

As for my dad, his favorite was a yellow layer cake with apple butter not only spread between the layers but also slathered on the sides and top. The thicker, the better. It was his favorite, first because he enjoyed baking it, and, second, because it was a quick version of the more complex and complicated apple stack cake that he enjoyed as a child.

As for my two brothers and three sisters, I am clueless.

As for me, I may be clueless about lots of things in life, but I am never clueless about my favorite cake. It's always the one smackdab in front of me, assuming, of course, that it's homemade from scratch or the one that I'm planning to bake next, always from scratch.

My siblings must have their favorites, too. I could ask, I suppose, but that straightforward approach would give me straightforward answers. What's the fun in that?

I prefer thinking and conjecturing and researching.

What cakes were the rage when I was born? My siblings? My parents?

Mind you. This is not original thinking at all. I have seen such articles before: "famous cakes the decade you were born."

The thing is that most of those articles don't focus on what matters to me: cakes before the 1950s. Apparently, people born before 1950 are no longer alive, or, if they are, they're too old to be baking cakes!

Well, excuse me. I was born before 1950, and I'll put my bakes up against the best!

So I decided to don my *toque blanche* and research cakes that were popular during the decade of the **Fighting Forties** when I was born! I have two older sisters and an older brother who were born in that decade, too.

I could simply tell you that the website *Desserts from the 1940s* included Carnival Marble Cake, Magic Peach Cake, Mincemeat Christmas Cake, and even a Chintz Cake.

But my 1940s siblings and I, though born in the same decade (and of the same parents) are as different as night and day.

So I decided to see what I could discover about birth-year cakes.

1947 was my year. A Chocolate Weary Willie Cake seems to have captured attention. It might interest you to know that "Weary Willie" was another name for a tramp. (Well, excuse me again. I've been called lots of things before, but never a tramp. Having made that disclosure, I'm confident that you will check out the link to that recipe. However, would you refrain from doing so until after you finish reading—and liking—today's post? Thank you in advance for refraining and for liking!)

Another 1947 cake was Jack Berch's Mahogany Cake. Berch was a radio announcer who chatted, whistled and sang for audiences from 1935 to 1954. "Keep a listenin' while I'm a whistlin'" was his motto. I like the backstory enough to try that recipe.

Now let's move back a few years to 1943 when my sister Judy was born. That year the Red Velvet Cake was a hit. The recipe had been around far earlier, but in 1943, Irma Rombauer's classic cookbook *The Joy of Cooking* introduced the Red Velvet Cake to America.

The year before—when my brother Stanley was born—America was grappling with war rations, and many cake recipes called for cheap pantry staples and far less sugar. This was the year of the Victory Cake.

My sister Arlene was born in 1940, the year of the Do Nothing Cake: "easy, takes no time to throw it together, and is so delicious." I'm sure that she will be quite insulted when she reads about "her" cake, because she is always busy doing something.

My two oldest siblings were born in the previous decade, the **Threadbare Thirties** following the Great Depression.

Little wonder that when my sister Audrey was born in 1935, an eggless, milkless Depression Cake was popular. Far better, though, would have been the Sun-Maid Raisin Nut Cake from the same year, with the recipe right on the back of the raisin box.

Moving back two years to 1933, when my brother John was born, a Chocolate Prune Cake was the favorite. If you don't like prunes, you might try the Doberge Cake, also popular that year.

Since I started this post by talking about my parents' favorite cakes, it seems fitting that I should end with something about the cakes that folks enjoyed during their birth decades.

My mother, Bertha Pearl, was born in 1912, the year that the Titanic sank. During her decade of the **Nineteen Tens/Teens**, lots of cakes were in the lineup. Chocolate Nut Cake. Sponge Cake.

But I think my mother would have given a nod to the Lady Baltimore Cake, described in Owen Wister's novel, *Lady Baltimore*:

> "'I should like a slice, if you please, of Lady Baltimore,' I said with extreme formality. I returned to the table and she brought me the cake, and I had my first felicitous meeting with Lady Baltimore. Oh, my goodness! Did you ever taste it? It's all soft, and it's in layers, and it has nuts—but I can't write any more about it; my mouth waters too much. Delighted surprise caused me once more to speak aloud, and with my mouth full, 'But, dear me, this is delicious!'"

Finally, we reach 1902 when my father, John Saunders, was born, at the start of the **Aughties** decade. Among a number of other chocolate-battered cakes, the first recipes actually dubbed Devil's Food appeared that year, "one in *Mrs. Rorer's New Cook Book*, and the other in *The New Dixie Receipt Book* in which it was slyly subtitled 'Fit for Angels.'"

Clearly, I could bake up my past forever, especially if I were to pursue cake backstories for grandparents, aunts, uncles, first cousins, and cousins twice removed.

Fortunately, I won't.

But rest assured. I will bake all the cakes that I have mentioned, knowing that I will continue to learn an awful lot about baking. Who knows: with a little luck, I might even stumble upon a recipe or two worthy of sharing with others.

As I taste my way along, I will stack up a rich and multi-layered appreciation of my family's past with every cake I bake ... with every bite I take.

MARCH 21, 2022

Heading Out

"My mother was always unfazed by my haircuts, however much they surprised (or mortified) her. She knew what many other mothers didn't. In time, I would get over my cut and move on."

Hey, folks! I got my hair cut last week on Saint Patrick's Day. No big deal. Right?

Wrong! It was a big deal for me. I hadn't had a haircut since March 17, 2020, right at the start of our fractured COVID world.

When I got that haircut, I was as hopeful as everyone else that COVID would fade away just as quickly as it had emerged.

But COVID continues to hang around longer than any of us expected. And you guessed it. During the last two years, my hair grew longer than I ever expected. No problem. I secured my little ponytail with a little rubber band, and it didn't look too bad at all. Really. It didn't. I kept the sides and top cut about as short as usual. I kept my hairline and neck trimmed, too. I did it all, all by myself.

With my new "do," whenever I walked toward people,

I always got the usual greeting. "Hey, how's it going?" But as I walked past, I always heard, "Oh, my God! You've got a ponytail. It's so you."

As my ponytail grew longer and longer, I decided to play it up with colorful hair ties for my longhairs. Purple. Blue. Green. Rainbow. Bling blings. Psychedelic. Celtic. They were the Raddest. On any given day, I'd usually pick my hair tie to match my shirt color. From that point forward, "That's so you" became music to my ears, always making me smile a little wider and a little longer.

Finally, the ponytail was hanging down below my shoulders. It didn't look that long because my hair has some natural curl. But, still, it felt just a little too long. Since I didn't want to cut the glorious mane that I could always feel but could never quite see, it seemed to me that a man bun was a perfect—perhaps even a trendy—solution.

Mind you: it wasn't much of a bun: I'm balding on top and the rest of my hair is thin. What mattered was the simple pleasure that it gave me. Actually, it pleased me a lot, so much so that I had every intention of celebrating the bun with a pair of hair sticks, ideally a little pair of sterling silver chopsticks. Sadly, I could not find any that were short enough.

Nonetheless, my ponytail/man bun made me feel more Rad than I had felt since my twenties and thirties when my Scandinavian stylist Hilda always whipped out her long matches after cutting my hair and horrified me as she singed the ends to keep my hair from "bleeding" and to encourage it to grow. Before that my mother sometimes used nothing more than her fingers and scissors to give me a feather cut. Both my mother and Hilda had an easy job, because in those days I sported a full head of hair. How can any stylist go wrong? Hair. Glorious hair. Those were the days, my friends.

In college, I flaunted a pompadour. In high school, a ducktail. In grade school, a Mohawk, and before that a buzz cut.

My mother was always unfazed by my haircuts, however much they surprised (or mortified) her. She knew what many other mothers didn't. In time, I would get over my cut and move on.

And so it was with my ponytail. I guess I got over it. Maybe. I'm not really sure.

But I am sure of this. I'm trying my best to believe—even if I can't do more right now than give my belief an elbow bump—that what seems to be a sharp decline in COVID numbers, at least in the United States, heralds better days ahead. Hopefully, it's more than a temporary lull before we move on to the next surge.

Either way, I'll be heading out with a new haircut to greet whatever awaits us.

MARCH 27, 2022

Get Behind Me, Satan!

"We kids were usually out the door already, long before my mother sent the Devil on his way with the broom in her hand."

My early childhood memories—I'm thinking now of my preschool years—are rich and vivid. My five older brothers and sisters would have been at school, weekdays, so I hung out with my mom, hanging on to every word that she said, especially when she prayed.

Her prayers were as beautifully worded as the verses in the King James Bible, which she knew forwards and backwards. Throughout the day, she prayed whenever the spirit moved her.

When my mother prayed—or, for that matter, when she preached—she never focused on the Devil. Instead she put the spotlight on the love of God.

Even so, she fully believed that the Devil was a real force to be dealt with, and she held him fully accountable whenever things went wrong.

When the forces of evil seemed to surround her and close in, she would rise up with the same King James linguistic power with which she prayed and preached, fully ready to take on the Devil who was causing her grief.

Big things. Small things. It didn't matter. My mother was armed and ready for proper spiritual combat. She never presumed that she had the power to rebuke the Devil. She knew better. She always did so in the name of the Lord.

Maybe the special-occasion cake that she was baking didn't turn out as it should. Into the trash it would go, all the while I could hear my mother saying, *"Satan, you may think that you'll keep me from baking this cake, but I'll show you a thing or two! In the name of the Lord, get behind me Satan."* Then she would tackle a second cake.

Or she might be sewing costumes for a school play and the stitching wasn't going the way that it should. *"Satan, in the name of the Lord, I command you to get out of this house right now and leave me and my sewing machine in peace."* Afterwards, she would make that sewing machine sing.

On weekends, with all of us at home, the noise might hinder her from praying or from collecting her Sunday-sermon thoughts. *"Satan, in the name of the Lord, go. Get out of here."* We kids were usually out the door already, long before my mother sent the Devil on his way with the broom in her hand.

To my young ears, the battles were real. Without a doubt, the Devil was right there in the room, with my mother looking him straight in the eye, determined to stare him down.

And it always seemed that her rebukes in the name of the Lord won. Peace and love and mercy prevailed, if not forever, then at least until the next battle.

Little wonder that I fell in love with one of her several Bibles: *The Illuminated Bible (The Good Samaritan Bible)*, published in Chicago by John A. Dickson Company, 1941.

It included not only the Bible but Index and Digest, Collation of Scriptures, Laws of the Hebrew People, Teachings and Sayings of Jesus Christ, Parables of Our Lord, Warnings and Promises, Concordance, Lives of Noted Bible Characters, Maps and Family Records, and, to my great delight as a child who had not yet learned to read: *Through the Bible with Pictures.*

Through the Bible with Pictures consisted of engravings, if not by Gustave Doré then definitely in his style. The green plate illustration of the Devil was the most frightening image that I had ever seen. It didn't keep me awake at night, but it scared me to death, and the thrill was such that I kept coming back for more, over and over again.

Recently my oldest sister Audrey sent me my mother's *Dickson Illuminated Bible*, used so extensively that the binding is gone and some of the preliminary pages are missing. Until now, I hadn't looked at that Bible in decades.

My mother's travels throughout the pages are still apparent.

Written in the margins of several surviving preliminary pages are faded pencil notes in my mother's hand for a sermon beginning, "The old track walker waved a broken lantern to stop the train."

Some pages are dog-eared, leaving me wondering: what verses captured her attention on those pages? On other pages, the verses are marked in large parentheses that I still recall as her signature notation.

Her travails and rejoicings are evidenced, too, by tear stains here and there, throughout.

As for evidence of my own travels throughout the pages of that Bible, I had hoped for some kind of childhood scrawl that I might claim as mine. I found none.

However, I may have found more. Something strange. Something surprising. On one of the pages in *Through the Bible in Pictures*, the lower right quadrant has been torn out. That's the exact spot where the Devil always stood with his pitchfork and his long serpent tail, waiting for my return visits. I do not recall tearing out that image of Satan. But since I was the youngest and the one most fascinated by that image, I had to be the one who did it.

Who knows. Perhaps as a child, I simply decided to take matters into my own hands and rebuke the Devil in my own way by destroying his image once and forever.

"Get behind me, Satan."

MARCH 31, 2022

In Praise of Bridge Builders

*Never to forget where we came from and always
praise the bridges that carried us over.*

— FANNIE LOU HAMMER
(1917-1977; Civil Rights Crusader.)

My life has been filled with people who have helped me succeed. People who have helped carry me over. I like to think of them—collectively—as my bridge builders.

BRIDGE BUILDERS—*MY PARENTS AND MY SIBLINGS.*
My parents, of course, started building the bridge upon which I still trod. They gave me life and empowered me to live mine to the fullest. They provided forever-tools—always to use, never to lose, ever. As a coal miner, my dad lived the life that he worked, and he preached it. As a preacher, my mother lived the life that she preached, and she worked it. They taught me to work hard at and see to the finish anything and everything that I started, fully believing that all work has dignity. They taught me the difference between working for a living and working for love. They taught me

to appreciate, value, and celebrate diversity. They taught me to embrace and accept everyone along my way. And, yes, they taught me that with an education I could be whatever I wanted to be and go wherever I wanted to go.

My five brothers and sisters played critical roles, too, in constructing the bridge that has served me so well. Since they were older, I didn't always understand the full dimensions of their lives: restaurateur; sales person and caregiver extraordinaire; medical technologist; mechanic; and postmistress. Yet, whatever they were doing always impressed me and sent me chasing my own dreams.

BRIDGE BUILDERS—*MY EDUCATORS AND MY BENEFACTORS*. Growing up in the coalfields of Southern West Virginia, I was blessed to have some of the best educators in the world. They knew the subjects that they taught, and they taught those subjects with passion. Perhaps more important, they loved their students and took personal interest in us. They were living witnesses: we could transform our lives through education just as education had transformed their lives.

My third grade teacher at Shady Spring Elementary School stretched my bridge by introducing me to Robert Frost's poetry. I fell in love—and remain in love—with poetry, and Frost remains my favorite poet. Bridge work continued as other teachers pulled me toward Scripps National Spelling Bee Competitions and Voice of Democracy Competitions. And I will always remember the teacher who got me hooked on the parts of speech and sentence diagramming. She knew that she had unleashed a wild child in love with the power of language.

My teachers at Shady Spring High School lengthened and strengthened the bridge still more. One showed me that powerful writing and hefty revision go hand in hand. Another helped me realize that typing and bookkeeping were solid backup skills that could open other career paths if my dream of going to college had to be deferred. And what a critical expansion my high school biology teacher provided by welcoming me and several other students to crash his desk every day at lunch, day after day, week after week, semester after semester, from our sophomore year all the way through graduation. Those lunch-time conversations were far more important than any lunch before or since. He gave us his time. He gave us himself.

As high school graduation approached and going to college became a reality, benefactors stepped up to help build my bridge. My parents and siblings didn't have a lot to give, but what they had, they gave. Similarly, the citizens of my hometown set up a scholarship fund to help college-bound students buy freshman-year textbooks. I was one of the first recipients. That $150 check meant my future to me.

My professors at Alderson-Broaddus University added wonderfully rich dimensions to the bridge. Most of them lived on campus—on Faculty Row—and our classes were so small that we were often their dinner guests. They helped me see the human side of the presumed academic ivory tower that years later I would strive to model. My advisor, though in her fifties, finished her doctoral degree while I studied under her and served as her Work Study. She gave me an appreciation of lifelong learning. Fortunately, too, benefactors made it possible for my life bridge to continue growing. Their endowed scholarships helped me fulfill my dream of becoming a college English professor.

As a graduate student at the University of South Carolina, phenomenal educators continued to enrich my life and build my bridge. I'm thinking of my advisor who turned me on to textual bibliography. Another professor introduced me to Mary E. Wilkins Freeman—the ongoing focal point of my scholarly research from then until now. I'm recalling the professor who lectured, literary work in hand and not a lecture note in sight, with fiery passion and exultant joy. He allowed himself to be slain in the intellectual moment just as my mother always allowed herself to be slain in the spiritual moment. Through his teaching, I saw the best of both worlds—his and my mother's. I had a vision of the educator that I would strive to be.

BRIDGE BUILDERS—*My Colleagues and My Friends*.
Just as I was blessed to have bridge builders throughout my educational life, so too have I been blessed to have them in my professional and personal life.

I would not be where I am today had it not been for my supervisor at the former Department of Health, Education, and Welfare. When I was a summer intern in his Division of Two-Year Colleges, he was the one who suggested that the Library of Congress might be the perfect place for me as an editor. He was the one who nudged me to Capitol Hill to submit an employment application.

Without his influence, I would never have had a twenty-five-year career at the world's premier research library.

During that career, I worked with the best professionals in the federal sector. They were awesome bridge builders for me and countless others. One—a pioneer in library automation, at a time when computers were still called machines—helped me move up from being an editor in the MARC Project to being an editor in the NUCPP-Pre-1955 Imprints, the bibliographic wonder of the world. Another made me believe that information is never lost: painstaking and dogged research can always lead to its discovery. Another made me believe that I had it in me to be the Training Coordinator for the United States Copyright Office. Then he led me from there to being the Director of the Library's Internship Program and from there to being Special Assistant for Human Resources, giving HR advice to department heads throughout the Library as well as to two Librarians of Congress.

After I crossed the bridge from the library side to the academic side at Lord Fairfax Community College, I was blessed to have still more bridge builders in my life. The biggest, perhaps, was the selection committee that recommended hiring me as a professor of English, thereby making my third-grade dream come true. Later, another bridge builder challenged me to teach dynamic 8-hour classes on Fridays and Saturdays. Another graciously asked me to co-advise the Alpha Beta Omega Chapter of Phi Theta Kappa—the International Honor Society of the Two-Year College. Other bridge builders challenged me to teach without walls: Virtual Learning. Still another, without books: free Open Educational Resources personally curated and designed by me. Then there was the seminal opportunity to co-author and edit the college's report for LFCC's Reaffirmation of Accreditation, Southern Association of Colleges and Schools (SACS). Add to that team teaching Leadership Honors Seminars and English Honors Seminars and co-presenting at conferences with mathematicians, artists, and psychologists. And I will always remember the growth opportunity afforded by co-chairing the Developmental English Curriculum Team charged with redesigning Developmental English across the Virginia Community

College System. Other bridge builders—colleagues, deans, vice-presidents, and presidents—championed me so successfully that, from time to time, I was in the limelight at the college, state, and national levels.

Fortunately, close friends have been there with me throughout my crossing—giving the support that only friends can provide. The "You can do this" pep talks! The "You did it" celebrations. The listening. The sharing. The "Here's a tissue" followed by "Better now?" The emailing. "What? You kept them all? Guinness Book of World Records? No way!" The texting. The calling. The nothingness. The silliness. The everything-ness. All the things that nurturing friends do...just because that's what friends do.

BRIDGE BUILDER—*MY SOULMATE.*
Words cannot describe one of the most important bridge builders in my life: my soulmate, my late partner. Allen journeyed with me across a large expanse of my bridge, quietly adding key components along the way. Gourmet cooking. Gardening. Hiking. Biking. Together we made the journey from who I was before, to who I am now. Together we witnessed the power and depth of love through surrender. Together our hands clasped tightly one another's, one last time, as he crossed his own bridge into eternity.

BRIDGE BUILDERS—*MY GOLDEN YEARS AND BEYOND.*
Today, I am in awe. I am standing on the bridge that others built for me, still strong after seven decades. I am standing on the bridge that others will continue to build for me, including my executors who will pay my bridge forward by strengthening the endowed scholarships that Allen and I envisioned and established.

Looking back, the distance from where I started—the coalfields of Southern West Virginia—to where I am today—the Shenandoah Valley of Virginia—is not that far: fewer than 300 miles. But the joys and triumphs that I have experienced while journeying across the bridge exceed by far the wildest dreams of my wild imagination.

Looking ahead toward my Golden Years—whatever they are; whatever they bring—I step forth confidently. My bridge is strong. My bridge is sturdy. My bridge will endure. Those who built my bridge made it according to the best specs.

Looking ahead further still to that time when I will cross from my earthly bridge into the Great Beyond—whatever it is; whatever it brings—I hope that all of my bridge builders will be there to welcome me. My Soulmate/Partner. My Colleagues. My Friends. My Educators. My Siblings. My Parents.

What a great gettin' up morning that will be as I rejoice in singing the praises of my bridge builders, the ones who carried me over.

APRIL 3, 2022

Get Behind Me, Satan—
REVISITED

*"A memoir forces me to stop and remember carefully.
It is an exercise in truth. In a memoir, I look at myself, my
life, and the people I love the most in the mirror of the blank
screen. In a memoir, feelings are more important than facts,
and to write honestly, I have to confront my demons."*

— Isabel Allende
(b. 1942; Chilean-American writer who calls her writing style
"realistic literature, rooted in her remarkable upbringing and
the mystical people and events that fuel her imagination.")

I have always been a staunch practitioner of Robert Frost's precept that "Talking is a hydrant in the yard and writing is a faucet upstairs in the house. Opening the first takes all the pressure off the second" (Letter to Sydney Cox, January 3, 1937).

That's why I rarely share anything that I am writing with others until I am reasonably comfortable that my "draft" is fast approaching my "fair copy."

But I would explode if I didn't share teasing tidbits about

what I'm writing with a select few along the way.

For example, when I was drafting "Get Behind Me, Satan," I shared the basic idea with a friend, telling her that my goal was to create a funny, humorous post that would mention not only the way that my siblings and I dashed out the door as my mother rebuked the Devil, broom in hand, but also the way that the *Flip Wilson Show* in the early 1970s caught my mother's comedic fancy. Whenever Geraldine did something wrong—and she loved misbehaving—her defense was always "The Devil made me do it." My mother loved it. She made it clear that she did not want to be bothered when Flip Wilson was on TV.

When I finished the first draft of my post, I texted my friend:

"Well, good grief! I just finished a crummy draft of 'Get Behind Me Satan,' and it slid off in a direction that I did not see coming at all! Any deliberate humor is gone. Flip Wilson is gone. And I'm not sure what the post ... IS. Well, it's crummy. But, at least, I have a crummy draft calling me tomorrow night!"

She texted me back instanter:

"Maybe you have 2 posts in this: the one you set out to write and the one that happened. Can they be two with different messages?"

I replied enthusiastically:

"Hmmm...maybe so! I like that idea a lot! I may use it and NOT give you any credit OR maybe you will become my 'Linden (VA) Correspondent.' Oh! I'm liking this a lot! 'Get Behind Me, Satan, REVISITED!' Yep! This is a winner!"

So now, dear readers, you have the first-hand backstory of the post that you are reading right now.

Obviously, since my Linden Correspondent paved the

way for me to explain my initial plan for "Get Behind Me, Satan," I'll go right ahead and do so.

I've already mentioned that my siblings and I would dash outdoors when my mother started rebuking the Devil.

I've already mentioned how my mother fell in love with Flip Wilson and Geraldine.

What I haven't shared, though, is something that I had intended to include in my initial post if it had not melted away in a different direction. Read on.

Who would have believed that after all these years—and just like my mother—I hold the Devil fully accountable for anything and everything in my life that's negative.

As you know, especially if you read my post "Baking Up My Past," I don't suffer baking failures lightly, and, fortunately, those failures don't happen often. But I have been known to toss a culinary dream right into the trash can, all the while rebuking the Devil with language not found in the King James Bible and not proper for this post. Nonetheless, the fervor of my rebuke is on par with my mother's.

And if you remember my post "The Power of Consistency and Persistence," you know that I take my biking even more seriously than I take my baking.

Without doubt, it's when I'm biking that Satan tempts me the most. Just imagine. I'm on my bike doing my best to get into my daily routine, and almost always after about twenty minutes into it, I hear that voice:

"This is tough, no? Never gets easier, does it? Hey, give yourself a break. Why not quit for today? You've done enough already. Just stop."

What a mell-of-a-hess that leaves me in, sitting there on my bike, Gospel music shaking the rafters, with that Devilish little voice doing its best: Stop. Hop. Off. Quit.

In Bed: My Year of Foolin' Around

But it's at that moment that my pedaling kicks into overdrive. I speed up from 20mph to 23mph, rebuking the Devil out loud, above the blaring Gospel music:

"Satan, you ole slew foot, you! You'd love for me to stop biking now. But I'll show you who's the master of this bike. With God's help, I'll bike the full sixty minutes, maybe more. So go. Leave me be!"

And for an extra punch, I pause just long enough to light up my Sage Smudge Stick to give my workout area another layer of cleansing purification.

At that point, my dog, Ruby, gives me her puzzled look, tucks her tail, and dashes off to safety, leaving me to fight my own battles.

My biking rebukes work well until the next day or so when inevitably the Devil returns to have another round with me!

So that's the direction my initial draft was taking, and it was moving along exactly as I had expected. That is, until my sister Audrey sent me my mother's Dickson Bible, the one that included *Through the Bible in Pictures*. The Gustave Dore images were marvelous, especially the one of the Devil that was the most frightening thing I had ever seen as a child.

After I had looked at that well-worn Bible showing heart-wrenching evidence of my mother's travels and travails, my next draft of "Get Behind Me, Satan" started to veer away from my intended humorous course.

Then, when I saw that the image of the Devil had been ripped from the lower quadrant of the page exactly where the Devil always stood with his pitchfork and his long serpent tail, waiting for my return visits as a child, it veered further still.

Needless to say when I realized that I must have been the one who destroyed the image as my guileless way of rebuking Satan once and for all, the draft veered into its own and claimed itself, triumphantly.

It became what it was supposed to be.

It became a reflection that captured the simple truth as I recalled it rather than a jazzed-up post aimed at entertaining readers.

If my mother were here, she would look at me, smile, and remind me of what she taught me all along, "The truth will set you free" (John 8:32).

APRIL 8, 2002

Glimpses of My Father's Hands

John Saunders Kendrick
(April 8, 1902–September 21, 1983)

Not long ago, I went searching for a relic that I thought I had stored in the loft. I looked and looked, but I never found whatever it was that sent me on my quest. Instead, I may have found more.

As I rummaged through heaps of possessions—some treasured; some not—I found an elegantly framed photograph that Sister gave me decades ago. (In true Southern fashion—at least in my family—you never call the oldest daughter or the oldest son by their first names. Audrey has always been Sister; John, always Brother.) Sister gave all five siblings copies of the same photograph. Hers is lighted and hangs proudly and prominently on the wall that you see when you walk into her dining room. It's a photograph of an old man—a very old man, head bowed, forehead leaning on clasped hands, and elbows resting on the dining room table. On the table, a loaf of bread, a bowl with spoon, a knife, and a cross-laden tome. At first glance, the photograph appears to be a copy of "Grace"—Eric Enstrom's famous 1918 photograph of a Minnesota miner. You may have seen it in a home, a church, or a restaurant. I've seen it everywhere.

The photograph on Sister's dining room wall is identical to Enstrom's in every detail save two. First, the old man in her photograph has no beard. Second, the old man in her photograph is not the Minnesota miner. He's a West Virginia coal miner. He's my father.

I'm rapt by the photograph, and I wonder now—just as I did when Sister gave me my copy—how she ever convinced my father to pose for it. My father knew neither artifice nor airs. More, though, I ponder an overarching question, "Why did Sister have my father sit for such a photograph?"

I had never seen my father's hands clasped in prayer as they are clasped in Sister's photograph. My mother was the one who always said grace at our table, with all of us joining hands. It was not until late in life—perhaps just a few years before Sister's photograph—that my father became a Christian. Certainly he would not have prayed at mealtime before then. By the time he became a Christian, I no longer lived at home. Sister, though, lived next door. Perhaps Sister had seen my father say grace.

I can't say what Sister saw, but, as for me, I remember my father's hands differently.

I remember my father's hands as strong hands. When but a child—no more than four or five, so small that I had to stand on a kitchen chair to watch as he butchered a fresh chicken—I reached out to ask, "What's that?" just as his cleaver—raised high in air—came thrusting down to sever the chicken breast. The cleaver could not stop. With equal speed, my father's hand grasped my nearly severed right hand and held it in place until the doctor arrived. Today, the scar that spans my hand authenticates the strength of his: holding on, not letting go.

I remember my father's hands as a coal miner's hands—fiercely strong, calloused, rough, knuckle battered, and sooty from coal that could not be scrubbed away. Those hands shoveled coal for fifty years, never missing a day, never suffering injury. Those hands provided.

I remember my father's hands as a gardener's hands—perfectly patient, tenacious, self-confident, and unswerving as he pushed the plow, laying rows as straight as the crow flies. "Don't look down," he prompted, when the time came for him to teach me how to plow a row. "Stay focused on one thing at the end." Those hands gardened longer than they mined, never missing a season, never losing a harvest. Those hands fed.

I remember my father's hands as a carpenter's hands—steady, certain, and capable as he remodeled our home and helped others remodel theirs, working with wood and wallboard, concrete and plaster. Those hands were untrained hands. "Just a jackleg carpenter," he'd say of himself. Those hands built.

I remember my father's hands as a thinker's hands. His walking carriage, always—whether in coal miner's "bank clothes" or in white starched shirt and khakis (always his at-home attire)—was with hands behind back, palms out, right resting in left.

Later in life—with our roles reversed: I, the caregiver; my father the one for whom I cared—I saw his hands as gentle hands. As age and illness weakened his body, softened his heart, and calmed his soul, I often held his hands in mine. One day, and I remember it vividly, I had a great curiosity—a compelling curiosity—to compare our hands, his and mine. I asked him to hold his hands out in front of him, and, as he did, I outstretched my hands to his, touching. Our hands were perfect matches—identical—his hands and mine.

And when my father lay in bed dying, I held his hands in mine until we both knew peace as death came with certainty and with finality.

The next day my mother and I made funeral arrangements. We both wanted understated elegance. The brushed, platinum-finished casket with a solid white silk lining—without tufting or design—seemed perfect.

When the evening of my father's wake arrived, I walked with my mother toward the open casket where my father lay. Even from the far end of the chapel, we could see something on the lining of the raised casket lid—a design.

Drawing closer, we were both taken aback as we looked inside the casket lid. It was not what we had ordered. It was not a solid white silk lining without tufting or design.

Instead we witnessed—together—a pair of praying hands. To the right of the hands, the words, "May God hold you in the palm of His hand until we meet again."

It was not what my mother and I had planned. It was not what we had ordered. And, yet, the praying hands were there, holding for me—and I believe for me alone—a lasting message.

My Father's hands.

My father's hands.

My hands.

Now, as I look back, I see Sister differently. Now, as I look back, I see her photograph of my father differently. Being older than I, Sister knew my father longer—and better. Living closer to my father than I, she had spent more time with him. Being more blessed than I, Sister had more than enough grace to glimpse my father's hands in ways that I would not see until the end.

APRIL 11, 2022

Fit as a Fiddle: The Inefficient Way

"Some of us wouldn't get much exercise at all if it weren't for the fact that the TV set and the refrigerator are too far apart."

— Joey Adams
(1911-1999; American comedian, vaudevillian,
radio host, nightclub performer, and author.)

I have had a Fitbit since 2013 when my late partner gifted me with a Flex, the first Fitbit tracker worn on the wrist. Allen wasn't certain that I would like this new gadget. To his great surprise and equally to his great delight, I became a Fitbit junkie, upgrading my device with every opportunity. I moved smoothly from the Flex to the Charge to the Versa and, most recently, to the Sense. All the upgrades made perfect sense to me!

My Fitbit is the first thing that I check when I awaken. I want to make certain that I made it through the night. Sometimes I pinch myself when I realize that I have made it, and, then I pinch myself again when I realize all the things that it tracks! Sleep score—duration, deep sleep and

REM sleep, and restoration. Exercise readiness score. Skin temperature. Resting heart rate. Breaths per minute. Heart rate variability. Blood oxygenation. My God! I have my own 24/7 Doc in a Watch.

I especially like the way that my Fitbit tracks my daily steps. It nags me every hour at exactly ten minutes before the hour if I have not gotten in 250 steps. And, when I meet my hourly quota, it rewards me with titillating vibrations, followed by the sweetest message: "Goal Complete! 250/250." That's just the encouragement that I need to get in at least 10,000 steps a day.

On my teaching days, achieving that goal is easy. I walk all around the classroom while I talk. Of lesser importance—but important, nonetheless—I try to schedule my classrooms as far away from my office as possible. That's a sure-fire way to rack up steps, going forth and coming back again. And to the extent that I decide not to have back-to-back classes, I can double or even triple the benefits of applying my fiddle-fit inefficiency principle.

Similarly, on my non-teaching days when I am at home, it's never a challenge if I'm outdoors. My gardens cover a healthy acre or two, so just walking around to see what needs to be done places me well above 10,000 steps. If I'm actually working in the gardens—let's say mulching—that usually takes me over 20,000 steps. But, sadly, I can't mulch and garden every day.

Many days, I am indoors, neither gardening nor teaching. I have found that the best way for me to reach and exceed 10,000 steps on those days is to be inefficient! I know that sounds counter-intuitive, but it actually works.

The principle is basic and elementary. Forget—absolutely forget—multi-tasking. Instead take any task, break it into as many sub-tasks as possible—the more, the better—and perform everything at the sub-task level.

Performing everything at the inefficient, sub-task level works so well that since the start of this year I have walked 782,356 steps. Yes. That's right. 782,356 steps. Based on my gender and my stride length, that's equivalent to 370.4 miles.

I made this remarkable discovery about the power of inefficiency quite by accident, just like so many other great scientific advances. Coca-Cola. Cornflakes. Velcro. Viagra.

I remember the exact circumstance when I had my breakthrough moment.

I had gone grocery shopping, but I was nowhere near getting in my 10,000 fitness steps. When I drove into my driveway, I started thinking. The distance from my Jeep to my kitchen door is about 75 steps. I could easily carry my four or five bags of groceries inside at the same time. But what the heck. I need steps. This is where inefficiency steps in. Let's see. If I leave the groceries in the Jeep and walk to the kitchen door, unlock it, and walk back to the Jeep, I add 150 steps. Then if I take one bag at a time, I will walk 150 steps every trip. Multiply that by four trips—one trip for each bag plus the initial trip to unlock the door—and suddenly my inefficiency has boosted my customary 75 steps to 750 steps.

My fit-as-fiddle inefficiency principle is equally efficient when performing routine household chores. Vacuuming is a good example. My vacuum cord easily reaches from the kitchen through the dining room and into the living room. If I didn't need steps, I could just vacuum all three rooms before unplugging and moving on. But I get more steps by using the kitchen electrical outlet while vacuuming the kitchen. Then I take the vacuum and plug it in to the farthermost electrical outlet in the dining room and continue vacuuming. Then I do the same as I move to the living room. That simple action earns me slightly more than an additional 100 steps above the 3,186 steps required to vacuum those three rooms. Imagine how many steps my inefficiency will help me achieve as I vacuum the entire house.

One of my favorite applications of getting fit through inefficiency involves dusting furniture. I never ever start the task with furniture polish in one hand and dust cloth in the other. No way. That's too efficient. I put both down somewhere as far away as possible from the furniture to be dusted. Then I step forth with just the polish. I apply it. Next I return the polish to the original staging area, pick up the cloth, and return. I wipe. I shine. Then I return the cloth to the original staging spot. I continue that process while dusting my entire home. When I finish, I am fit or fit to be tied. Sometimes, both.

And I simply must share with you how remarkably efficient I am with kitchen inefficiencies. For example, if I'm standing at the sink and I need something out of the cabinet immediately to my left, I could walk a step or two in that direction and get it. Far better, though, is to walk to my right and go all the way around my kitchen island in order to get to the cabinet that was within arm's reach to my left. That gives me 45 steps. Imagine all the stepping opportunities that I can take advantage of, just by preparing breakfast alone. Add to that lunch and dinner. Gracious me! I just had a brilliant idea! What if I apply that same principle to drying and putting away dishes! Inefficiency can step up any meal, any time of day.

Here's another thing that I do. Phone calls—whether incoming or outgoing—provide a perfect time to get fit through inefficiency. Instead of sitting down and sipping a cup of coffee while talking, I get up out of my chair and walk. I have tried walking around one room and that's good. Better still, though, is walking back and forth between two rooms. Best of all is walking all around the house. That's especially good for me since I have a two-story home. That boosts my steps and my heart rate at the same time. I admit that when I apply my fit-as-a-fiddle inefficiency principle to phone calls, I have to watch my steps as well as my phone manners.

If I really need more steps in a day, I never—absolutely never—return anything to its rightful home. I put them all in one place, ideally as far away from where they belong as possible. Then, when I have time—but always before the end of the day—I step my items back to their homes, item by item by item. Those steps accumulate quickly, and I enjoy the double joy of seeing my home as uncluttered as it should be.

Another one that I like is walking from my office to take my coffee cup back upstairs to the kitchen for a refill. En route, I saunter past my aquarium and realize that I need to turn on the light. Rather than do it right then and there, I continue to take my coffee cup upstairs and set it down. Then I walk back downstairs and turn on the aquarium light. Afterwards, I go back upstairs to refill my coffee cup, and walk back downstairs to my office, thereby gaining a total of 312 inefficient steps.

Or if I want to get downright physical about it, when I'm lifting weights at home, I don't just stand there between sets looking in the mirror at the muscles that I hope to see. Instead, I find something to do. Sometimes I just step over to another mirror on the far side of the room to look at the muscles that I hope to see. Then I run my comb through the hair that I don't have as much of as I used to have. Here's a sweet trick: if I swing my Fitbit arm sufficiently while combing what I wish I had more of, I add a few more steps to my day.

I have so many more examples to share that I could step this post out to the length of an entire book. But why tell all at once? Maybe I could find a co-author—another inefficient Fitbit stepper—and make it twice as long. And, frankly, on days when I am desperate for steps, group authorship has even crossed my mind.

So what if it takes me longer to get to wherever it is that I am going? So what if it takes me longer to do whatever it is that I am doing? Whenever I arrive wherever—for whatever—I'll step out as fit as a fiddle.

APRIL 18, 2022

Take Two | Fit as a Fiddle: The Intentional Way

"Intentional living is about living your best story."

— John C. Maxwell

(b. 1947; one of *New York Times* best-selling motivational authors, having sold more than 24 million books in 50 languages.)

After I published last week's post—"Fit as a Fiddle: the Inefficient Way"—I brushed up against a fear that stopped me dead in my steps! What if my readers thought that I actually believed in my principle of fitness inefficiency? Or, worse. What if they thought that I actually applied all of those inefficiencies to my fitness routine, day after day?

I won't lie: I have used those inefficiencies from time to time to reach or exceed my steps-per-day goal. How else could I have come up with such outlandish strategies for getting in more and more steps. Obviously, too, my inefficient method actually does increase daily steps. As I mentioned last week, since the start of this year I have walked 782,355 steps. Yes. That's right. 782,356 steps. Based on my gender and my stride length, that's equivalent to 370.4 miles.

And, obviously, too, other folks do similarly outlandish things. Thank you, Chris, for owning up to the fact that you have even stopped "the car on the side of the road [to] jump up and down and walk around for ten minutes to make up for the lost steps." I will remember that strategy!

Little wonder, then, that I felt compelled to post a "Take Two" so that I could seize the opportunity to make perfectly clear what everyone hopefully knows already. **Fitness takes work. Hard work. Consistent work. Intentional work.**

Trust me. I know firsthand. I'm a straight shooter when it comes to my overall fitness game, and I play it with intentionality.

Ironically, down through the years I thought that I was enjoying overall success. But a decade or so ago, my dentist discovered—during a normal checkup—some surprising and not-so-normal numbers. My blood pressure was elevated. One week later, my doctor confirmed that I had joined the ranks of one in three Americans who have high blood pressure and do not even know it.

She minced no words: I had to play my numbers better, smarter, and with greater intentionality. I suddenly realized: this is no lottery, where the odds are far too high against my winning. This is my life, where the odds are good that I can control some numbers and turn this game around.

Some numbers, I can't control. Like my age: 74. Like my height: 5' 8".

But I can control other numbers. Generally, I want them low.

Like my weight. My current 181 isn't bad, but the low 170s is my best wager. I'd like to get my body fat below 23 percent. I want to hit a range of 18 to 22. I'm getting there, slowly but surely, by eating fewer calories. By cutting 500 calories daily, I can lose one pound weekly. What a payoff!

Generally, I like my cholesterol numbers low. I want my total well below 200 mg/DL and my LDL—the bad stuff—below 100. That's optimal. I want my triglycerides—the fat—lower than 150. But I want one number high: my HDL. Hot tip: aim for higher than 60.

I want some other numbers high, too. Like fiber. Most Americans consume 14-15 grams daily. I'm getting 30 grams plus, by eating at the bottom of the food pyramid: 6-11 daily servings of bread, rice, and grains; 3-5 of vegetables; and 2-4 of fruit. Dividends? Less body fat, reduced colon cancer risk, and lower blood sugar. Keeping my blood sugar below 120 mg/DL but no lower than 70 is keeping me from developing diabetes.

Since that initial diagnosis, I've been playing my exercise numbers with greater intentionality, too. 60 minutes—every day. Every other day, I go for 90. No bluffing.

With my new approach to exercise and diet—and with one pill a day—my blood pressure numbers have plummeted. I stay in a normal range of 120/80. Most days, lower. My resting heart rate is low, too. 60-100 is normal. Mine runs 60. Jackpot!

My doctor remains astounded: my blood pressure, cholesterol, and blood sugar numbers continue to be spot-on, back-to-back wins. In fact, my numbers are so incredible that she's always asking me for insider information! Go figure!

I'm going to keep on playing my numbers not only by the book but also with intentionality. I believe in life, and I want mine to be long, healthy, and productive. I want to hit those higher double digits: 80s and 90s. Who knows—triple digits might be grand.

It may be a long shot, but the way I look at it: if I don't live longer, I'll live better. Intentionally.

APRIL 25, 2002

The Joy of Weeding

*"Look deep into nature, and you will
understand everything better."*

— Albert Einstein
(1879-1955; German-born physicist who developed the special and general
theories of relativity and won the Nobel Prize for Physics in 1921.)

Personally, I hate weeding! It's tedious. It's time consuming. It's tiring. It's never-ending. Absolutely. Never-ending.

I would much rather harness myself to a weed whacker, clearing great swaths of wilderness with every swing to my left, with every swing to my right, and with every step thrust frontward as I charge ahead to tame the untamable. I reckon a weed whacker is a reckoning force.

Yet, some folks (so I have been told) actually enjoy weeding. Apparently, they like to pull up weeds, one by one by one. Apparently, they never grow tired or weary of pulling up weeds, one by one by one. Their mantra? You guessed it: "One by one."

My late partner, Allen, was one of those folks. He liked pulling up weeds and did so with the same care and precision that he used as a surgical technologist.

He would plan his weed work a week in advance. The conversation below shows how it all came to pass. I see no reason to say who's saying what. The differing approaches to weeding—mine and Allen's—are abundantly clear without naming either of us and without calling either of us names.

"*Thank God! The weekend is nearly here. What would you like to do on Saturday?*"

"*Weed.*"

"*How about doing something fun? You really want to weed?*"

"*Yes. Weed. I just need some quiet time.*"

"*Well, okay. Sure. While you weed, I'll weed whack. We'll get a lot of yard work done.*"

On reflection, I'm not certain that my part of the bargain provided quiet, especially since we usually played Gospel music in the background, full volume, while we worked in the yard. And when the music stopped, no problem. I would fill in by singing at full throttle the handful of words that I knew from some Gospel song that I liked, over and over and over and always painfully off key, though never deliberately so. Soon thereafter, Allen would slip inside and slip back out again, protected fully by his smartphone and earbuds. He never said a word.

But, hey. I'm no dummy. He made his point loud and clear. Quietly. Immediately. I got it. But since he was now listening to his own music with his own earbuds stuffed into his own ears, I just kept right on singing, as loudly and as off key as ever. It made me feel good. Besides, I take the Bible literally when it says, "Make a joyful noise." And, equally important, I take folklore seriously, too. I have always heard that making noise while doing yard work keeps snakes away! So there! Even if indirectly, Allen still reaped the benefits of my singing: all the snakes disappeared into the woods, all except for the black snake that loved my off-key singing and slithered all around the yard to stay close to me, but that's copy for a future post.

When it came to weeding, it was no big deal that Allen and I listened to different music while applying different weeding methods. Working together, we always accomplished a lot within four or five hours.

I mowed down an acre or so, and I was covered from head to toe with vestiges of grass and leaves and dust. But, hey! I got my weekly weed whacking joy.

Allen removed every single, solitary weed from an established flower bed, perhaps 20 feet by 15 feet, and, sometimes even refreshed the mulch. He would be drenched in perspiration, with muddy jeans from butt to hem. But, hey! He got his weekly weeding joy.

Inevitably, as we admired what we had achieved individually and collectively, we would mutually agree to a quick shower (individually, not collectively) and a backroad drive (collectively, not individually) to a farmers' market, followed by lunch!

The after-joy of weeding and weed whacking meant as much to us (collectively and individually) as the actual joy itself.

Since Allen's death, though, I have often wondered what those treasured weeding days meant…to him. What was it that he experienced deep down inside?

Recently, I decided to re-create, as nearly as possible, one of Allen's typical Saturday weeding days.

I won't bore you with all the pre-weeding details, like getting up at 4am, reading the *New York Times* and *Washington Post*, both online, cup of coffee in hand.

Or, having leftovers for breakfast, from dinner the night before.

Or, putting on blue jeans and a favorite flannel shirt—plaid, with sleeves far too short—and always a baseball cap from somewhere memorable like Geneva Falls, NY.

And I'll not mention heading out to start weeding almost always at exactly 7:30am.

Those were the things that Allen did. So I'll skip right over all those details and commence with Allen's weeding tools.

A black plastic yard bag, for sitting and kneeling. An old dull kitchen knife for cutting out the roots of each weed. And a yard basket for collecting the weeds and their roots. And, yes: no gloves. He liked his fingers and hands to be one with the soil.

That was it. A simpler array of tools for such a noble task cannot be imagined.

Sometimes, as he weeded, it was as if he were descending into the earth that he tended, rising up from time to time, carrying to the compost pile the red yard basket filled to the brim with weeds and their roots. And so the cycle continued—descending, rising, and carrying—until he was done for the day.

That was it. A simpler approach to such a noble task cannot be imagined.

On my appointed day for re-enacting Allen's day of weeding, I did not need to think about method or tools or pre-weeding activities. All those were so ingrained in my memory, my heart, and my soul that everything fell into place naturally.

My morning—this past Saturday, in fact—started with cool temps in the mid-fifties, gradually warming to the upper seventies. A mix of clouds and sun. A gentle breeze. Low humidity. Just right.

As soon as I positioned myself with intentionality on my black plastic bag, I felt grounded—no pun intended. I knew that I had sat down exactly where I chose to sit. I knew that I had nowhere else that I wanted to be. I knew that I had nowhere else that I wanted to go. "In the moment" vibrated with new meaning.

And then I felt totally in control. I knew that I could do as much or as little as I chose to do. I knew that I need move no further in any direction than the limits of my reach. Suddenly, I no longer felt overwhelmed by the enormity of totality. I could sit right where I sat, forever and forever and forever, and work my own postage stamp of mountain earth.

To my surprise—and, again, with no pun intended—I could smell the coffee that my neighbor higher up on the mountain was brewing, and I could nearly taste the bacon that he was frying. Closer to home, I could smell the lilac in my upper yard, just beginning to perfume the air, but even now its purply fragrance was so heavy that it nearly took my breath away.

To my great surprise, I could hear tractor trailers racing seventy miles an hour up and down the interstate, their roaring engines muffled to a monotonous drone by ten miles or so of puffy clouds and winding river. Closer still, I could hear the chirping of robins, never alone, always calling one to the other, always with the other returning the song.

And I could hear and feel the rustle of dry decay as my hands grabbed and bagged leaves from yesteryear. I could even hear the blue buzz of a horse fly as it circled my head, and, more joyous by far, the whir of a ruby-throated hummingbird—my first of the season—as it helicoptered all around me with quizzical uncertainty, darting deliberately, continuing to hover nearby, singing its high-pitched chips.

To my greater surprise, I started seeing things at the granular level. The grit in the soil. The veins in the weeds.

The spidery whiteness of roots. The leaves and blooms on nearby plants. The house looming ever so large above my grounded perspective. The trees towering above the house. The clouds and sky arching over all, including me.

To my greatest surprise, one hour slipped into two. Two melted into three. Three faded into four. Four, into forever.

By then, the sharp, cutting edge of my morning angst had become as smooth as well-worn marble stairs.

By then, my hope had heightened beyond my reach, stretching as far into the future as my senses could carry me.

By then, I had experienced deep down in the inner recesses of my soul what Allen had experienced in his.

By then, I knew the joy of weeding.

MAY 2, 2022

Oh, No! Sourdough!

"Can I bring you some of my sourdough starter. Would you like that?' Hattie raised an eyebrow at me. 'I don't know,' I said. 'It is quite a commitment. I had some before and I didn't look after it. It died and I felt terrible.'"

— Sally Andrews
(author of the *Tannie Maria Mystery* series;
The Milk Tart Murders, 2022.)

When I was a graduate student at the University of South Carolina (Columbia), I became a sourdough master, partly because I lived the life of a starving grad student but largely because I loved practicing a culinary art with spores going all the way back to ancient Egyptian times. And whenever I wanted, I could fast forward to the more recent and better-known traditions of the California Gold Rush miners who were known as "Sourdoughs."

With equal speed, I could shift my focus from sourdough histories to sourdough geographies. Did you know that the flavor of sourdough differs from region to region? It does. The reason is simple. Microbes differ from place to place. Plus, bakers in different regions have varying flour preferences and differing ways of starting their starters.

Working with my own sourdough was so fascinating and my baked goods—primarily bread and pancakes—were so delicious that I kept my sourdough culture alive and well throughout grad school and throughout my subsequent career at the Library of Congress.

Oddly enough, when I moved from Capitol Hill to the Shenandoah Valley, my sourdough starter died. Maybe it didn't like fresh country air as much as I. I doubt it. I probably got so blown away by country air and country living that I neglected to give my sourdough culture the care, attention, and regular use that it requires, even in the country.

Obviously, without my own starter, I had to stop baking my own sourdough bread. No big deal. I could easily buy some pretty good sourdough loaves in my local grocery stores. I say "pretty good" because store-bought sourdough bread always smacks of commercial yeast. A real sourdough aficionado would never, ever—absolutely never, ever—use commercial yeast to boost a sourdough starter that wasn't strong enough to rise up on its own. No way. The beauty of working with sourdough is slowing down, taking time, and letting Mother Nature work her own Poppin' Fresh, Pillsbury Doughboy magic. Rise up. Rise up.

But a few weeks ago, I got a hankering to bake some sourdough bread. So I decided to make room in my life once again for sourdough starter.

No big deal. It's simple and straightforward. Using a wooden spoon, I mixed up 120 grams of whole wheat flour with 120 grams of water in a glass jar, covered it with cheesecloth, put it in a warm kitchen spot, and waited for my mountain spores to start their mountain magic.

By day two, little bubbles bounced gleefully up and down and all around. The magical sourdough dance of life had begun!

At that point, I knew exactly what to do. Discard half of the starter. Then feed the remaining starter 120 grams of all-purpose flour and 120 grams of water. As always, mix it all up with a wooden spoon, cover with cheesecloth, and return the jar to a warm kitchen spot.

However, I ran smackdab into a major crisis of monumental magnitude, ethical and economical.

Here's the ethical part. The "discard" starter is filled with living microorganisms. While I had absolutely no qualms whatsoever about baking it to death for my own betterment and joy—not to mention the joy and betterment of those with whom I share—I was distressed thinking about throwing it out—discarding it—as of no worth.

Here's the economical part. I am a big believer in "Waste not, want not." I can't throw away something that I might be able to put to good use. The mere thought makes every fiber of my being quake.

My compound crisis that day resulted in two jars of starter on my counter, instead of the single jar that I should have had.

On day three, I suffered just as much as I had the day before. Yep. You guessed it. Now I was parenting and feeding four jars of sourdough starter.

Day four doubled my joy and my responsibility: eight jars.

Day five, sixteen jars.

Now, come on folks. This is getting serious—alarmingly so—because it takes seven days or longer for a starter to mature and be so full of vim and vigor and little yeasties that it can transform any kitchen into a Sourdough Sanctuary.

You do the math. (After all, I teach English. What do I know about math?) But as near as I can figure, by day seven—if I continued to adhere to my high standards of sourdough ethics and economics—my counter would be covered with 64 jars of sourdough starter, each one needing love and feeding. I could manage the love. I could manage feeding. But what the heck! I don't even own that many Weck jars. Besides, I don't need all that sourdough. Neither baker nor bakery am I.

Thank God, I came up with a brilliant plan: reach out to friends and offer up my precious sourdough starters for adoption. Surely my friends would save me from myself.

Thus began my noble quest to rid myself of my own madness.

ME TO A FRIEND. *"If you have any interest in adopting a jar [of sourdough starter]—with a full commitment to having it bring you baking joy for years into the future—I'll be glad to share with you, and I will even forego the customary adoption process that I am told is customary in matters of bake such as this. Just let me know!"*

FRIEND TO ME. *"Well, I'd love to know about that 'adoption process' for hand-reared sourdough, but I daren't risk actually adopting any cuz I have a feeling it would die before I got any use out of it and I don't want to risk experiencing any ritualistic unpleasantness that might have made up part of the adoption process. If you want to give me a loaf or a waffle, though, I'd be entirely grateful!"*

Well, phooey! How's that for a friend? She wants all the gain without any of the pain. Hmpff!

At that point, I knew that my efforts to place my starters up for adoption were going nowhere fast.

Here's what I came up with as an alternative. Rather than

watch jars of sourdough starter double every day, why not bake with the sourdough discards?

I love to bake, you know. You definitely know that if you read and remember my post "Baking Up My Past." (And if have not read it, read it. And if you have read it but don't remember it, I won't say, "Shame on you." But, really! Shame on you. Re-read it to lessen the shame that you're surely feeling.)

But returning to the serious matter of turning my sourdough discards into delights rather than tossing them into the compost heap as of no worth, I did as my friend—the same one who chose not to adopt one of my starving starters—always reminds me to do whenever I share with her one of my many and endless brilliant ideas: "Google that."

And that's just what I did! I googled "Baking with sourdough discard."

Dare I share with you my utter shock and amazement when I discovered that lots and lots of other folks had stolen my brilliant idea—just as lots and lots of folks have stolen my other brilliant ideas in the past—and had posted hundreds of recipes without giving me even the slightest crumb of credit, not even in Baking Notes. Well, I have never. (But rest assured: I have.)

The only thing that lessened my shock and amazement was the fact that some of those sourdough discard recipes sounded so good that I decided to try them.

I knew just where to start. Sourdough bread. I had made it before. Easy peasy, lemon squeezy.

Next? Sourdough pancakes. I had made them before, too, but these would be super special because I could open up my last bottle of Brattleboro (VT) Maple Syrup that I bought in 2019 when I was guest speaker in the town where

Mary E. Wilkins Freeman launched her distinguished writing career. Oh, my! I was not disappointed. Those pancakes were well worth the wait.

Then came sourdough waffles. Vanilla, one day. Chocolate, the next. Both days, Brattleboro maple syrup presided.

Then came sourdough muffins, lots and lots of jumbo, bakery-style muffins. Morning Glory. Blueberry. Triple Chocolate. Lemon White Chocolate Chip. Banana Chocolate Chip. To my great joy, the sourdough muffins proofed to be exceptional. My neighbors, friends, colleagues, students (and one stranger) gave rave (and ravenous) reviews.

I knew, though, that I needed to move past breakfast. How could I use my sourdough for dinner? Of course! Pizza. Imagine your favorite pizza, and I'll guarantee that it will be better with a sourdough crust.

My sourdough chicken and dumplings were heavenly. I confess that I had some major doubts about sourdough cornbread, but it proofed to be the best ever.

And you can't have dinner without dessert. How about Sourdough Chocolate Orange Bundt Cake? You want some? Excellent! You won't be disappointed. What's that? With ice-cream? Sure thing. Vanilla. Homemade. On the house.

I am happy to report that I have baked the good bake so successfully and so frequently that now I am the proud parent of sourdough-starter triplets. All three jars are in the fridge where they can chill with one another for an entire week before I have to care for them again.

At this point, I have a plan. That's right: you guessed it. It's brilliant. Here it is. I'll spend this coming weekend having my own sourdough bake off.

To start, I will use one entire jar of starter—every last drop of it—for making several loaves of sourdough bread.

Then I will use the second jar—every last drop of it—to make assorted sourdough muffins.

"What about that third jar?" I hear someone asking. Don't worry. It will be an "only," but it won't be lonely. I will love it and nourish it and use it forever and forever and forever, and I will bake really good bakes, bake by bake by bake.

Better still, every time I bake with it, I will do so with an abundance of bubbly joy, knowing that I saved myself from parenting the 64 jars of little yeasties that I nearly found myself parenting.

And, best of all, I will no longer walk into my kitchen sighing under my breath, "Oh, no! Sourdough."

MAY 9, 2022

Directions to the Magical Land of Ideas

"My ideas usually come not at my desk writing but in the midst of living."

— Anaïs Nin
(1903-1977; French-born American diarist, essayist, novelist, and writer of short stories and erotica.)

Without doubt, I love all of the English classes that I teach, but my Creative Writing classes always tug a little tighter at my heartstrings. I think I know why. We write. We draft. We workshop. We revise. We share. We bond. Together.

Aside from valuing writers' bond, I like writing with my students because I want them to see that seasoned writers struggle perhaps as much as fledgling writers. I want them to see that writing is work. No, I want them to see that writing is hard work. More, I want them to see that with lots and lots of mental lifting they can become agile writing gymnasts.

Here's another reason why I like to write with my students. As an educator, I want to experience, as nearly as possible, what my students experience: coming up with a topic to meet someone else's requirements; developing a draft; workshopping the draft with peers; revising the draft based on peer feedback and personal afterthoughts; and sharing with the class the woven words of heart, mind, and soul.

Also, as an educator I want to feel the pain of jumping through the same deadline hoops that "the good professor" imposes on his students. It's a much-needed lesson in humility, one that I can experience every two weeks, since that's the allotted timeframe for each writing assignment: drafting; workshopping; revising; and sharing. Spread over a 14-week semester, I am humbled seven times.

In the past, I've done my "writing-with-my-students" stint once or twice each semester, eventually bowing out as the semester progressed because of the full range of my professorial responsibilities, namely commitments to other classes. And that is true. Can any full-time professor be a full-time writer? I doubt it.

My students, generally, are full-time students with the full range of their own full-time student responsibilities, and yet I expect them to be full-time writers, too.

This semester I promised myself that I wouldn't bow out of writing with my students. Actually, I established more rigorous requirements for me than for them. I decided to write and publish a blog post every week.

I did not make known my personal commitment. Nonetheless, week by week, I chatted with my students about my writing. I wanted them to know that I was writing and that I had my own self-imposed goals and Monday deadlines.

At the end of this semester, we celebrated and reflected on our growth and accomplishments as writers. During my reflections, I projected my blog so that the class could see it on the big screen. Several students follow the blog and others are regular visitors, so they knew already that I had published 24 posts this semester. But those completed posts weren't at the heart of my sharing. Rather, I wanted to watch their faces when my 17 drafts—at various stages of completion—popped up on the screen.

When I finished, one of my students pinned me to the wall with a pointed question: "Where do you find those ideas?"

How do I answer a question like that? To answer assumes that I can provide directions—a map, if you will—to the magical land where ideas reside.

I wish that I could. Sadly, I can't.

I'm not certain that I even understand what it means to "find" ideas. Where do I look? And how shall I begin? And how do I know when I've found one?

As for me, I don't go around looking for writing ideas. However, I do go around listening to the world. My world. Inner. Outer.

When I listen—when I am attentive—ideas seem to "find" their way to me. This post is a good example. My student's question captured my fancy: "Where do you find those ideas?" And in response to his question, I shared with the class a writing idea that found its way to me that very morning.

Its working title is "Growing Up More than Once." While driving to campus, I had been thinking about Fall 2022 as my last semester of teaching. In the midst of my reverie, I had an insight. I've grown up three times. Once in the traditional way that we all grow up and launch our own lives. Next was growing up as a researcher and scholar at the University of South Carolina and the Library of Congress.

Now I've grown up as an educator at Lord Fairfax Community College. And as this phase comes to an end, another phase will open, giving me an opportunity to grow up once more! I will share no more for now. Otherwise, I won't have anything more to say when I get around to writing that post.

But here's my point. I didn't go looking for that idea. Seemingly, the idea came looking for me. And as soon as it found me, I captured the tentative title and a barebones outline in a WordPress draft as soon as I walked into my office and turned on my computer. Some might call it journaling. But it's not. I don't journal. For me, it's simply listening. It's being attentive. Then it's taking the time to honor an idea that found its way to me.

The same thing holds true for this post. It found me during class when my student asked, "Where do you find those ideas?" Perhaps equally important, the question continued to abide with me as I drove home. Now here I am extending my answer to Morgan through this post. The idea found me; called for—no, demanded—exploration; and I'm honoring the call.

I've just shared how one idea found me while teaching and how another idea found me while driving. Other ideas find me when I least expect to be found. Biking, indoors and out. Listening to gospel music. Taking a shower. Pulling weeds in my garden.

For me, it seems that whenever I lose myself—whenever I'm doing something that takes me away from me—a door opens and an idea enters, hoping for home and for honor.

Those are the best directions that I can give to the magical land of ideas.

MAY 22, 2022

In Praise of Work

"If it falls your lot to be a street sweeper, go out and sweep streets like Michelangelo painted pictures. Sweep streets like Handel and Beethoven composed music. Sweep streets like Shakespeare wrote poetry. Sweep streets so well that all the hosts of heaven and earth will have to pause and say, here lived a great street sweeper who swept his job well."

— MARTIN LUTHER KING, JR.
(1929-1968; American Baptist minister and activist, one of the most prominent leaders in the Civil Rights Movement.)

Hey, folks. Listen up. We need to do something about the bad rap that work seems to be getting! Witness what happened to work in 2021: The Great Resignation. The Big Quit. The Great American Walkout.

But even before the Pandemic, job satisfaction wasn't the greatest. A comprehensive study conducted jointly by the Lumina Foundation, the Bill & Melinda Gates Foundation, Omidyar Network, and Gallup found that more than half of U. S. workers are unhappy in their jobs.

That's unacceptable. That's downright dreadful, especially since we spend about a third of our life working. It seems to me that what we do for a third of our life ought to make us happy.

As for me, I must be blessed. No, I must be super blessed because I have always loved my work, whatever it happened to be at the time that I happened to be doing the work that I was doing. And believe me: I've worked far more than one third of my life.

I've worked my entire life. In fact, just the other day, I said to a friend, with no hint of whining, with no intent of complaining, and with no lament of exhaustion: "I was born working."

Exaggerated? Perhaps. All right. Of course. It is.

Nonetheless, I'm betting that I did something to help my mother speed up my birth so that I could get into the world and begin my world of work. Since she's no longer alive, she can neither verify nor dispute my claim, so I'm safe with my exaggeration.

Nonetheless, I'm here to give work a better rap. I'm here to sing work's praises.

Lots of songs focus on work. Who doesn't know "Heigh Ho" in Disney's *Snow White and the Seven Dwarfs*? Or Dolly Parton's "9 to 5"? Or how about "Workin' for a Livin'" by Huey Lewis and the News? Or "She Works Hard for the Money" by Donna Summer? Or "Five O'Clock World" by the Vogues. Or, finally, "Hard Hat and a Hammer" by Alan Jackson.

If those folks can sing about work, why can't I blog about it? Besides, work is what I've always done, and work has always worked for me.

Read on, work with me, and you'll see for yourself.

I have vivid pre-school memories of scrabbling up and down and all around the slate dump behind our West Virginia home, looking for scrap iron. The "Iron Man" paid a good price for our finds. I say "our" because my brothers and sisters joined in as did most, if not all, of the kids in our coal camp.

After my family moved away to another West Virginia town when I was seven, I discovered that the citizenry there could not only afford bottled soft drinks—Coke, Dr. Pepper, Pepsi—but also could afford to toss the empty bottles thoughtlessly out of their vehicles onto the side of the road. That's when I discovered that one man's trash is another man's treasure. I collected those bottles, washed them up to their original sparkle, returned them proudly to the local general store, and walked away with three cents per bottle, fully believing that I was fast becoming the richest kid in town.

Around the same time, one of my older brothers found out that folks in our new town loved to fish, especially with night crawlers—large, slimy, segmented worms, with a wide reddish purple band just behind a large head and a body tapering back sometimes as far as 10 inches to a flat tail. Luckily, our yard seemed to be a breeding ground for the anglers' preferred bait. Weekend nights would find me and my older brother and my older sisters out in the yard with flashlights, searching for nightcrawlers. We became experts in pulling them ever so gently from the ground, ever mindful of increasing our collective earnings by a nickel for each live worm. Before long, we had a nightcrawler monopoly with our local bait shop. We had hit pay dirt, and we knew it.

I branched out to another work endeavor: mowing neighbors' yards. It didn't pay much—a quarter a lawn. But it wasn't as much about growing rich as it was the rich satisfaction that I derived from seeing my beautifully landscaped yards. I remember one in particular. I would spend the entire day cutting the grass, edging around the garden beds and walkways, refreshing the mulch, deadheading and pruning. Sometimes when day was done, I would sprawl out in the grass and play out in my mind the answers that I would give the interviewer who would one day seek me out before featuring my client's yard in *Better Homes and Gardens*.

Those work stints joyed me all the up to, through, and out of high school. The summer after graduation, I worked at an explosives company, high up on a mountain, a mile or so from the nearest town. All by myself, I managed an office of one—me. I did it all. Bookkeeping. Typing. Answering the phones. Monitoring the scales and recording weights as trucks went out with explosives and came back empty. In my starched shirt and full Windsor-knot tie, I was the master of all that I surveyed all alone on a mountain top, a mile from nowhere.

When I went to college in the fall, I continued working for the next four years. Work Study. Dorm Counselor. Summer Discovery English tutor. Mail carrier—United States Senate. Intern— former Department of Health, Education and Welfare (Division of the Two-Year College). In all those positions, I enjoyed the work, I enjoyed my colleagues, and I enjoyed the networking.

Work continued through graduate school. Research Assistant for one of the world's most respected textual bibliographers. Teaching Assistant in one of the country's best university English departments. Again, the work, those with whom I worked, my students, and my research on Mary E. Wilkins Freeman all brought joy beyond measure. Some days I pinched myself because it all seemed too good to be true.

We're nearing the end of my working man's chronicles, so keep working with me.

After graduate school, I kept right on working. First at the Library of Congress (LOC), where I had a rich, twenty-five-year career. Editor, MARC Project. Editor, National Union Catalog, Pre-1956 Imprints. Training Coordinator, United States Copyright Office. Director, Internship Program. Special Assistant, Human Resources. Little wonder that I still consider the LOC to be the best agency in the entire federal sector.

After retiring from the LOC, I became a professor of English at Lord Fairfax Community College (becoming Laurel Ridge Community College). For twenty-three years (teaching twelve months a year, every year), "Professor" has been music to my mountain ears, the completion of a melody that I first started hearing as a coal camp kid. Little wonder that I consider Lord Fairfax/Laurel Ridge Community College and the thousands of students I've taught to be the best community college and the best students in the Commonwealth of Virginia.

At the end of this fall semester, I will retire. But guess what? I will keep right on working at something.

Teaching: visiting professor doors may open and I may enter. Research: visiting scholar doors may open and I may enter—my work on Mary E. Wilkins Freeman is ongoing. And how about my love of gardening (see my "The Joy of Weeding") and my love of baking (see my "Oh, No! Sourdough!" and "Baking Up My Past") and my love of company (see "My Imaginary Guests").

But here's the bottom line. Whatever work comes my way, I will work to make sure that I'm enjoying the work that I'm doing!

OMG! Do you mean to tell me that you had to work with me all the way through this post just to hear me blurt out that we have to work at enjoying the work that we do? It's so true that it's worth repeating. We have to work at enjoying the work that we do.

Maybe—just maybe—the attitude that we bring to our work determines, as much as anything else, the praises that we are able to offer up.

MAY 30, 2022

The Circle Is Unbroken

Bertha Pearl Witt Kendrick
(May 16, 1912–May 30, 2010)

Freud was not the only one who took dreams seriously. My mother did, too.

Admittedly, her belief was more Biblical than psychological. Nonetheless, my mother could—and often would—quote Scripture verbatim and at length—verse after verse, from Genesis to Revelations and many books in between—to convince her husband and six children that dreams could hold profound messages and meanings; that we could interpret dreams; and that dreams could take us inward—to our psychological, spiritual, and physical selves—and outward—to a collective consciousness linking all the ages and bringing us all together.

Dream talk was part of our daily ritual, though never before seven in the morning, lest the dreams might come true. We could share any dream, but mother focused on those that lingered in the psyche as the ones possessing possible significance and meriting analysis. Rarely did my mother proffer interpretations of other people's dreams.

Instead, she listened and redirected us to discover how our dreams made us feel. I was fascinated by her dream analysis—nearly self-psychoanalysis—and by the uncanny way that so many of her dreams tapped into profound spiritual truths.

Early in my life, my mother made a believer out of me. I remain so, especially since her death twelve years ago today. Two nights prior, I had three dreams in quick succession, with short-lived awakenings and instantaneous interpretations.

DREAM ONE. Mom was home, observing how hot it felt inside the house. She got up out of bed and walked out on the porch where it was so much cooler. As she reached her arms up toward a blue, blue sky, the wind blew her hair upwards and furled the skirt of her gossamer dress all around her. Mom started smiling and laughing and twirling—around and around and around.

Interpretation. Is Mom dead? No longer paralyzed? For the first time in six years, she's out of bed—walking and dancing. She's ecstatically happy.

DREAM TWO. Mom, costumed as a white mouse, performing. Her audience, amused by her antics. Their reward? An encore—more frolics, much laughter.

Interpretation. Freed from the journey, freed from the maze, Mom blissfully celebrates her new path.

DREAM THREE. Mom entered a softly lighted room. Dad was sitting in a recliner, as was his practice before his death. Beside him, a table with lamp; to the right, another chair. Mom walked over, sat down in the chair, smiled at my Dad, and turned off the lamp. The room slowly—ever so slowly—fell into warm darkness.

Interpretation. It is finished. Mom and Dad are reunited. The circle is unbroken.

When I awakened, my dreams lingered, vibrant and vivid. I felt—no, knew—deep down in my soul that my mother, who celebrated her ninety-eighth birthday two weeks before, came to me in those three dreams to prepare me for her death.

Two days later, Mom died.

God called her home. Forever dancing with a heavenly host of saints and angels, Mom finished the circle.

JUNE 6, 2022

OHIO on My Mind.

*"If you find it hard to laugh at yourself,
I would be happy to do it for you."*

— Groucho Marx
(1890-1977; American comedian, writer, and performer: stage, radio, television and vaudeville. He was the most famous of the four Marx Brothers.)

One of my all-time favorite essays is Suzanne Britt's "Neat People vs. Sloppy People." It's perfect when I'm exploring the structure of compare/contrast essays in my College Composition classes, especially as I explain a subject-by-subject approach. The first half of her essay focuses on sloppy people; the second half, neat people.

But what I like far more than the essay's rhetorical structure is Britt's unexpected humor.

Obviously, it's not unexpected humor for me because I have taught the essay for decades, and, for what it's worth, the essay is as fresh and as funny today as it was when I first read it in her *Show & Tell* (1983).

But it is unexpected humor for my students. Here's why. Britt sets the stage brilliantly with nothing more than the essay's title. Tell the truth. In your own mind, don't neat people always win out over sloppy people?

Of course! Neat people always come out on top. And in her essay, they even come out first in the title. We're all programmed to value neatness over sloppiness. My students are, too.

So I like to build on the assumptive beliefs that Britt puts into motion with nothing more than the title. When I assign the essay—but before my students have read it—I ask them to jot down whether they are neat or sloppy.

Also, I ask them to jot down whether I am neat or sloppy. I know fully well that they will put me into the "neat" category. When I am at the college, I always wear a shirt and tie (or jacket, shirt, and tie) and real, polished dress shoes. (Mine are real because they have genuine leather soles.) My students are convinced that's how I dress when I'm weeding or when I'm weed whacking or when I'm splitting wood with a maul. Shirt. Tie. Real shoes with genuine leather soles. No doubt about it. I'm in the "neat people" category.

My students read the essay. When they come back to class prepared to discuss both categories—neat and sloppy—they are gobsmacked.

Let me explain.

Britt is soft—really soft—in her discussion of sloppy people, and, indeed, she defends their sloppiness: "Sloppy people, you see, are not really sloppy. Their sloppiness is merely the unfortunate consequence of their extreme moral rectitude. Sloppy people carry in their mind's eyes a heavenly vision, a precise plan that is so stupendous, so perfect, it can't be achieved in this world or the next. [...] Someday is their métier. Someday they are planning to alphabetize all their books and set up home catalogs. Someday they will go through their wardrobe and mark certain items for tentative mending and certain items for passing on to certain relatives of similar size and shape."

And in the second half of her essay, Britt comes down hard—really hard—on neat people. She's exaggerating, of course, but my students aren't expecting her extreme exaggeration, even though they all chime in, announcing that someone in their family is "just like that." Here's an example: "Neat people have cavalier attitudes toward possessions, including family heirlooms. Everything is just another dust-catcher to them. If anything collects dust, it's got to go and that's that. Neat people will toy with the idea of throwing the children out of the house just to cut down on the clutter."

Her exaggerated ending is just as comical: "Neat people [...] are so insensitive. After they've finished with the pantry, the medicine cabinet, and the attic, they will throw out the red geranium (too many leaves), sell the dog (too many fleas), and send the kids off to boarding school (too many scuff marks on the hard-wood floors)."

It goes without saying that my students remain 100% convinced—really convinced—that I'm in the "neat people" category.

However, their eyes widen and their mouths open when I disclose that I am unequivocally in the "Sloppy People" category. I offer up solid evidence. I have every personal letter that I have ever received. I have every canceled check that I have ever written. I have all of my federal and state income tax returns. I have my father's last bottle of cologne (Avon—Wild Country, still fragrant after 40 years). I have my mother's last tube of toothpaste (Close-Up, still squeezable after 12 years). I have my late partner's last pack of chewing gum (Spearmint—Rain, still tempting after one year and six months). Need I go on? I agree. Thank you. I'll spare you and me.

Needless to say, down through the years as I gathered up all of these treasures (and, let me add, they are treasures)—evidence of lives lived; of lives well lived; of stories in the making; or of stories waiting to be written—my motives were pure and noble. And they still are as I continue to gather up treasures.

But a few months ago, I started seeing tell-tale signs of a type of sloppiness that has nothing at all to do with my extreme moral rectitude—the underlying reason why I keep all the things that I can't bear to toss away as of no worth.

I wonder sometimes whether some of my emerging, non-moral sloppiness isn't downright laziness.

I mean, like … maybe everyone does some of the things that I discovered that I was starting to do. I hope so, but I doubt it.

Let me toss out some examples. You decide.

In early spring, I pruned an evergreen tree outside my bedroom window. When I finished, I returned my shears to the basement, but I had the brilliant idea that since the ladder was out, I should go ahead and polish the windows on that side of the house. Unfortunately, I didn't have time right then. So I folded the step ladder and left it on the edge of the walkway. Sadly, way led on to way, and well over a week later, I was still walking around the ladder lying on the walkway, still somewhat in my way.

Here's another example. Emails. Yes. I keep all of the personal, meaningful ones in virtual folders. No problem. But what about all of the other ones that I could delete and be done with? Why don't I just go ahead and delete? I don't, and I don't know why. Or what about the ones that require—and will get—a straight forward response? Why not respond right then? Your guess is as good as mine. I have a tendency to wait until the next day so that I can think about the response that requires absolutely no depth of thought at all and that will get no depth of thought at all.

And then there's the real mail, the printed stuff that I find in my mailbox. Most of it is junk mail, of so little interest to me that sometimes I let it accumulate and ride along for several days as the passenger in my Jeep before bringing it into the house and tossing it into the trash where it belonged in the first place.

And what about the real estate tax bill that I discover when I sort through the stack of junk mail that's been riding along with me? I always look at the due date and inevitably decide to wait a few days or so before paying. Why? I have no idea. It would be so simple to just write the check and check that item off of my to-do list.

This self-discovery, folks, was troubling and troublesome. Somehow, I knew that I had to reconcile the sloppy side of me that Britt celebrates with this sloppy/lazy side of me that causes crimson as I cringe.

Fortunately, I remembered a perfect solution that had been hiding out in my cluttered mind—yes, it's sloppy, too—all along. Years ago, when I was the Training Coordinator for the United States Copyright Office, I worked closely with Copyright's executive officer. Her office was lean, mean, and sparse. Nothing was out of place.

"How on earth do you manage to keep your office like this?"

Her response? "Only handle it once."

I have always remembered her approach even if I have not always applied it.

But as I thought about this post, I did some quick research to see what else I might find out about the wisdom that Grace Reed shared with me.

Come to find out, "only handle it once" is a well-known management tool that's been around for decades and decades.

It's commonly referred to as **OHIO: Only Handle It Once**.

Guess what? I've been using it to save myself from becoming the sloppy/lazy person that I am hell bent on not becoming.

Guess what else? It's working really well.

Let me prove it to you. Hang on a sec. I'll be right back after I do a quick walk through of my home.

That didn't take long, did it? Thanks for waiting.

I am ecstatic because I only found three things that I had not disposed of properly when I handled them the first time. A can of spray paint by the kitchen door leading to the deck. (Later today, I'll throw the can away after I paint the table on the deck.) A brush cutter replacement blade at the top of the stairs leading to the utility room downstairs. (I would have been back sooner, but you will be pleased to know that I took the time to put the blade on its designated hook in the utility room.) A post card eye-exam reminder smack dab on the edge of my dining room table. (Voila! I made it disappear. Who needs it now, anyway? My appointment is bright and early tomorrow.)

My efforts to avoid toppling into the abyss of lazy sloppiness have made me so ecstatic—so euphoric—that I may well have reached a near state of mystic self-transcendence, and I want to stay in that state. For that reason—and that reason alone—as I move ahead, rest assured that I will keep OHIO on my mind.

JUNE 13, 2022

The Final Drive: The Chilling Backstory

"Truth is stranger than fiction, but it is because Fiction is obliged to stick to possibilities; Truth isn't."

— Mark Twain

(1835-1910; American writer, humorist, entrepreneur, publisher, and lecturer. *Following the Equator: A Journey Around the World*, 1897.)

Do you remember "The Final Drive"—my post about the sudden and unexpected death of my 2013 Jeep Wrangler?

If you do, I daresay that you will enjoy the backstory just as much, if not more, than the original post. The first part of the backstory is straight forward. Even so, it requires close attention. The second part is chilling—never before shared except with a few close family members and a few close friends. It requires even closer attention.

I started the original essay with my Creative Writing students in March of 2020, just when COVID-19 started showing its nastiness. I needed a topic, something to write about. I was up against one of my own "good-professor" assignments with one of my own "good-professor" deadlines. I knew that I had to deliver the goods or suffer class embarrassment.

I had lots of ideas, but I wanted to write a humorous essay.

At the time, the only thing remotely funny to me was what I did when my Jeep's sound system failed. A mouse or a chipmunk or some other critter had gotten under the hood and had chewed unseen wires in unseen places. The repair cost was far pricier than I chose to pay. Instead I figured out with great speed and with zero cost how to jerry-rig my iPod to a Bluetooth speaker. Voila! I had perfect surround-sound gospel music wherever I went.

For me, that was funny. Here I was a college professor who could have afforded the repair. But here I was choosing to do what I had often chosen to do throughout my life: make do with making do, especially with things that are of little consequence in the greater scheme of things.

But my chosen course of action became funnier to me when the day came that I forgot to recharge my jerry-rigged sound system and I had no music at all. Instead, I had the sounds of silence. I started hearing an unusual noise coming from under the hood. The noise was hard for me to describe. Knocking? No. Pinging? No. Tapping? Yes. Tapping. A rhythmic tapping, tapping, tapping, growing louder and louder and louder as I climbed my mountain, homeward. Neighbors stared. Dogs ran. This was a palpable noise that required reckoning.

I knew the very moment that I watched the dogs run—the very moment that I watched my neighbors watching their dogs run—that writing about the reality of what was happening to my Jeep might elevate my essay to the humorous level that I desired. I had an angle that I thought would work.

But when I took my Jeep in for service, the humor

started to lessen. The lesson that I would come to learn took on a more serious tone.

My mechanic's fear was that the Jeep had faulty hydraulic lifters.

"How could that be?" I questioned, especially since the Jeep had relatively low mileage and especially since I had followed the service plan to the letter.

"Sometimes those things just happen."

Despite his fairly certain preliminary diagnosis, he suggested that a heavier oil with an additive might reduce the friction, lower the noise, and extend the engine's life. I tend to trust experts, so I followed my mechanic's advice.

Sadly, his remedy didn't last long. The tapping grew louder and louder. Eventually, he told me that the hydraulic lifters had to be replaced. But before the job was even finished, my mechanic delivered worse news. The engine was shot. Nothing could be done. That was it for the Jeep that I had loved so much and had taken care of so faithfully.

As these things were unfolding with my Jeep, I was drafting my essay with my students. I shifted my angle to a more serious one.

I focused on the simple observation that what was happening to my Jeep paralleled, in many ways, what happens to human beings, especially as we grow older. Even if we faithfully follow the most recent and up-to-date edition of life's unpublished user-manual, we all reach a point where even the experts can't fix our brokenness.

I liked that angle a lot and set about revising the essay to make the parallels between a Jeep's engine and a person's heart as clear as I could without hitting my readers over the head with a skillet.

To my surprise, when I workshopped the essay with

my students, their comments made it clear that they had not gotten my intended message. I had not delivered the message clearly, even though I thought that the takeaway—wrangling with mortality: the Jeep's; mine; yours—was abundantly obvious. It wasn't.

As I continued to revise, I did two things.

First, I decided to end the essay with some email snippets, exchanged with a friend.

"Does this mean your poor Wrangler is in the shop getting that rattle fixed? Or worse …???" she probed.

"Worse," I answered. "It looks like the engine is shot."

"Aww. I'm sorry. Jeeps are sort of human, aren't they?"

"Yes," I mused. "Both are wrangling for the final drive."

Second, I decided to change the title. "The Wrangler" became "Wrangling" and that became "Wrangling for Life." Then I changed the title one last time so that it mirrored the last three words in the essay: "The Final Drive."

"The Final Drive." I liked that title a lot. It worked for me. By then, the semester was over, I had given the essay all the thought and energy that I cared to give it, and, besides, Allen—my partner—and I were enjoying my new, four-door 2020 Jeep Sahara.

From this point forward, what I am about to share with you today—right here in this post—will be met with full belief or full disbelief. A middle ground cannot be taken because it does not exist.

I never discussed that essay—or any of my essays—with Allen. Nor did I ever share that essay—or any of the others—with him.

We were so immersed in all the other rich dimensions of our daily lives together that my private-time writing always struck me as comparable to his private-time reading: *The New York Times*, *The Washington Post*, and *The Wall Street Journal*.

Be that as it may, toward the end of 2020—the week before Thanksgiving—Allen thought that he had a cold or maybe pneumonia. Unfortunately, our family doctor discovered otherwise. Her diagnosis, to our mutual alarm, was Stage 3 Lung Cancer. Allen's cancer team developed a comprehensive treatment plan: thirty days of chemo and radiation. A month later, they would operate to remove the upper left lobe of his lung.

The treatments were aggressive, taking a far heavier toll on Allen than anyone expected. Naturally, when we got back home after his last treatments on January 25, 2021—struggling to make our way from the driveway to inside—we hugged and hugged and hugged, tearfully celebrating the fact that chemo and radiation were over.

The very next day, however, I had to call the rescue squad to rush Allen to the hospital where he was placed in intensive care.

At that point, he and I both knew the seriousness of his condition, but we were optimistic, so much so that we talked about his surgery scheduled for late February, and we even chatted about new linen drapes for the living room and about renovation plans for the guest bathroom.

I spent most of the next day at the hospital with Allen before coming home for dinner.

When I returned for my evening visit, Allen looked at me and said:

"When you come back tomorrow, bring a can of gasoline."

"Gasoline? What on earth for?" I asked.

"We need to make sure that we have enough gas in the Jeep to go for the final drive."

Allen died suddenly and unexpectedly the next morning.

JUNE 20, 2022

Wrapping My Head Around Age

*"Age is a matter of mind over matter.
If you don't mind, it doesn't matter."*

— Ascribed to Mark Twain
(1835-1910; American writer, humorist,
entrepreneur, publisher, and lecturer.)

Come on now. Tell the truth. Are you aware of your age? Do you feel your age?

I know. I know. You could really nail me on that question. It's far too vague.

I agree. But, after all, talking about age is always vague, and it's sometimes downright uncomfortable if not painfully disquieting.

I'm guessing that you immediately thought about your chronological age.

That's a solid and smart place to begin, but it's only one type of age.

What about your appearance age?

Or your biological age?

Or your psychological age?

Do you have an awareness of those ages? Are they all in sync? How do you feel about those different ages when you think about yourself?

While you're processing those thoughts—don't think too hard or too long, though; spontaneity works as well with that question as it does with maneuvering life itself—let me toss out some other ways that we can look at or avoid our age.

Let's start with life stages. I like a fast pace, so we'll skip right over pre-birth, birth, infancy, early childhood, middle childhood, and late childhood.

Let's move right on to subsequent stages, the ones that matter most to me and this post.

You probably know them all already, but in case not, I'll toss them out with a word associated with each stage.

Adolescence (12-20): passion. **Early adulthood (20-35)**: enterprise. **Midlife (35-50)**: contemplation. **Mature adulthood (50-80)**: benevolence. **Late adulthood (80+)**: wisdom. And **death/dying**: life.

In case you're wondering—and I certainly hope that you are—I fall into the "mature adult" stage. It's great being in a stage with 30 years to fool around with, whether I'm 50 looking toward 80 or 80 looking back at 50. And it's great knowing that I am benevolent. (I knew that already. But reinforcement always works well.) More important, "mature adult" is far more melodious to my ears than the ageist "Sweetie" or "Dearie" that I and other mature adults suffer far too often by far too many people who should know far better.

With those life stages behind us, let's have some linguistic fun. Let's explore some single words for each decade of our lives.

Brace yourself. They're dreadful words. Just dreadful, especially when they're all hanging out in the same place together all at the same time. Any one of them makes me scratch my balding pate, trying to figure out who on earth would use such words in regular talking or in regular writing. (Don't tell anyone, but I just checked. The terms that I just dissed—and am about to diss more fully—are used in the medical field. I might have known it. But, again, don't tell.)

I'll start with the one coined most recently. 1991. **Supercentenarian—110** years or older.

Then **Centenarian—100 or more**. I like that one a lot, especially since I completed an Estimated Longevity Test a few days ago. It was free. So why not? I didn't even have to give an email address. It calculated the results right on the spot. According to the test—which, btw, seemed medically well-grounded and super scientific—I should live to be 105. Imagine that! I'll take it, especially if it comes with good health, a sharp mind, good spirits, and faithful family and friends lifting me up. (I had to pause here to correct a plethora of typos. Glasses go hand in hand with aging and I've had my multifocal lenses since midlife. OMG. I wonder whether I made typos on the Estimated Longevity Trst and that's why ut told me that I wuld live to be 501. I'm absoluty sur thet I did knot.)

I'll combine the next two. **Nonagenarian—90s**—and **Octogenarian—80s**. I lump them together because when people ask me my age, I sometimes tell them that I'm 88. At other times, I tell them that I'm 98. It just depends on my mood and how much I need to be pumped up. I love looking at them as they look at me. They smile. They beam. Then they declare, "My goodness, Professor Kendrick! You sure don't look that old. And to think that you still manage to teach. How on earth do you do it?"

What an ego trip those comments give me, all because of my playful exaggeration. Of course, I still teach. Of course,

I don't look 98 or 88—well, hopefully I don't—because I'm a **Septuagenarian—70s**. I exaggerate my age for a very good and highly legitimate reason. When I tell folks that I'm 74, I get puzzled looks or no comments at all. What can I say? I've left folks looking puzzled and speechless more than once in my life. Trust me. It never had anything to do whatsoever with my age.

Then we have **Sexagenarian—60s**—and **Quinquagenarian—50s**.

Oddly enough, the terms **Quadragenarian—40s**—and **Tricenarian—30s**—are not in common usage. Somehow that strikes me as an affront to both groups.

The same can be said of **Vicenarian—20s**—and **Denarians—10 to 19**.

All that I can say is this. Perhaps it's not an affront after all that those terms are not in common usage for those age groups. I should know. When I was someone in those age groups, I wouldn't have wanted to be called those things either, any more than I would want to be called a Septuagenarian now. I mean, come on. Who wants to be called something that the person doing the calling can't even pronounce, let alone spell.

I warned you nine paragraphs ago that these terms were dreadful. Candidly, they ended up being more dreadful than I ever dreaded that they would be dreadful.

Nonetheless, I suppose those terms might come in handy from time to time to add an *aere distinctionis* to what, in reality, are downright insults. And we might just get away with it. Let's see.

"He's an old geyser" might morph into "He's a sexagenarian geyser." That might even be mistaken for sexy.

"She's just an old broad" might become "She's just an octogenarian broad."

In Bed: My Year of Foolin' Around

Truthfully, though—and I am all about truth and transparency—I'm not sure that either insult works any better, all garbed and garbled in Latin as they are.

No doubt, you're still pondering your varying awarenesses of your various ages.

In case you're wondering what I'm pondering—Please tell me that you are wondering. You are, right?—let me tell you that it's not my age.

Actually, I've never pondered my age because I've never had a clear awareness of my age at any age.

I guess you might call me an Age Chameleon. (Go ahead. I've been called far worse.) How old I "feel"—regardless of how I slice it and dice it—changes based on those who are around me.

When I was a kid, surrounded by older folks, I felt wise beyond my years.

Now that I've grown up to be one of those older folks who surrounded me when I was young, I feel like one of the younger kids who surround me now that I am older. (I know what you're thinking, and you can just stop it right now. I have not become my own grandpa.)

Let me explain. When I'm teaching traditional, right-out-of-high-school students, I feel exactly like I felt in my late teens. Independent. Not averse to risks. Extraverted. Romantic. Confident that a full lifetime lies ahead. Confident that my full head of hair will always be full. I like feeling like that.

Sometimes—especially since I teach in a community college—I have some students who have been out of high school for a while. With them, I feel exactly like I felt in my twenties: strong bones, strong muscles, ready to run life's marathons, and ready to make lots of moves—career or otherwise. I like feeling like that, too.

Sometimes, my students are in their thirties, and, around them, I feel just as I felt then: hitting some high notes in my career; thinking about settling down. Or maybe they're in their forties, making me feel as I felt then: climbing toward career peaks; reaching financial security; discovering the power of progressive lenses.

Hopefully, you're getting my point. I see myself pretty much the same age as those with whom I interact.

Dare I tell you the truth? Of course, I will. I always do. I interact with me more than I interact with anyone else in the entire world. And in those interactions, I feel just as I felt when I was 27. Unstoppable. I feel that way, that is, until I walk past a mirror. I hate mirrors because they shatter the unreality of my 27-year old self. I do not blush at all to tell you that I have considered removing all the mirrors in my home, but if I did, how on earth would I manage to comb the hair (that I have less and less of) or check to see that all the wispy strands (that I have more and more of) are in place?

But let me bring me and you back to my point before you and I both drift off to parts unknown.

I like the fact that I am an Age Chameleon. I think that it might be a blessing in disguise.

It gives me the best of all the ages. Potential. Hope. Vitality. Playfulness. Imagination. Ingenuity. Passion. Enterprise. Contemplation.

Toss in to that fantabulous mix two more things. Benevolence. Wisdom.

I don't mind at all that I am not aware of my age and that it doesn't matter to me.

Here's the way I see it. As I work at wrapping my head around age, maybe—just maybe—I'll end up wrapping my head around life.

JUNE 27, 2022

Living with a Writer

"Blessed are the weird people: poets, misfits, writers, mystics, painters, troubadours, for they teach us to see the world through different eyes."

— JACOB NORDBY,
(b. 1973; author of *Blessed Are the Weird: A Manifesto for Creatives*, 2016.)

Writers have been the mainstay of my intellectual life since childhood.

It's safe to say that I know more about writers than I know about anything else. I know not only the breadth and depth of their literary canons (especially those writers whose works I enjoy and teach) but also the breadth and depth of their lives (even those writers whose works I do not enjoy and do not teach).

Taken as a whole, I suppose that writers are a hard lot to live with. (Taken as a whole, I suppose that we are all a hard lot to live with.)

But writers seem to be harder to live with than most of us, and they have more quirks and more eccentricities in their lives and relationships than most of us. Or, maybe it's simply that they are more in our faces because they have achieved literary fame, the consequence of which is having the world look at all the foibles of their lives through painstaking, unforgiving, and unforgetting research.

A few examples of writerly quirks and eccentricities will suffice. Then you can decide for yourself.

One of the first writers to pop into my mind is Oscar Wilde. He had many eccentricities, but can you imagine living with someone who once walked down the street with his pet lobster on a leash, as he supposedly did on at least one occasion?

Or what about Lord Byron who, when at school, kept a pet bear in his room, walked it around campus on a leash, and even tried to get it a fellowship.

More alarming, still, is Mary Shelley who wrote with her 23-foot boa wrapped around her shoulders. Supposedly, she would write until the boa started to squeeze, at which moment she would stop for the day. Perfect timing, no?

Shelley and Byron and Wilde make Edgar Allan Poe look rather sane if not downright boring. So what if he wrote with his Siamese cat on his shoulder as a double source of relaxation and inspiration? No big deal.

At least two writers had a thing for apples and water, separately not together—the apples and the water, not the authors. Friedrich Schiller kept rotten apples in his desk drawer, claiming that the smell motivated him. And to keep from falling asleep while writing, he dipped his feet into ice water. For her inspiration—a century or so later—Agatha Christie chose to eat the apples rather than let them rot. She did so while taking a bath.

At least one writer wrote wearing nothing but his ideas and his underwear (John Cheever). Another exercised naked in front of the window (Franz Kafka) and enjoyed going to nudist camps. He always stood out in the crowd. Go ahead. Guess. Nope. You're wrong. He was the only guy wearing swimming trunks.

Some writers stand out in other ways: their writing quarters. Dylan Thomas had a writing hut on his estate. Roald Dahl visited Thomas and was so impressed by the hut that he made one for himself based on the exact same dimensions. George Bernard Shaw's writing hut was truly unique. It was built on a turntable so that it could be rotated to let in the sun.

And let's not leave out some really strange quirks that writers use to achieve quotas or to meet deadlines. I am most impressed by Demosthenes who shaved half of his head, knowing that his embarrassment would keep him at home and on task. Victor Hugo was far less dramatic: he met his writing quotas simply by having his valet hide his clothes.

Unrelated to the preceding examples of writers having hard-to-live-with quirks are two writerly snippets too good to not snip and include here. I must. I can. Therefore, I shall. Did you know that John Steinbeck's dog Toby ate nearly half of the first manuscript version of his *Of Mice and Men*? I cannot help but wonder whether that culinary delight is the origin of the student lament that educators hear over and over again, "My dog ate my homework."

All right. I cannot leave you or me in such intellectual limbo. I will be right back to report my findings after I consult the *Oxford English Dictionary (OED)*.

I'm back. What a fun journey, though I confess that my speculation was in error. The phrase first appeared in print in the *Manchester Guardian* (July 1929): "It is a long time since I have had the excuse about the dog tearing up the arithmetic homework."

While consulting the *OED*, I decided to go ahead and verify the second snippet that I am about to snip and share since I was not certain of its accuracy. Did you know that Samuel Taylor Coleridge coined the following: *selfless, psychosomatic, bipolar, bisexual,* and *suspension of disbelief*?

All right. I was wrong about *selfless*. It first appeared in J. Godolphin *Holy Arbor* (1651): "I leave this Memento with all selfless Christians." Coleridge did not use it until 1825 in his *Aids to Reflections* 112: "Holy Instincts of Maternal Love, detached and in selfless purity."

I was right about the other words. *Psychomatic* first appeared in Coleridge's *Shorter Wks. & Fragments (1834)*: "Hope and Fear..have slipt out their collars, and no longer run in couples...from the Kennel of my Psycho—somatic Ology." *Bipolar* appeared in 1810 in his *Friend*: "Philosophy being necessarily bipolar." *Bisexual* appeared in 1825 in his *Aids to Reflection.* 252: "The very old Tradition of the *Homo androgynus, i.e.* that the original Man ... was bisexual." And my favorite of all—*suspension of disbelief*—first appeared in his *Biographia Literaria* II. xiv. 2: "A semblance of truth sufficient to procure for these shadows of imagination that willing suspension of disbelief for the moment, which constitutes poetic faith" (1817).

Obviously, I am fascinated by writers' quirks and eccentricities. What is not so obvious is the fact that I would have been able to tolerate and be amused by the quirks and eccentricities if I had actually lived with a writer.

For better or for worse, I never had the opportunity.

But I have been blessed to live with one writer for most of my entire life, 24/7. Vicariously.

That's exactly what I have done with Robert Frost since 1955 when he took up his residence with me, vicariously: heart, head, home.

It's been easy living with him as I have done. In fact, I would say that I have had the best of all possible Frostian worlds. I have enjoyed all the good. And I have been spared all the drama—mainly a thread of depression that seems to have plagued the entire family. I have been able to read about it rather than live with it.

I started living with Frost when I was in the third grade. My teacher, Marie Massie, introduced me to literature, and she started with Robert Frost. She hooked me with his poem "Birches." I still recall reciting the entire lengthy poem—59 lines—not only before the entire class but also mid-air, alone, as I too "subdued my father's trees / By riding them down over and over again / Until I took the stiffness out of them." It did not matter to me then that I had not caught the deeper meanings of the poem and that I had missed the ambiguities. I simply liked the sounds, the word play, the associations. And I wanted more. My teacher obliged, not just with poems, but also with Frost's "The Figure a Poem Makes." I dare say that very little of the essay made sense to my third-grade mind, but I warmed up from the start to Frost's notion that poetry, like a piece of ice on a hot stove, should ride along on its own melting.

From that point forward, Frost has served as my own literary touchstone, constant companion, and friend. Every day, at least once a day, sometimes more, something always seems to happen that reminds me of something in Frost's poetry. And off I go on my poetic flight. Or perhaps it is that every day, at least once a day, something in Frost's poetry reminds me of something else. And off I fly. Whichever way it happens, it's a journey of constant joys and surprises and poetic feats of associations.

On more than one occasion, Frost has been my dream companion.

It's usually the same dream, over and over, capturing the stereotypical—and erroneous—image of Frost, the farmer poet. Frost and I are always in a garden. It's always summer. I've always worked up a heavy sweat, always pushing a hand plow, always tilling the soil between rows of plants while he always sits all relaxed and all leisure-like on a stump as he recites some of his poems.

That recurring dream started when I was in grade school. I still dream the dream from time to time, and I love it because I am always young and thrilled to be laboring in the presence of my very own poet.

I try, as best I can, to forget the one spat that I had with Frost. Thank God, it was a vicarious and momentary falling out, a literary lovers' quarrel of sorts. I remember the details vividly. They still pain my memory.

It was the morning of January 20, 1961. Robert Frost had been asked to write and read a poem at John F. Kennedy's Inauguration. For the occasion, Frost wrote "Dedication." I watched as televised Frost entered the homes of Americans and others throughout the world. It was an historic occasion. Kennedy was the youngest president to be elected at the age of 43. Kennedy was the first Catholic to be elected president. And Frost was the first poet to be invited to read at a presidential inauguration.

It was a cold, blustery, snowy day and the sun was shining so glaringly on Frost's manuscript that he fumbled and fumbled and fumbled. Yet he kept trying. Finally, he decided—wisely—to abandon the manuscript of the poem written for the occasion and instead to recite from memory his "The Gift Outright." Both poems are so similar in spirit that I am not certain the shift in text mattered.

Frost was clearly embarrassed by the turn of events and his struggle, but the audience roared with approval and Frost stole their hearts.

He made my heart fall. I remember commenting to my parents, who were watching television with me, that the crowd cheered simply because they were glad that the fiasco was over and that laws should exist to keep old people from embarrassing themselves in public that way.

To this day, I cannot believe my youthful unkindness on the occasion. I have shared my reaction down through the years, hoping that open confession would lessen the pain of my thoughtlessness.

It has not.

On a more positive note, on more than one occasion, I've nearly brushed up against fleeting moments of Frostian fame.

As an undergraduate, I decided to prepare a concordance of Frost's poetry. Without consulting anyone, I spent two years building the concordance on index cards. At that point, I was emboldened to propose the publication to Frost's publisher, Holt, Rhinehart, and Winston. Their reply brought a crushing blow: they had entered into a contract with Edward Connery Lathem to develop a Frost concordance. It was published several years later in 1971.

Another close brush with Frostian fame came a year or two later when I reached out to the United States Postal Service suggesting a Commemorative Postage Stamp on the one hundredth anniversary of Frost's birth: March 26, 1974. Unfortunately, work on the commemorative stamp was underway already. Nonetheless, my enthusiasm earned me a Frost Commemorative Postage Stamp Poster, and it has graced every office that I have occupied since then. I always hang it so that it's the first thing anyone sees when they enter my office. Measuring three feet by four feet, it is commanding, and it makes a commanding statement. To the right of the crusty old bard's portrait—seated and writing at a makeshift desk—is a quote from his poem "Mending Wall": "Before I built a wall I'd ask to know / What I was walling in or walling out, / And to whom I was like to give offense. / Something there is that doesn't love a wall…"

I value the poster not only because of my personal—albeit ever so slight—connection to the commemorative postage stamp but also because the quote captures a critically important lesson in human relationships and gives each of us an ongoing admonishment about the folly of building walls that separate us from ourselves and those around us.

Decades later, I brushed against Frost in the flesh, if you will, when I had the honor of introducing his granddaughter, Leslie Lee Francis, as part of a 2002 Distinguished Lecture Series co-sponsored by Shenandoah University and Lord Fairfax Community College. She spoke on "Education by Poetry." It was a special treat for me to meet and chat extensively with Dr. Francis, daughter of Lesley Frost, the eldest child of Robert and Elinor Frost. When the evening ended, she gifted me with an inscribed copy of her book *The Frost Family's Adventure in Poetry: Sheer Morning Gladness at the Brim* (University of Missouri Press, 1994.) In the book, Dr. Francis traces the family's adventures from their years on the Derry Farm in New Hampshire through their nearly three years in England, bringing Robert Frost to the brink of recognition as a poet. Her gift brought me to the brink of tears.

Who would have ever dreamt that a third-grade teacher in the mountainous coalfields of West Virginia would have turned me on to a poet with such fervor that he would become my constant companion for life? But she did. I have never forgotten the magic that she worked, and it's that same kind of magic that I hope to perform whenever I enter a classroom to teach a literature course. I always have in mind certain goals, objectives, and outcomes that I hope my students will achieve. But deep down in my heart I have one goal that surpasses all of the pedagogical ones. And I share it with my students. My hope for them is that somewhere during the course they will find a writer—a poet, short story writer, playwright, novelist—any writer who from that point forward will serve as a touchstone in their lives—a friend; a companion; someone who will be there with them always; someone they can live with forever.

Living with a writer, especially vicariously, might just be the best of all possible worlds.

JULY 5, 2022

Take Two: Living with a Writer—More Frostian Moments

"All thought is a feat of association; having what's in front of you bring up something in your mind that you almost didn't know you knew."

— Robert Frost
(1874-1963; one of America's most celebrated poets.)

L ots—and I mean lots—can be said about last week's post "Living with a Writer." I'm not talking about the number of views. The post enjoyed the usual readership. (I will note, however, that it had more readers than usual from foreign countries, including Bosnia & Herzegovina as well as Ecuador.) I'm not talking about **Likes**, although I was pleased that it had a few more **Likes** than usual. (It might interest you to know that "Fit as A Fiddle: The Inefficient Way" has the distinction of being my most **Liked** post of all.)

What's really important about last week's post relates to the mileage that I'll be getting—this week and continuing for several weeks beyond—from reader feedback! I am listening. I hear you. I thank you. And trust me: I'm going to run with the ideas that you tossed my way. I always do.

Some feedback came as emails; other feedback came as comments published to the post.

Here's my plan. This week I will focus exclusively on readers' emails, since my responses to them are rather straightforward. I will reserve responses to last week's comments until next week's post. Actually, the comments are so rich that I might even get still another week's post from their richness. Everything is copy. (See my "Directions to the Magical World of Ideas.")

In one email, a faithful reader wanted to know what Lesley Francis—granddaughter of Robert and Elinor Frost—wrote in the copy of her *The Frost Family's Adventure in Poetry: Sheer Morning Gladness at the Brim* that she gave me on April 9, 2002, when I introduced her as part of a Distinguished Lecture Series co-sponsored by Shenandoah University and Lord Fairfax Community College.

I was thrilled to get that email query because I had wanted to include the inscription in my initial post. Unfortunately, I could not because the book was in my office at the college, and, as you know, I work on these posts at night on my smartphone while lying in bed. If you don't know that, you might want to read my "Spaces and Habits of Famous (and Not-So-Famous) Writers".

Since last week's post, though, I went to the college, I pulled the volume from my shelf, and I nostalgically read the inscription:

"For / Brent Kendrick, who / has let Frost lead him / 'knowing how way leads on to / way.' With best wishes from the author and granddaughter / Lesley Lee Francis / 4/9/02 / Lord Fairfax CC".

The quote within her inscription, of course, is from the third stanza of what, without doubt, is one of Frost's most popular poems, "The Road Not Taken":

> And both that morning equally lay
> In leaves no step had trodden black.
> Oh, I kept the first for another day!
> Yet knowing how way leads on to way,
> I doubted if I should ever come back.

The same faithful reader wanted to know whether I had mentioned any specific Frost poems when I introduced his granddaughter. Splendid question. Indeed, I did. Throughout the afternoon on the day of Dr. Francis' lecture—"Education by Poetry"—showers passed intermittently through our area, and I had been reciting in my mind a Frost poem that appeared in his book of poetry, *A Boy's Will*. I recall wishing that the rain were a little heavier, that the winds were a little more fierce, and that the time of year were not quite so much into spring—perhaps a patch of snow here and there—so that the realities of the day would match more closely those of the poem that I had been reciting. Even though the poetic conditions and the natural conditions that day didn't enjoy a one-to-one correlation, I included Frost's "To the Thawing Wind" as part of my introduction. The poem welcomes spring rains, the return of birds and flowers, as well as flowing streams. But equally important is the desire for spring to:

> Burst into my narrow stall;
> Swing the picture on the wall;
> Run the rattling pages o'er;

Scatter poems on the floor;
Turn the poet out of door.

    Quoting the poem seemed perfect for the season and the occasion.
    Another reader wanted to know some instances when something happened that made me think of a Robert Frost quote.
    Actually, it happened most recently just a few minutes ago while I was writing. When I wrote "I nostalgically read the inscription," I thought immediately of how Frost likened poetry to homesickness and love sickness:
    "Poetry begins with a lump in your throat; a homesickness or a love sickness. It is a reaching out toward expression; an effort to find fulfillment. A complete poem is one where an emotion has found its thought and the thought has found words" (Frost to Louis Untermeyer, 1916).
    Here's another instance. A few nights ago, when I had my nightly phone chat with my sister Audrey, she mentioned that she was rather taken aback when she went to swat a fly, and it seemed to pause and look at her. As she shared her experience with me, I was reminded of Frost's "A Considerable Speck." In the poem, the speaker encounters a speck on his manuscript page—still wet with ink. Just as he was about to *"stop it with a period of ink,"* he has a profound realization:

> Plainly with an intelligence I dealt.
> It seemed too tiny to have room for feet,
> Yet must have had a set of them complete
> To express how much it didn't want to die.
> […]

> I have a mind myself and recognize
> Mind when I meet with it in any guise.
> No one can know how glad I am to find
> On any sheet the least display of mind.

And for one final example. Just this past Sunday, as I worshipped outdoors while weed whacking along my mountain road to pretty it up for July 4th, I happened upon a small clump of storybook sweet peas with tenacious tendrils and a subtle, alluring fragrance. I had not planted it. How it had gotten there was a mystery to me. But it was so exquisite all alone—showcased midst briar and bramble and honeysuckle—that I spared it. I had not the heart to level it to the ground from which it sprang. I mowed around it, fully confident that it would bring joy to at least one passerby, perhaps more. And, if none, the seeing and the sparing had brought hefty morning notes of joy to me, equal to cathedral tunes.

As soon as the sweet pea stole my fancy—as soon as I saved it—my mind fragranced off to Frost's "A Tuft of Flowers." In the poem, the worker who has come to turn the grass after it has been mown, looks and listens unsuccessfully for the one who had done the mowing:

> But he had gone his way, the grass all mown,
> And I must be, as he had been,—alone,
> "As all must be," I said within my heart,
> "Whether they work together or apart."

At that moment, a butterfly drew attention to a tall tuft of flowers beside a brook:

> The mower in the dew had loved them thus,
> By leaving them to flourish, not for us,
> Nor yet to draw one thought of ours to him.
> But from sheer morning gladness at the brim.

As the poem continues, the speaker comes to the belief that he has stumbled upon a message from the dawn:

> And dreaming, as it were, held brotherly speech
> With one whose thought I had not hoped to reach.
> "Men work together," I told him from the heart,
> "Whether they work together or apart."

Frostian moments such as these may be small. They may be fleeting. They may be seemingly insignificant. But one thing is for certain. They stand as extraordinary reminders of why literature matters: it has the magical power to transport us from our ordinary worlds to unforeseen spiritual realms.

JULY 11, 2022

Take Three. Living with a Writer: Owning Up to My Own Eccentricities

A civilized society is one which tolerates eccentricity to the point of doubtful sanity.

— ROBERT FROST
(1874-1963; one of America's most celebrated poets.)

You may take great pleasure in knowing that this may be my shortest blog post ever. The operative word here is *may*. I won't know how short this post will be until I reach the end. That, I suppose, is **my first writerly eccentricity**. My writing—very much like Robert Frost's—rides along on its own melting, like a piece of ice on a hot stove. It goes where it wants to go, and it moves where it wants to move.

But I suspect this post may be my shortest because I will be sharing my eccentricities. Goodness, no. Not those. How on earth did you know about those, anyway? They're far too personal to share with the world at large. Besides, a post focusing on them would take years and years to share. Not really. But, on the other hand, maybe.

But since I have slid off course already, let me go ahead and share one—just one—of my personal eccentricities before attempting to get back into the flow of writing about my writing eccentricities.

Here it is. I have a tremendous fascination with numbers. Doesn't that strike you as odd, especially since I am an English professor? It does me. Maybe it will strike you as less odd when I tell you that my fascination is limited to certain types of numbers. Like palindromes. You know. The ones that read the same, forward and backward. **11, 22, 101, 111, 666, 999**. I don't have anything against palindromes, mind you, especially if I only see one every now and then as I go about my day. But some days it seems they won't go away, especially when they take up residence in my digital clocks and glare at me. **1:11. 3:13. 3:33. 7:07.** (Thankfully, they never take up residence in my Grandfather Clock. Palindromes are as much visual as they are numerical.)

What's even more fascinating are mirror hours. **10:10. 11:11. 12:12.** You see them, right? Well, if you don't, from this point forward, you will. And when you do, you will sit up and take notice, just as I do.

Depending on the combinations and the frequencies, I tend to believe—as many people do—that palindromic numbers and mirror hours signal the presence of messenger angels. I do my best to be attentive to their messages, too, especially if I see the same number repeatedly in the course of a day. A few days ago, for example, I couldn't escape **555**. It was everywhere. I even saw it on my Fitbit. After doing a timed, 6-minute morning meditation, my Fitbit showed that the session fell 5 seconds short, coming in at **5:55** minutes.

But I didn't mind. **555** is an intriguing Angel number heralding adventure, change, liberation, and intensity. Bring it all on. I'm revved. I'm ready.

But this is neither the time nor the place for me to discuss my personal eccentricities. I would be lying if I told you that I don't have any more, just as you would be lying if you told me that you weren't dying to know what they are. Forget it. I'm not telling. (Well, maybe a double Martini—extra dry, up, with a twist of lemon—could encourage me to tell a thing or three. Maybe.)

Let's see. Let me do my best to slip-and-slide my way back a little closer to the melting ice cube of my original intent: my eccentricities as a writer. It occurs to me that this might be the perfect place to thank one of my faithful followers who, after reading my "Living with a Writer," commented: *"You are a published author that continues to educate and amuse us on a weekly basis. I'm sure we would all love to know what your quirks and eccentricities are when it comes to writing?"*

I hope that you love what you have read so far so much that you will continue reading to the end as I continue to put into full public view my writerly quirks.

My second eccentricity as a writer bears close kinship to the first. Unlike Edgar Allan Poe who needed to know the last line of what he was writing before he put his pen to page, I need to know the first line of what I'm writing before I touch the first letter on my smartphone. (Yes. I write my blog posts on my smart phone. See my "Spaces and Habits of Famous—and Not-so-Famous—Writers.") Once I get that first line, the rest melts along all on its own.

My third eccentricity as a writer relates to the first two. With the first line that I write, I like to get a rhythm going, usually a slow and easy one. It's the sort of rhythm that gospel singer Rev. F. C. Barnes gets going in his "He Was There Just in Time to Rescue Me." He opens his rendition by saying, *"You know. This song is kinda like me: slow. But ya'll don't mind, do you?"* Then he continues by working the title line and one or two other lines, over and over and over again, for a soothingly rhythmic song stretching out for **8:18** minutes. It's much the same thing that the Barrett Sisters do in their "Jesus Loves Me" as they milk the rhythm and richness of just three words for a commanding **5:15** minutes. It's the same thing that Lucille Clifton does in her "won't you celebrate with me" as she rocks us in a world that has tried to kill her every day but has failed. Those rhythms—and other similar ones—bounce around and around and around in my head and sometimes carry more meaning than the actual words that I spit out. Frost would call it the sound of sense. In my own writing, I am never quite sure what the rhythm is or whether I am achieving it. Often it is more felt than seen, but it pulls my thoughts forward and piles them, like little pillows one atop another, and I like to think that it has the soft sound of sense.

My next eccentricity as a writer—my fourth—is one that I outgrew a long time ago, but it has such quirky quirks that I will memorialize it here for the record.

In the late 1970s and early 1980s when I was working on my *The Infant Sphinx: Collected Letters of Mary E. Wilkins Freeman*, I drafted the general introduction and the introductions to each of the five sections in longhand.

But wait. It gets better.

I wrote them on a note pad. Not just any note pad. It had to be a yellow, legal notepad.

And it gets even better, if such be possible. I had to write using #2, yellow pencils. No erasers. Read on. Discover why.

If I made a mistake on a page, I could not erase. I could not scratch through and move on. I was compelled to rip out the blemished page and start over on a brand-new page, proving my mastery of ideas if not my mastery of time well spent.

I continued that approach to writing for a long, long time.

When PCs came along, however, I shifted with great joy because I discovered that I didn't need to throw any of my drafts away. I could keep them all, simply by giving each a unique revision number. Keeping all of my drafts, I suppose, is **my fifth eccentricity as a writer.** I enjoy going back to see how an essay changed over time, from start to finish. More often than not, I will revise anything that I write a dozen or more times. (Let me add here that I love—absolutely love—preparing my posts in WordPress. It automatically tracks and keeps all the changes that I make for each and every post. Right now, for this post, WordPress has captured **22** revisions. I work hard for the money. Thank you very much.)

At this point, I have a huge decision to make. It involves an eccentricity that is personal, but it will have an impact on the writerly eccentricities that I do or do not share with you from this point forward. It, too, has to do with numbers. I do things in odd numbers only. For example, when I'm gardening, plants get planted as single plants or in groupings of **3, 5, 7, 9** and so on. I just don't do even numbers. Right now, then, I have two choices, and choices are always good. I can stop my post here with five writing eccentricities. Or I can give you a sixth one and then be forced to end with a seventh.

Well, bless you, for shouting out that you want more. I am glad to continue, especially since **7** is one of my favorite numbers. Think about it for a minute. 7 Days. 7 Seas. 7 Brides. 7 Sisters. 7 Dwarfs. 7 Wonders of the Ancient World. And 7 Horsemen of the Apocalypse.

Without further rhythmic delay, let's start exploring my sixth eccentricity.

Those who know me, know that I do not like being told what to do (well, that's generally true) especially when it comes to writing (and that's always true). But I love telling others what to do, especially when it comes to writing. Here's the backstory. It all started on a wordy, wordy day when I was a sophomore in high school. My teacher Anna Mae Collins would march into our classroom, always wearing prim and proper dresses that generally looked like a nurse's uniform regardless of the color or the fabric. But that didn't matter. Mrs. Collins loved the parts of speech and sentence diagramming, and since I loved both as well, I loved her all the more. For a typical writing assignment—given usually on a Friday—she would provide the topic and the word length for the essay. She had lots of topics—so many that I don't remember any. But I remember that she loved essays that were 1,200 words long. More, she loved giving us a structural formula that we had to follow. Here's how it might go. 9 paragraphs. 10 compound sentences. 6 compound-complex sentences. 4 complex sentences. 1 interrogative sentence. 1 exclamatory sentence. And 1 imperative sentence. We had to underline each of those various types of sentences and identify them in the margin.

We would work our proverbial little butts off all weekend. Well, that's rather presumptuous of me, isn't it? Let me revise that claim. I would work my proverbial little butt off all weekend. Ms. Collins would march into class on Monday. I'd be sitting right up front, all smiles because

I had met all of her requirements, each and every one of them. I was pumped with pride. She would clomp up and down the aisles, collecting our essays one by one, sizing them up as she clomped.

With measured tread, she would advance to the front:

> Class, I am fully confident that your essays are excellent. But you can make them better. Take them home tonight and cut out all the huff and puff and fluff. Watch out for those nasty prepositional phrases. Adjectives will work just as well. You must keep the content of your original essay. However, your revised essay can only be 700 words long. Exactly 700 words. Also, you must use the same formula that I gave you on Friday: 9 paragraphs. 10 compound sentences. 6 compound-complex sentences. 4 complex sentences. 1 interrogative sentence. 1 exclamatory sentence. And 1 imperative sentence.

Folks. Folks. Folks. We're talking the Dark Ages of the 1960s. We had to handwrite those essays on lined paper. We had to count the words, word by word. And here we were having to go home and do it all over again. The moans and groans were loud enough to be heard in the principal's office which is precisely where Mrs. Collins would have marched us if we had challenged her assignment. The more often she gave us assignments like that, the more often I fell in love with Anna Mae because through her I fell in love with the power of revision, especially the powerful revision that takes place when writers have to follow precise guidelines, including word counts.

My sixth eccentricity as a writer, then, is my belief that less can be more. (I believe that everywhere, of course, except in my blog posts. For those, I fantasize that I am being paid by the word. For those, I fantasize that I have **1.41** million followers.)

It will come as no surprise, then, when I tell you that one of my favorite writing assignments for my students—in College Composition and in Creative Writing—is to have them write an essay that is exactly 500 words, excluding the title. Not 499. Not 501. Exactly 500. (Oh, my! I just had a wonderful idea. I can combine this quirk with my numbers quirk and change the length to exactly **555** words. It's a done deal. Please do not tell prospective students who might have signed up for my classes this fall.)

Further, it will come as no surprise when I tell you that students never change. Mine moan and groan as much as my classmates did in 1963. Unlike them, however, my students come to class with their 500-word essays and thank me profusely. They truly do.

I'm not sure what just happened, but my sixth writerly eccentricity was remarkably longer than any of the previous ones.

I promise. My seventh will be shorter. Hopefully.

Anna Mae Collins was not my only English teacher who insisted on eliminating huff and puff and fluff through tight and rigorous revision.

In college, my freshman English professor Barbara Smith required us to analyze everything that we wrote using the Gunning Fog Index. It was developed by publisher Robert Gunning who theorized that people could not read because newspapers and periodicals encouraged writing that was far too complex. I was fascinated by the Fog Index and discovered readily that my 25-word sentences did nothing but hide the soul and spirit of my message. It was then that I started using smaller words and shorter sentences.

The Fog Index is still used, but today our computers can measure the fog level for us automatically. MS Word calls it Readability Statistics. Those metrics provide a word count, a Readability Score, a Grade Level, and more.

Here's my seventh and final eccentricity as a writer: I run Readability Statistics on everything that I write. What's that? You want proof? Sure. Here are the stats for this post: **Readability Score: 76.4%.** (The higher the percentage, the easier the read.) **Grade Level: 6.1.** (The lower the grade level, the easier the read.) I'm pleased with those stats. Maybe I'm slightly puffed. Maybe I'm slightly full of it. But I simply must tell you that former Presidents Barack Obama and Abraham Lincoln's best prose have comparable Readability Statistics. I cannot think of better company.

Clearly, this post did not end up as one of my shortest. It *may* end up as one of my longest.

What can I say? Blame it on the ice. Blame it on the hot stove. Blame it on Robert Frost. Better still: thank my faithful reader who asked me to write about my writerly quirks and eccentricities.

JULY 18, 2022

Take Four. Living with A Writer: Modern Applications of Ancient Writing Artifacts

"We are always yapping about the "Good Old Days" and how we look back and enjoy it, but I tell you there is a lot of hooey to it. There is a whole lot of our past lives that was not so hot."

— WILL ROGERS
(1879-1953; American vaudeville performer, actor, and social commentator.)

Hey, everyone! Listen up! Make certain that you keep a copy of this post in a safe, virtual folder. Maybe even the Cloud. It is destined for fame. It is destined for greatness. It is destined for glory. It will go down in the annals of history as the most historic and historical blog post ever published.

You will discover why as you continue to read. But let me start with one reason and that one reason alone will earn this post its deserved historical distinction. For the first time in my life, I am at a loss for words. I am. My students would be thrilled beyond thrills because they consider me to be exhaustive and, no doubt, exhausting when I start talking about anything that is near and dear to my heart.

No doubt, you—dear reader—are wondering why on earth I am at a loss for words. Let me explain. My post last week focused exclusively on me: "Take Three. Living with a Writer: Owning Up to My Own Eccentricities."

One of my eccentricities that I felt comfortable sharing was the fact that I had drafted the general introduction and the introductions to the five sections of my *The Infant Sphinx: Collected Letters of Mary E. Wilkins Freeman* on yellow legal pads, using #2 pencils without erasers. The really quirky part of that eccentricity was that whenever I made a mistake, I ripped out the page and started over.

One of my faithful followers challenged me to write my next post on a yellow legal pad, using a #2 pencil, and to share with you what happened as I wrote. Dear reader, you are so undeserving of the suffering that you will surely suffer as you continue to read. But please do continue to read. Remember: no pain, no gain. (Because I love you so much—whoever you are and wherever you are [including you, Mrs. Callabash, wherever you are]—I have timed the read-time for this post. You are now 6 minutes and 36.3 seconds away from full fatigue and brain drain.)

It was a commendable challenge, so much so that I really should quote it verbatim, and I would, but I can't. I am lying in bed writing my post on a legal pad, using a #2 pencil, as challenged—I am such a sucker for challenges—so I don't want to lose my grain of thought by switching over to my Smartphone to look at last week's post so that I can quote the comment in its entirety the way that it deserves to be quoted.

Therefore, starting with the next paragraph I will use placeholders for anything that I would normally have the good sense to look up instanter on my Smartphone. I will use this placeholder convention throughout this post. My very first one follows.

Placeholder for When I Return to My Sanity and My Smartphone: Insert faithful reader quote from last week. I believe the reader signed herself **"J."**

I responded to **"J's"** challenge by asking whether yellow legal pads were even manufactured these days. I noted that if they had fallen out of usage, not to worry: I had seen such writing artifacts at the Smithsonian Institution and, perhaps, I could arrange for a Docupost: **Modern Applications of Ancient Writing Artifacts.**

My reply to **"J."** was far more brilliant than it appears here, but, again, I can't easily switch over to my Smartphone.

Placeholder for When I Return to My Sanity and My Smartphone: Insert my dazzling reply to **"J."** Make sure to capture the correct title of the Docupost that I plan to propose to the Smithsonian Institution.

Not long after **"J's"** comment, another faithful follower—**"soyfig"**—informed me that she had some yellow legal pads and #2 pencils that I could have.

Placeholder for When I Return to My Sanity and My Smartphone: insert **"soyfig's"** actual comment, especially since, as I recall, she used some figurative language.

I responded, of course. I respond to everything, seen and unseen, heard and unheard. But, sadly, I do not remember my exact reply, but I am sure that it was a beauty.

Placeholder for When I Return to My Sanity and My Smartphone: Insert my beauty-of-a-reply to **"soyfig"** who writes so figuratively.

Obviously, I accepted the challenge because, as I noted earlier, here I am writing about what it's like writing a blog post on a yellow legal pad, using a #2 pencil, while lying in bed.

I should be euphoric, I suppose, because I am certain—and history will confirm my certainty—that what I am developing right here and right now is **a new Creative Nonfiction genre**. To mirror its counterpart in the world of fiction, I hereby announce—with all the power and authority that is not vested in me—that this new genre will be dubbed **Creative *MetaNonfiction.***

Placeholder for When I Return to My Sanity and My Smartphone: Check the *Oxford English Dictionary* (*OED*) to see whether the word and the genre exist already. If not, notify the editors immediately. *"by gorry by jingo by gee by gosh by gum,"* fame awaits.

I believe that I have said so already, but I will say so again: writing my post on this yellow legal pad, using a #2 pencil, is not making me euphoric. I can't speak for you, but I can speak for me. My bed is a place of immense pleasure. Trust me. This is not pleasurable. I've got a stupid yellow legal pad—six times larger than my Smartphone—propped up on my knobby knees and the stupid pencil does not have the same quality graphite that I recall. Yes: I still recall the quality—or lack thereof—of everything going all the way back to the cold and snowy day of my November birth. If that be true—and it is—then fast forward with me and you will know that I speak the truth when I say that recalling something from the 1970s is a piece of graphite for me.

Morever, lean in and listen carefully: the damned yellow legal pad is not backlighted. Why am I whispering? For one good reason. I'm whispering because I don't want anyone to steal my idea! If an ancient writing artifact like a yellow legal pad is going to continue to plague us, at the very least it should be backlighted so that it will not plague us in the dark.

Placeholder for When I Return to My Sanity and My Smartphone: Check the dictionary. Backlighted? Backlit?

I just heard someone ask, "Why does it matter if your yellow legal pad is not backlighted?" [**See above Placeholder.**]

Well, that's a splendid question. It matters a lot. It's starting to get dark outside. My overhead light makes a glare on the yellow legal pad, so I can't use it. My nightstand lamp is not bright enough, so I can't use it either. I must be blunt. I can no longer see what I am writing. And, like my pencil, let me be blunt again. If I can't see what I'm writing, how do I look into the heart of what I'm thinking?

Thank you very much for your suggestion. I expected it. But, as much as I appreciate it—and I do—I will not run out tomorrow to buy a lamp to attach to my headboard. Simply explained: I won't be needing it. I will never write another blog post on a yellow legal pad, using a #2 pencil, while lying in bed at night. Never. Never. Never.

However, I will figure out a way to finish this post since I accepted the challenge, sucker that I am.

Already I can think of three possible solutions.

Solution 1. Fill a Mason jar with fireflies. They might illuminate my yellow legal pad sufficiently.

Solution 2. Jerry-rig a flashlight to the headboard of my bed, with the light beaming down on the yellow legal pad propped up against my knobby knees.

Solution 3. Go to bed at 6pm so that I can work on my post for several hours before it gets too dark for me to see.

"Too dark for me to see" reminds me of Emily Dickinson's first-person account of death, "I Heard a Fly Buzz." The poem ends, I believe, with: "And then I could not see to see."

Placeholder for When I Return to My Sanity and My Smartphone: Find the Dickinson poem and make sure that my quote above is accurate.

I am back to report that my tentative solutions—even though brilliant—were abysmal failures. That's too kind. They were duds.

Firefly Solution. It was fairly easy to catch a jar full: they are everywhere in my yard. And, oh, my! Such a golden glow as they put out. For a while my bedroom looked almost like a nightclub dance floor with strobe lights. But it didn't last long. The glow became dimmer and dimmer and dimmer. And, even more quickly, I grew a guilty feeling for having captured all those helpless little fireflies and for having put them to work against their will *Contra Naturam*. I set them free. Shine bright. Shine far.

Jerry-rigged Flashlight Solution. I thought for sure that this solution would work. However, I couldn't figure out a way to mount the flashlight to my headboard, especially at the required angle. I considered duct tape which seems to work for everything, but when I recalled what I had paid for my Henkel Harris bed, I froze with tape and flashlight in mid-air. It took me hours to free myself.

Going to Bed at 6pm Solution. Forget it for one reason only. I have worked long and hard to earn the reputation that I now proudly hold as a wild, night-owl party animal. My friends and my colleagues have grown so proud of me as I have, over time, extended my bedtime from **8:00pm** to **8:30pm** to **9:00pm**. And I have now, after years of practice, mastered the **10:00pm** hour. When a party's going down,

I want to be found, and I certainly won't be found if I am in bed at **6pm**.

But I have come up with **another solution** that had not occurred to me initially. I will take the first hour of my morning routine to write my blog post on a yellow legal pad, using a #2 pencil.

Well, I tried it. Let me just say that this is not what anyone might *hooey* it up to be. Now I am wishing that I had challenged my two faithful followers to this challenge. Thankfully—and luckily for them—I am not that cruel. *Absit iniuria.*

They wouldn't like all these disruptions either. Up until now, I have made perfectly good and methodical use of a sensible and calming way of writing my post in bed on my Smartphone. Even though I have willingly taken on a momentary stay against my ever-so-sane method, I will remind myself—in *mantra manner*—that I am blazing new trails into **Creative MetaNonfiction**. History and literature demand that I continue. History and literature demand that I see this stupid stint through to a stupendous end.

Placeholder for When I Return to My Sanity and My Smartphone: Look up **Creative MetaNonfiction** to see whether such a genre exists. Oh, no. I remember that I have placed this placeholder in the post already, but since I cannot erase or scratch through, I will build upon the redundancy and puff it up as best I can. Have I actually stumbled upon—simply by stupidly accepting a challenge—a new genre? Oh, joy! Maybe I will enjoy a footnote in the annals of something—anything, please—after all.

Placeholder for When I Return to My Sanity and My Smartphone: Revisit Charlotte Perkins Gilman's "The Yellow Wall-Paper." As I recall, the unnamed narrator who goes insane—always be suspicious of unnamed narrators—may have written HER journal on a yellow legal pad, using a #2 pencil. Well, I am fairly certain that she did not, but look it up anyway. Adding that twist to the original story would be masterful for an updated version. The narrator escaped from the yellow wallpaper. But I wonder: would she be able to escape from her yellow legal pad as masterfully as I am about to do, soon and very soon. You're welcome.

What's ironic about all of this is that when I accepted this challenge, I did so fully expecting fun, even if nothing more than hearing my pencil graphite its way across the page.

Placeholder for When I Return to My Sanity and My Smartphone: Can *graphite* be used as a verb? Well. Duh. I just used it as a verb in the preceding paragraph. Therefore, it can be. Therefore, I really do not need to follow through with this placeholder. I will keep it anyway in the interest of not ripping out this yellow page which is otherwise perfect.

But verbs notwithstanding, my pencil is not making those nostalgic sounds that I had longed for, not even when I bend my ear way down close and personal to the page. Instead, it glides along like a waxy crayon. And, in fact, my box of pencils is labeled, on one side of the box, *Crayon*. Oh, dear. I forgot. *Crayon* means *pencil* in some language. An esteemed English professor—a colleague—took great joy in beaming that to me when I showed the box to her. Well, never mind.

I do mind, however, that the only yellow pads that I could find anywhere were 8 1/2 by 11 inches, even though they were marked *Legal Pad*. Well, excuse me. If it's not 8 1/2 x 14 inches, it's not legal, and shorties like the ones that I ended up with ought to be illegal.

Placeholder for When I Return to My Sanity and My Smartphone: (1) What companies still manufacture these so-called legal pads? (2) Do they come in true legal size? (3) Is it true, as I seem to recall, that courts no longer allow 8 1/2 x 14-inch legal pads because they do not fit readily into filing cabinets—not even virtual ones?

Placeholder for When I Return to My Sanity and My Smartphone: Do a comparable search into #2 pencils. Focus especially on what kind of graphite manufacturers are using for these crayons—I mean pencils—these days.

Placeholder for When I Return to My Sanity and My Smartphone: I need a pull quote for this post. What's the one about a sucker is born every minute? How perfect would that be!

Okay. I need to wrap this post up—Maybe in a yellow graphite bow?—but before I do, I simply must achieve a sense of order with this post—the very first example ever of **Creative MetaNonfiction**. The annals of history await my final word. I do, too.

I know exactly what I will do. I'll number the pages that I have written on this yellow legal pad, using a #2 pencil. And while I'm doing that, I'll write **AMDG** just to the right of each page number, just as a Jesuit lawyer friend of mine did on all his labor relations notes, always written on a genuine yellow legal pad, using a genuine #2 graphite pencil.

Placeholder for When I Return to My Sanity and My Smartphone: Look up **AMDG** to see what that acronym means. Marty had a perverse sense of humor, but, surely, he would not have penciled anything obscene or scandalous, especially since he knew that I would see what he was writing because I almost always leaned over him at the bar. But be sure to look it up anyway before publishing this post.

Wow! I have written 11 pages already about nothing more than what it's like to write my post on a yellow legal pad, using a #2 pencil, while lying in bed. Maybe this **Creative MetaNonfiction** thingy is not as bad as I have *graphited* it up to be. Well, if I can type it up, I can certainly graphite it up. But lo and behold! Here I've gone and coined still another word: *graphited*. Who knows? Maybe a **Creative MetaNonfiction Novel** looms in your future.

I suppose the only thing that might have been more fun than numbering the pages would have been ripping each one out and then taping them all together. I seem to recall a writer who typed one of his books on a continuous roll of paper, created by carefully taping each page together. This would have been, of course, back in the good old, *hooey* typewriter days.

Placeholder for When I Return to My Sanity and My Smartphone: Try to find out the writer who did this. I think that it was Jack Kerouac. I am certain. Yes. I recall it as vividly as if I had helped him! (Oh, how I wish.) He sellotaped enough pages to create a 120-foot roll when he wrote his *On the Road*. Check just to make sure. I would never dare publish anything without verifying all the facts before I spew forth. And also look up *hooey*. It looks like *phooey* to me.

As for any rhythm that I might be achieving while writing on a yellow legal pad, using a #2 pencil, forget it. Forget. It. Trust me. This post is not riding along on its own melting like a piece of ice on a hot stove. Frost itself wouldn't work. And Frost himself wouldn't be able to make it work either. I am so focused on paper and pencil that any semblance of thought has wisely flown far, far away to someone sensible enough to write a blog post sensibly on a Smartphone.

Worse, perhaps, I feel as if I am straddling an immeasurable and unfathomable chasm between the 1970s (when I enjoyed writing on a yellow legal pad, using a #2 pencil) and day before yesterday (when I lost my sanity and sold my writerly soul to the Devil by selling myself on the idea of accepting this challenge). To be certain, the image of such a straddler is an intriguing one. Conjure it up if you can. I double dare you. You will see for yourself. But let me assure you, post haste, that my legs—metaphorical or otherwise—are not nearly long enough to bridge such a chasm, and even if they were, I would not stand for it. I would object vehemently for all the world to hear, as, hopefully, all the world is hearing now.

Hear me and hear me well. What I am about to say is quotable, so go ahead and quote me: ***Phooey to all this hooey.***

I object to it so much that I will end it all right now, in one final declaration!

This is a nonsensical challenge up with which I will not put.

FINAL Placeholder for When I Return to My Sanity and My Smartphone: As I recall, Winston Churchill came up with the above quip as an objection to an editor who wouldn't allow sentences to end with prepositions. Churchill's retort memorialized the folly of editors who foolishly adhere to grammatical rules rather than to common sense and to the sense of sound. Try to find the specifics. Was it in a memorandum? I'm sure that it was, perhaps in 1941?

Halleluiah! I have freed myself at last from this yellow legal pad and from #2 pencils. I have returned to my sanity. (Wisely, however, I will not change one thing—not one *hooey-phooey* word—that I have written so honestly and so painfully as I soared my way to and through the heights of this challenge. *"The moving finger writes, and having writ, moves on."* (No. I will not put a placeholder for that non-Shakespearean quote. You may kindly—if you please and if you need—google it yourself to discover the real author of that quote.) And, thankfully, I have just returned to my Smartphone where I have just had joy beyond measure restored to every fiber—and even every *fibre*—of my being by doing nothing more than tap touching this post through to completion—one character at a time, using just one finger. Is that inefficient or what?

But the greatest joy ever is the knowledge that I have just written—and you have just read—the first example ever of **Creative MetaNonfiction**. May it not last forever in the annals of history and literature. May I be spared such notoriety. May I be remembered in far better ways. But, hey. What the heck. If you insist, I accept: better to be remembered for something, I suppose, than for nothing. Either way, it's all *hooey* to me.

JULY 25, 2022

Gr!t 'R Done!

*"The man who moves a mountain begins
by carrying away small stones."*

— CONFUCIUS
(c.551-c.479 BCE; Chinese philosopher,
politician and teacher; *The Analects*)

Needless to say, I need not even ask what I am about to ask. But I will ask it anyway.

Do you ever feel overwhelmed?

"Who? Me?" I just heard someone ask.

Yes. You. Maybe. But let's edge our way in to this just a little more before you decide, lest you decide too hastily.

I'm not talking about the way you feel when that last straw is headed right toward you, and you know fully well that it's the one that will break your proverbial camel's back.

If that's the mell of a hess you're grappling with, I'm really sorry for your streak of bad luck.

The *overwhelmed* that I have in mind is when you have a mountain smackdab in front of you. It's ginormous. And you have to move it, and you have no idea how you will ever get it done.

Maybe, in reality, it's nothing more than a mole hill. But perceptions are perceptions. If that mole hill is a mountain to you, then it is indeed your mountain.

Aren't we masterful at turning our mole hills into mountains?

I am. You are. We all are.

And, at the same time, let's acknowledge that all of us face real life mountains, too, that we have to move.

It's when we're facing our mountains—the real ones and the mole hills that we have turned into mountains—that we feel overwhelmed. That's when we sigh or cry or moan or groan because at that moment we just don't see how we will ever move that mole hill. We just don't see how we will ever move that mountain. We just don't see how we will ever get it done.

To feel overwhelmed before the mountains of life—real or overblown—is to be human.

This week, I'm feeling superhuman. *Overwhelmed* is on my mind a lot: it's the next to the last week before my summer classes end. Also, *overwhelmed* is on my students' minds a lot this week: they have reading assignments and a final discussion board forum this week and a final reflection essay next week.

(A word to educators who would be wise: abandon those ridiculous final exams. Replace them with meaningful final reflection essays. Reach out to me, and I will share proven strategies that have worked for me during the last four years.)

My apologies for that digressory jab at defunct final exam practices that continue to plague the hallowed ivory halls of learning. I couldn't help myself.

Where was I?

Oh, yes. My students are feeling overwhelmed by end-of-semester assignments and by final reflection essays.

Guess what?

I am, too. It's a mountain of work right in front of me, so close that I can smell the virtual submissions, so close that I can hardly breathe. And I have to get it done.

Let me define the preceding "it." I have to grade all of that student work that's closing in on me and smothering me, because I have to submit final grades two days after those final reflection essays are submitted. My mountain seems even larger.

Oh. Yes. I understand how it feels to feel overwhelmed.

I know, too, that my students always feel overwhelmed at the beginning of the semester. They have so much to do before the end.

I do, too. I'm their learning coach. I'm their learning cheerleader. I'm there to help them move those mole hills. I'm there to help them move those mountains. I'm there to help them get it done.

I always suggest some strategies that they can use to see themselves through to the successful conclusion that they hope to enjoy and that they can enjoy if they work at it.

Ironically, the strategies are always the same whether it's the beginning, or, as it is now, the end.

Ironically, the same strategies work for me, at my beginnings and my endings.

Ironically, the strategies will work for you, at your beginnings and your endings.

Following these strategies can help all of us—me, my students, and you—feel less overwhelmed as we tackle our mole hills and our mountains.

A good place to start is by realistically measuring our

grit. Please tell me that you know about grit. You do, right? Sometimes I have to explain it to my students, so let me explain it here for everyone's benefit.

And yes: after the explanation, you will have a quiz! Don't worry. (1) It's optional. (2) Anyone who takes the quiz will pass.

Grit has nothing to do with IQ. It has nothing to do with talent. It has nothing to do with luck. It has everything to do with your willingness to roll up your sleeves and do the hard work always required to achieve any goal, usually a long-term goal, but it applies as well to short term goals. Grit is all about perseverance and passion.

I have always known about grit, but Angela Duckworth is the one who turned me on to the power and awesomeness of grit. She has turned lots of folks on to it, too, and when you get turned on to grit, get ready to get it done, whatever you need to get done.

I start my semesters by having my students take Duckworth's 10-question Grit Quiz. It's everywhere on the Internet. Why don't you take it, right now? **Hot Tip:** Be honest. No need to fool yourself! Not now. Not ever.

After my students find out how gritty they are, I invite them to share their grit score with the class if they wish. I am always amazed by the fruitful and honest conversations that follow. I just heard someone whisper, "What's your grit score?" Thank you, but no need to whisper. I'm proud of it. I scored a 5. Did you hear me? Let me shout it again. **I'm a 5. I'm as gritty as they grit. My grit is awesome.** When I start it—whatever the "it" is—I'm going to stick with it until I get it done. Count on it.

After our class discussion of grittiness goes wherever it goes—and wherever it goes is always exactly where it ought to go: learning is always spontaneous, and spontaneity is always all right with me—I get my students hooked on Duckworth's TED Talk: "Grit: The Power of Passion and Perseverance." It's powerful. It's motivational. It makes you want to get down and get gritty. Go ahead. Watch it. It's had 26,997,225 views. With any luck, this post might take it up to 27 million views! So come on! Let's gr!t 'r done.

As my students and I get deeper and deeper into the semester, I am always mindful that the journey that I am trying to make a fun and fulfilling one for them might start looking more and more like a mountain. Then I love to share with them little proverbs as little reminders that a little strength applied consistently and for a sustained period of time can bring staggering results. Maybe it's as simple as "The man who would move mountains must begin by carrying away small stones" (Confucius, *The Analects*). Or maybe "Little Strokes Fell Great Oaks" (Benjamin Franklin, *Poor Richard's Almanac*).

Then as research papers start to loom on the horizon, I up the ante still more and share with my classes the backstory for Anne Lamott's classic book on writing and living, *Bird by Bird*. In the introduction to her book, she tells the story of her brother who had waited until the last minute to write his paper that was due the next day. Interestingly enough, the paper was about birds. Lamott's father told him to write the paper bird by bird. Looking at the component parts and completing one part of the paper at a time made the whole project seem less intimidating and less overwhelming.

What Lamott and Franklin and Confucius and a gazillion others are offering up as a pearl of wisdom is a lesson in incrementalism: progress comes gradually, in small steps.

It works for my students. It works for me. It will work for you.

As the semester progresses and end-of-semester fatigue raises its nasty and unnerving head, I can see in my students' faces the reflection of their mountains right in front of them. Then I know that I have to up the ante once again. I play for the class one of my favorite poems by Rita Dove—"Maple Valley Branch Library, 1967." It's an incredible tribute to learning and to libraries and to librarians and to getting it done. It has an even more special meaning for me because Rita Dove read that poem at the White House on May 11, 2011. Former President Obama—who believes that poetry and the arts matter (and they do)—provides a masterful introduction to the power of poetry, with wry, charming humor as only he can do. Afterwards the poet reads her poem. Both the former president and the former United States Poet Laureate are genuine charmers. I'll provide the link in just a second. Watch the video, please. (But not until you finish my post, or, if you insist on watching the video before finishing my post, go ahead. Just come back. I'll be lost without you.) "Rita Dove: 2011 White House Poetry Evening — introduction by Barack Obama."

Without exception, my students always love watching this video. Sometimes they even applaud. Sometimes they even applaud without mention of extra credit. The video inspires. It motivates. It makes them know that they can get it done.

Here's how Dove empowers my students—and all of us— to come to that understanding. The stanzas that follow are directly from her poem. They recount the poet's journey home, as a 15-year-old, carrying six volumes of knowledge— six books that she selected on her learning journey:

> "I carried [the books] home, past five blocks
> of aluminum siding and the old garage
> where, on its boarded-up doors, someone
> had scrawled:
>> I can eat an elephant
>> if I take small bites.
> "Yes, I said, to no one in particular: That's
> what I'm gonna do!"

Overwhelmed? My students? Me? You? All of us?

Of course, we are. To be overwhelmed is to be human.

Thankfully, we're not overwhelmed all of the time. But when we are, isn't it great to know that we have wisdom as our ally—all the way from Confucius to Franklin to Lamott to Dove? Isn't it great to know that we have wisdom cheering us every step of the way? As we carry away our stones. As we fell our oaks. As we write our birds. As we eat our elephants. As we get it done.

Isn't it great knowing that a little gr!t will gr!t 'r done?

It certainly calms me. And just as soon as I finish grading end-of-semester assignments and final reflection essays, I'm going to polish that nugget of truth as I face my next mountain: gardens (right here on my mountain) overtaken by a gazillion weeds, all reaching for the stars.

And guess what else? I will pump myself up just as I try to pump up my students—just as I have tried to pump you up here, so that you can face your own mountains, whatever they might be—and believe you me: I will tackle my mountain, and I will gr!t 'r done.

AUGUST 1, 2022

The Story of Angel Falls

"Hope" is the thing with feathers —
That perches in the soul —
And sings the tune without the words —
And never stops — at all —

— EMILY DICKINSON
from *"Hope is the thing with feathers"* (1830-1886; one of
America's greatest and most original poets.)

This is a story about a weeping pine.

But it's not just any story. It can't be just any story, because this isn't just any weeping pine.

This weeping pine is a special weeping pine. It's one of a kind. It's unique.

I bought it about four months ago. Actually, I bought it on March 17. In case you're wondering why I remember the exact date, here's why. It was my late partner's birthday.

I had not planned to buy anything that day. I was just browsing the local nursery's new arrival of plants, mainly West Coast conifers.

As I walked past one conifer, it looked like a stunning, younger version of a stately, older weeping pine right outside my kitchen door. "Gorgeous!" I thought. "But no need for another one."

At about the same time, the manager walked past and saw me looking. Lingering. Pondering. Wondering.

"You don't want to miss out on this one, Dr. Kendrick. It's super special. We only have two, and they'll go fast."

I've known John since he was a youngster, when his dad owned the nursery, and I trust him just as implicitly as I trust his dad.

"Oh, yeah?" I teased. "What makes it so special?"

John started telling me all the details, reassuring me that it's mature size would be perfect for the small area where he knew that I wanted a unique conifer.

I leaned in close to take a closer look at the tag, and as soon as I saw the name—Angel Falls—I knew that this tree was going home with me. It had to go home with me. Aside from being Allen's birthday, I had written a blog post about him two months earlier, "Honoring an Angel." But this story is not about Allen. This story is about a special weeping pine.

I had an immediate plan. This tree would become one more focal point in the garden that I had designed for Allen. But, again, this story is not about him. This story is about a special weeping pine.

I had just one concern. Even though the tree was small—no more than three feet tall—it was in a large tub, the size, perhaps, of a bushel basket. I knew that John would help load the tree into my Jeep, but could I manage to unload it alone?

I decided to figure out the logistics after I got the weeping pine home.

And figure it out I did. I stacked bags of mulch below my Jeep's lowered tailgate. I slid the tubbed weeping pine onto the top bag, and, then I continued stepping it down onto the ground.

From that point forward, I knew that dragging it downhill to its intended destination would be as easy as stepping into the future.

And, for a second, I stepped off the sharp edge of now into the softened expanse of tomorrow. I stood there—looking beyond the spot where I would plant the weeping pine—gazing ahead into years, each stretching beyond the next, further and further and further into the memory of forever.

And there it stood, as majestic and as grand and as unique as I ever dreamt or hoped that it would become: days, months, seasons and years melting into fluid time.

Then, suddenly, a March wind blew me back to my present reality, and I pushed the tub right beside the spot where, tomorrow, I would dig the hole that would become forever to my Angel Falls weeping pine.

The next day, I did the early, chilly morning needful. I dug the hole. I measured it precisely, making certain that it was the perfect width and depth. I added loam to loosen and enrich the soil. And I had my water hose at the ready to give a good soaking once the weeping pine was in place. I wanted to make certain that I did everything within my power to get the weeping pine off to the right start.

Then I locked the unsheathed blade of my utility knife and cut the sides of the tub so that I could free the weeping pine and anchor it to its new earth home.

The heave-ho that I gave was far more than needed. I found myself standing there with the weeping pine mid-air, with little more than a 5-pound ball of clay securing the roots of its foundation, the roots of its future, the roots of my hopes.

Where was the balled-and-burlapped bundle that I had always seen before whenever I gave a heave-ho to lift a tree from its tub? Where were the tender, wondrous roots pushing through the burlap? Where were the reassuring signs of life?

As I stood there, decades of gardening whispered to me, telling me to take this one of a kind, unique weeping pine back to the nursery and get a refund. The root ball was wrong. All wrong.

But I had dug the hole. I had freed the weeping pine from its tub. And I really wanted that tree in that spot. Now. Forever.

I sighed a sigh of hope, and I planted it. Now it was mine. All the worry about its well-being. All the responsibility of taking care of it. Today. Tomorrow. Beyond. Mine. All mine.

Nonetheless, I was so convinced that my weeping pine was a loser that I stopped by the nursery the next day and told John all about my experience and my misgivings. He was more optimistic than I, but he agreed to put my name on the second weeping pine as a replacement, just in case.

When I drove back home, I stopped beside my weeping pine. It looked stunning with its twisting, green-needled, falling branches contrasted against the fresh mulch.

As I looked, I wondered whether my morning assessment had been too harsh. I wondered whether my morning conversation with John had been too direct. I wondered whether I had been too stern.

Confident that my assessment was correct and my conversation on target, I drove a little further up the hill and turned left into the driveway.

March melted slowly into April. Every day I visited my weeping pine. I was so proud. I wondered whether my neighbors admired it, too, as they drove past daily.

No one had said a word. Not one neighbor. Not one word. Finally, I asked one neighbor what he thought.

"You just planted it? You're joking. I thought that it had been there all along."

I thanked him for what I took to be a compliment. It was a compliment in my mind, because I like my garden plants to look as if they are growing in forever.

It was too early in the season for me to see new growth. But even so it was now my responsibility to water my weeping pine weekly during times with no rain or no snow. And that's just what I did.

By mid-May, my world was a mountaintop of spring growth and spring blossoms. Bleeding hearts. Clematis. Daffodils. Dogwood. Peonies.

More important, all of my specimen evergreens were putting out new-growth candles, especially my white pine outside my kitchen door: candles six inches long, if not longer.

Sadly, my Angel Falls looked exactly as it looked the day that I planted it.

"Well," I thought, "at least its needles are still green."

I checked, every day, attentively. It became my routine.

By the start of June, something started happening: yellowing, browning needles appeared on the lowest branches of my weeping pine.

Armed with a cell-phone photo, I stopped at the nursery the next day to show John the death that I was living.

He grimaced. "Not good."

"Yeah. I know. Maybe I should go ahead and replace it with the one you're holding?"

"Hmmm. Not yet. Try cutting off the dead branches and wait two weeks."

My weeping pine looked better with the dead branches removed. Actually, it looked rather healthy once again. I was cautiously hopeful.

One of my neighbors agreed, reminding me that my weeping pine was probably in shock just from being transplanted from the West Coast to here.

"But you know," he said, "It's gonna do what it's gonna do. It will all work out the way it's supposed to work out. That's how life is."

Two weeks later, more branches had died.

Armed with more photos, I went back to the nursery.

"Should I give it some fertilizer?"

"That would just stress it more. It's probably a goner, but let's wait a couple more weeks, just to see."

I had never lost a tree before in all my years of gardening. I kept replaying everything that I had done since planting my weeping pine. I couldn't help but wonder whether what was happening was my fault. What had I done wrong? What could I have done better?

When I weeded the garden where I had given my weeping pine a home, I talked to it, encouragingly and out loud, especially as I sadly cut off more and more branches.

When neighbors walked past, I lowered my voice, hoping that they would lower theirs. I didn't want my weeping pine to hear them as they bluntly asked whether I had noticed that it was dead. Dead. That's exactly what they said. I was shocked.

"I'm not so sure. It's still trying. It's a fighter. You'll see." I know how to put up a front when I need one.

My weeping pine kept fighting, all the while that its branches kept dying.

"How long do I hold on?" I pondered.

Two more weeks passed. My weeping pine was an embarrassment, to me and to neighbors who, by then, didn't know what to say. Sometimes, saying nothing is the best thing to say.

I resolved to take one final photo, show it to John, and drive back home with the replacement weeping pine.

The next morning, when I got up close to my weeping pine, I witnessed a few short candles, no longer than an inch. Not many, but enough to make me believe that my weeping pine was alive, that it really was fighting. I zoomed in really close on those candles, determined to capture their bright green.

"Dr. Kendrick, you're holding on to false hope. Let's get that replacement loaded into your …"

"But look!" I took my fingers and stretched the image as far as John was certain that I had stretched my hopes. "Look at how green those candles are. See? Look. Right here."

"All right. If you insist. Maybe give it another couple of weeks."

Every day, I visited my weeping pine, witnessing more and more green candles of life in the midst of more and more brown needles of death.

A little more than a week after that, I was ecstatic when I made my daily visit and discovered that all the green candles all over my weeping pine had unfurled into short, stubby, vibrantly green needles. At this point, my weeping pine was certainly not much of a specimen. In fact, it was just a shadow of what it had been. But it was a living witness to life's fierce determination to keep on holding on, against all odds.

By then it was near the end of July. One morning, I stopped by the nursery just to check out their inventory.

John approached and inquired about my weeping pine.

I beamed as I shared the recent turn of events. Beam begets beam.

"Here's the deal, John. Go ahead and sell the replacement pine that you've been holding for me."

"You're sure?"

"I'm absolutely certain."

"Okay. I will. One thing's for sure. If your weeping pine doesn't make it after all this, at least you have a story."

"You bet," I thought, as I walked away. "It's a story of survival."

AUGUST 8, 2022

Ten Guaranteed Tips to Increase Blog Traffic | Top-Rated and 100% Unproven!

How far that little candle throws his beams!

— WILLIAM SHAKESPEARE
(1564-1616; poet, playwright and actor, widely regarded as the greatest writer in the English language; *The Merchant of Venice [Act 5. Scene 1].*)

Without a doubt, you will recall my post from several weeks ago: "Take Four | Living with a Writer: Modern Applications of Ancient Writing Artifacts."

It was characterized as "destined for **fame** ... for **greatness** ... for **glory** ... the most **historic** and **historical** blog post ever published."

It received **rave reviews**:

"*Hilarious!*"

"*Hysterical. I would have laughed harder if I hadn't been so horrified at your undertaking.*"

"*This is one of your most entertaining, funniest posts, and I thank you for ... sharing it with the world.*"

And it was **LIKED** by a comedian and a college president—two entirely different people, with two entirely different occupations, although the college president knows that humor is a close ally to successful and dynamic leadership.

All right. In the interest of partial disclosure and full but muddy transparency, I'm the one who characterized my post as "destined for **fame** … for **greatness** … for **glory** … the most **historic** and **historical** blog post ever published."

And it was just **one faithful follower** who called it **hilarious**.

And it was just **one faithful follower** who called it **hysterical**.

And it was just **one faithful follower** who said that it was my most **entertaining** and **funniest** post.

But I believe in the **power of one**. If it's good enough for a bank, I suppose it's good enough for me, especially cents that bank does not have one cent of my money.

The good thing, however, is that those three rave reviews came from three entirely different followers with three entirely different occupations.

But enough of my noncents. I will, *post mortem*, return to my serious side instanter.

A stand-up comedian really did **LIKE** that post. Thank you! Please: feel free to sit down. (And, just as an aside to the stand-up comedian: I'm giving up my 25-year teaching gig at the end of this coming fall season. Do you need a jokester—I mean a writer? You know. Just hinting.)

And a college president really did **LIKE** that post. Thank you! Please: feel free to preside. (And just as an aside to the college president: I'm giving up my 25-year teaching gig—I mean professorship—at the end of this coming fall season—I mean semester. Do you need a Visiting Professor? A Visiting

Scholar. Both? I'm good at wearing two hats at the same time as long as they don't mess up my hair. You know. Just hinting.)

And again, just as an aside to the comedian and to the prez—who must be reading this post, right? I mean, you just don't **LIKE** 'em and then **leave** 'em, do you?—it's not like I'm desperate or anything, because, hey, I've got this blog, and after today's unviral post, I'll have talent scouts unlined up my ungraveled, rutted country road all the way to my no-parking space in the uncleared forest, assuming, of course, the scouts have four-wheel drive. Good talent these days is not easy to get to.

And let me not forget to mention what **one other faithful follower** advised me to do: "**Perhaps you shouldn't discard the legal pad and #2 pencil. ... To help your nightly challenges of writing in this manner, I can offer you ... a backlit pen.**"

Well, as you know from many previous posts, I listen to my followers. So I immediately ordered myself two backlit pens from Amazon. You can get anything these days from Amazon, yesterday. Someone told me day before yesterday that I could even get a husband from Amazon, as soon as tomorrow or three days before. **Dayum!** Imagine that. I checked immediately. Unfortunately, Amazonian husbands are backordered. Unfortunately, too, they are not backlit.

My pens, on the other hand, were not back ordered, and they are backlit. They arrived just when I started writing this post, so what you see here was written in bed at night on a yellow legal pad that isn't legal, using a pen that is legally lit.

Wow! Using this pen to write in bed in the dark is amazing. I am transfixed if not transformed. If I had known about these backlit pens decades ago before they had never been invented, by now I would have written the Great American

Novel that has never been written. Or not. I'll be dealing with that topic in a future post.

But I can't deal with any of that right now. Right now, I am so enamored of this little backlit pen that all I can think about are little light quotes. Most are from songs, so I'm humming—can you hear me? Let me give you the links (below, in unalphabetical order) in case you want to hum along or sing along. It's a **FREE** perk for being a **FREE**loader—I mean follower! Get someone else to follow, and I'll let you hum along or sing along forever, for **FREE**.

"This Little Light of Mine."

"Glow Little Glow Worm, Glimmer, Glimmer."

"How far that little candle throws his beam."(Shakespeare, *The Merchant of Venice*. Act 5. Scene 1)

"Let the Lower Lights Be Burning.

"Light My Fire."

"A light unto the world." (John 12:46)

Well, good grief. Why on earth did Euterpe muse me up like that? Your guess is as good as mine.

So let me **hie** myself back to the business at hand—sharing with you my ten guaranteed tips to increase blog traffic, top-rated and 100% unproven. Is that a deal or what? But before I do, don't you just love that word: ***hie***. I do. I love verbs and verbiage. (But I shudder to think about conjugating ***hie***.) Anyway, I love that word. I'm not sure why. Maybe I saw it somewhere once, probably in a romance novel that I never read. Clearly, then, I have no idea who was doing what to whom in the novel that I did not read. I don't think that anyone in the novel uttered the word either. But I happened to think of it just now, and I thought that it would be an awful lot of fun for me to use it right here. Now I feel funfilled.

Well, gracious me. Now I have to **hie** myself back once

more. I guess all this is going down because my muse likes the fact that my pen is lit. That's right: my pen.

As I was saying, the initial accolades calling my post **historic** and **historical** and the initial reviews hailing it as **hysterical** and **hilarious** and **entertaining** and **funny** got me all pumped up and gave me great expectations that my viewer stats would jump off the charts.

I had such high hopes, especially since the views on the day that I published the post were 555% higher than the day before. Talk about being pumped. I was beyond pumped. I had such heightened expectations that I set my alarm clock to awaken me hourly throughout the night for the sole purpose of watching my stats skyrocket.

Sadly, nothing skyrocketed. Nothing. Not one thing. Except my blood pressure and my stress from waking up every hour to check on my stats. My blog stats, mind you. I don't need to check my personal stats. My Fitbit does that for me without even asking. And let me tell you: my personal stats dropped big time, especially my sleep score and my readiness to exercise score.

They were so low that I vowed that I would never do such a wired stunt again. I doubled my vow—**Never, Never**—when I charted my blog stats over the course of the next few days. It goes without saying that you can't increase your blog traffic unless you chart it. Right?

So that's precisely what I did on a flip chart—using royal blue and royal purple magic markers—to capture how the traffic plummeted. Those lines went so low that they fell all the way down to the floor where I continued to chart them all the way across the room.

When I finished the chart, I taped the unfloored part of it to my office wall—I write my blog in bed; I chart it in my office—and since then I have been waiting ever so patiently for my blog traffic to increase. It should. Right? I just charted it, and as I said in the preceding paragraph—or somewhere—you can't increase your blog traffic if you don't chart it.

And if you don't believe me, you surely believe Kevin Costner. Who doesn't? I know that I sure do, so much so that emblazoned on my chest—not too unlike Hester's scarlet letter **A**—is the famous line from his *Field of Dreams*: "If you chart it, they will come."

Now, listen up. Without further adieu—you wish, but not yet!—I am proud to share the ten hollow tips that lured you here, just like a moth lured to a flame. Yep. Ten tips. Guaranteed to increase your blog traffic. Top rated. 100% unproven. Trust me. They are unreal doozies.

Tip #1. *AERIAL ADVERTISING*. I cannot guarantee that this would work for you, but I am fairly uncertain that it would work for me because my mind is always up in the air. Why not skywrite my blog URL up there, too, maybe all up and down the California coastline where folks are more unwired than they are on the East Coast.

Tip #2. *BILLBOARDS*. Again, this might not give you more blog traffic at all. But, after I float down from my aerial habitation and walk once more upon *terra unfirma*, I am fairly certain that billboard advertising will be worth the cost. I plan to keep it short and simple, the same way that I keep my weekly blog posts short and simple.

I'm thinking something along the lines of:

> **Feeling WIRED???**
> Me, too. I'm here to help! Check out:
> ***thewiredresearcher.com***
> ***FREE*** **Life*line*** **Subscription**

Tip #3. *DOLLAR BILL PROMOS*. This tip would probably work for everybody, but only the bold and courageous should try it. Actually, it's been around for years. I'll bet you've seen one: a dollar bill with a Biblical reference written on it? Maybe even a phone number—call me? What I'm thinking is simple: Write your blog URL on the edge of a dollar bill. A dollar bill changes hands about 110 times a year. Wow! Write your blog URL on the edge of lots and lots of dollar bills and see how your blog traffic increases. I wonder, though, whether your increased blog traffic will be following you directly to jail. If I am not mistaken, writing on money is considered defacement under *Title 18, Section 333* of the *United States Code*. Blogger beware!

Tip #4. *BUSINESS CARDS*. These can't be just any business cards. They need to be all glamour and glitz and gimmick. Maybe something like: <u>Limited time only</u>. **FREE Access** to a blog destined to be featured in the *New York Times*, the *Wall Street Journal*, the defunct *Saturday Evening Post*, *True Grit,* and the 1931 first edition of *The Joy of Cooking*. But it won't be enough to just have those cards printed. You'll need to find someone to hand them out. In my case, my Linden (VA) and Front Royal (VA) correspondent—Yes. No *s*. She's one and the same person—has been given the right of refusal to pass them out at all the unlarge stores in our unmetropolitan area as well as at the five churches located at each corner of a four-cornered crossroads in one of our unknown villages near us both.

Tip #5. *FOOD TRUCK*. This one seems perfect for me since I like to bake. You might get a rise out of it as well. I'm thinking about renting a food truck for a few weeks and customizing it, using temporary paint. A pale tan, maybe, about the color of lightly browned, crusty bread. With a slight stretch of anyone's doughy imagination, the food truck might look like a loaf of bread. And for those who don't have a doughy imagination to stretch, I plan to paint on one side of the truck, **Oh, No! Sourdough**. And on the other side, **Baking Up My Past**. On both sides, of course, I'll paint my blog's URL. I'll offer up my full range of sourdough baked goods—regular sourdough bread, multigrain sourdough bread, as well as parmesan and black pepper sourdough bread, along with doughnuts, scones, biscuits, and dinner rolls. I'll also offer up my full range of cakes including, but not limited to, my Chocolate Weary Willie Cake and my Chocolate Prune Cake. But here's where the sweet part comes in. On both sides of the truck, **FREE** will be prominently lettered. Yep! Anyone who stops, gets one of my goodies **FREE**, with absolutely no wires attached—absolutely none, not one—other than signing up as one of my blog followers right then and right there on the spot while I watch. If this works, I promise to keep the **FREE** in *subscription*. (**"Say *whaaat*? Are you lit?"** Nope. See Tip #1.)

Tip #6. CHAIN EMAIL. Chain emails go all the way back to ye olden days of 1990. They waned but then returned with a boring resurgence during the pandemic. Their predecessor, of course, was the famed, infamous, and ancient artifact known as the *litterae*. Chain letters go all the way back to the 1930s when people included a dime in their chain letters. Later, they included recipes. And one of my Virtually (Anywhere) but nonetheless trustworthy correspondents tells me that chain emails these days often focus on sourdough starters and that she is certain that she unraveled the original Egyptian sourdough starter recipe cryptically hieroglyphed in the soon-to-be-famous post "Oh, No! Sourdough." Well, to be honest and to be as transparent as the windowpane test that dough must pass, I'm not sure how a chain email could be used to promote blog traffic. I'm told, though, that chain emails are "Unstoppable." If you figure it out, come back to my blog and send me a reply. **Ka-stats, ka-stats, ka-stats!**

Tip #7. *CHALK WALK.* I like this one a lot. It's so cheap that it's nearly **FREE**. Plus, it brings out the kid in me. Chalk my blog's URL on sidewalks, using glow-in-the-dark chalk. It would bring an unsensational light unto an unliterary world. (I'm just kidding.)

Tip #8. *CUSTOM BUMPER STICKERS.* I am probably the only one alive who remembers this. But maybe not, so I will ask. Do you remember the streaking craze that struck the nation in the 1970s? I'm reminiscing about one super special, balmy spring evening in 1975. I had a hard time keeping up with the others—1,000 or so, all of us students—streaking ~~our~~ their stuff across the USC campus. It's a wonder that I didn't get trampled or worse. The best part came a few days later. It was hilarious to see genteel Southern ladies and gentlemen in their 70s and 80s driving around Columbia, totally unaware that a **"I'm a Streak Freak"** sticker had been proudly stuck on their rear ...

... bumpers.

I've often wondered how they got there. (I probably still have one of those stickers somewhere in my loft.) Mind you: I'm not suggesting a streaking revival, but bumper stickers promoting a wired blog would certainly stop some traffic. (Hopefully, not the traffic headed to your blog.)

Tip #9. *PENCILS PACKAGED WITH YELLOW LEGAL PADS.* This is another one that would be perfect for me. I could go to all the bookstores at the colleges and universities where I don't teach and hand out #2 pencils embossed with my blog's URL packaged with a yellow legal pad, referencing my "Take Four. Living with A Writer: Modern Applications of Ancient Writing Artifacts," destined to go down in the annals of history as the most historic and historical blog post ever published, all because it was written in bed on a yellow legal pad using a #2 pencil.

Tip #10. DO NOT SEARCH FOR GUARANTEED WAYS TO INCREASE BLOG TRAFFIC. This is the most important tip of all. That's why I saved it for last. Articles claiming to have ten guaranteed, top-rated but 100% unproven tips for increasing blog traffic are nothing more than bogus attempts to increase traffic to their own blog. Such hyped-up, sensational articles seem to be the unnormal norm these days. Don't look for them, and, for God's sake, if you do look for them, don't tell anyone that you looked. Such articles lack the unmuddy transparency needed to be included in Wikipedia.

Please, though, finish reading this post before you wisely decide to follow my advice.

And—please, please—if you enjoyed this post, send the link to seven of your unfriends and ask them to do the same, starting with you at the top.

And—pretty, pretty please—if you enjoyed this post, share it via **WordPress**, **Twitter**, **Facebook**, **Email**, and **Reblog**. And, for God's sake, **LIKE** it. (I'm Beggin'.)

Go now with heartfelt thanks from the bottom of my blog. May the traffic be with you.

AUGUST 15, 2022

Why an Education Matters: The Softer Side

"If a man empties his purse into his head, no man can take it away from him. An investment in knowledge always pays the best interest."

— BENJAMIN FRANKLIN
(1705-1790; American writer, scientist, inventor, statesman, diplomat, printer, publisher, and political philosopher; Poor Richard's Almanac.)

This week I'm thinking about education, far more than usual. The reason is simple. Exactly one week from today, I'll be meeting a new group of community college students who have decided wisely that getting an education is their best move. With them, I'll be standing on the brink of now and the future. It's a new beginning for me and a new beginning for them.

As an educator, my role is to provide students with the knowledge base they need in English, especially American Literature, Appalachian Literature, and Creative Writing.

Aside from equipping them with the needed knowledge base, my goal is to turn them on.

"*Turn students on to English? No way!*"

"*When pigs fly*," someone else squealed.

I understand. I have understood since I started teaching. From the first day that I enter a classroom at the start of a brand-new semester, mine is an uphill battle. But that's perfectly all right. I love challenges. I have every confidence in the world that by the end of the semester my students will see that language and literature can help them discover their own worlds and the worlds around them. I have every confidence in the world that by the end of the semester my students will see that language and literature matter. "He can inspire a rock to write," wrote one student in my early teaching career at Laurel Ridge Community College.

Nonetheless, I am aware that I may not have one student who is majoring in English. So, while I am passionate about language and literature and while I know that I can turn my students on to those subjects, I feel an equal responsibility to be passionate about education. I want my students to believe that education—their education—matters.

Sometimes getting them to believe that is an even greater challenge than turning them on to English.

I have to meet that challenge, too, right from the start, because I know that the community college graduation rate nationwide is about 62%.

I celebrate the students who make up that percentage. And I celebrate the 30% of community college students nationwide who transfer to four-year colleges and universities.

Yet, while celebrating all those students, I want to do my best to reach out to the others who might not be part of the 62% graduation rate or the 30% transfer rate unless I convince them that an education—their education—matters.

Why an education matters is abundantly clear to those of us who are educated. Career options. Job security. Expanded earnings. Networking. Professional connections. Increased happiness. Friendships. Better health. Even longevity.

I could include statistics to support those claims. I won't. Candidly, they don't do much for me.

And, candidly, when I talk about the practical benefits of an education—and I do—eyes glaze over and my students search for imaginary exits, especially when I start bringing in statistics to support my claims.

On the other hand, when I switch my focus to the softer side of why an education matters—the side that allows me to be personal and passionate—vision returns to glazed eyes and students return to the classroom that they just fancifully exited.

Sometimes—actually almost always—I'll start the soft-side conversation by asking my students how many of them are the first in their family to go to college.

Usually about one third of their hands go up—a response that's consistent with national data for community college students.

They seem to take notice when I tell them that I am a first-generation college student, too. They really take notice when I share some personal information about me. Son of a West Virginia coal miner and his wife, a Pilgrim Holiness minister. Grew up with three books in my home—the King James Bible, Webster's Dictionary, and Sears Roebuck Catalog. Made it to the halls of the Library of Congress, which for 25 years became my home, with more than 20 million books. Then to the halls of Laurel Ridge Community College which for the last 23 years has been my home, where I've taught more than 7,000 students. Without being boastful, I want them to hear and see firsthand how an education transformed my life. I want to convince them that an education will transform their lives, too.

They get turned on more when I tell them that with an education they can go anywhere because they will be experts in their field. These days, I seem to have more and more students in health sciences, so I make a point of emphasizing that they can go wherever their credentials are recognized. Their eyes light up when I talk about the option of being a traveling nurse or a traveling surgical technologist. Their eyes really light up when I talk about the bonuses and salary increases that go hand in hand with adventuresome, free travel.

I remind them as well that an education empowers them to become their own knowledge navigators. I share with them what Robert Frost once wrote: *"We go to college to be given one more chance to learn to read in case we haven't learned in High School. Once we have learned to read the rest can be trusted to add itself unto us"* ("Poetry and School," *The Atlantic Monthly*, June 1951). Frost, of course, is talking about developing critical reading skills and critical thinking skills, both at the heart of all education.

Or perhaps I help them understand that an education matters because books matter. Emily Dickinson says it best:

> There is no frigate like a book
> To take us lands away.

Some days I emphasize that an education matters because it emboldens you to follow your passion. I share with them my own undergraduate struggles as English, Pre-Law, and Pre-Med messed around with my head. One day, after switching majors several times, I allowed my passion to take hold of my heart. From that point forward, English prevailed.

Or what about the notion that an education enables us to be anchored and hopeful amidst the storms of life that are certain to come our way? I'm thinking again about Robert Frost and his poem "One Step Backward Taken." The speaker in the poem is shaken by a universal crisis:

> *But with one step backward taken*
> I saved myself from going.
> A world torn loose went by me.
> Then the rain stopped and the blowing,
> And the sun came out to dry me.

And how about this one that I like to use when students wonder whether an education is worth the cost, especially as their student loans grow larger and larger. I remind them that an education is one of their best investments. No one can take it away, ever. Perhaps even better is the way that the investment keeps on growing through lifelong learning.

Those are just a few of the "soft" reasons why an education matters to me. They are the ones that are on my mind this week as I anticipate next week's new beginnings.

There's one more, though, that's always on my mind. It's the University of South Carolina's motto surrounding the seal on my doctoral class ring. It's a quote from Ovid, **"Emollit Mores Nec Sinit Esse Feros,"** which translates to **"Learning humanizes character and does not permit it to be cruel."**

AUGUST 22, 2022

Piecing Together the Pieces of a Tale

"What matters even more is that a Southern woman's generosity in the face of her own starvation—"You can have the honey, but please, please don't break my jar"—ricochets through the ages together with the Union soldiers' noble act of harming neither the old woman nor her treasured wedding jar."

In Remembrance of Mary "Polly" Conner Slaughter (August 17, 1806–April 10, 1891)

1. Relic, *n*. [1] Something kept as a remembrance, souvenir, or memorial; a historical object relating to a particular person, place, or thing; a memento. —*"Luther's…apartment…contains his portrait, bible, and other relics."*

Piecing together the pieces of a tale is never easy. Like shards from a broken vessel, the pieces are rough edged and resist coming together again. Yet, with loving care, a craftsman can piece together the pieces, yielding—once again and for all eternity—remembrances of that which was.

May the piecing of these pieces bring forth such a tale.

2. *Marriage, n.* The action, or an act, of getting married; the procedure by which two people become husband and wife.
—*"Euery Minister shall keepe a faithful...Record...of all Christnings, Marriages, and deaths."*

On Thursday, August 11, 1825, Mary "Polly" Conner (daughter of John David "Daniel" Conner and Lucy Fox Robertson) married Martin Slaughter (son of John Slaughter and Mary Handy). They exchanged vows at home in Elamsville, Patrick County, Virginia. Mary was eighteen, just a week shy of nineteen. Martin was twenty-three, just a few weeks shy of twenty-four. Mary's father, an elder in the Primitive Baptist Church, gave surety, he performed the marriage ceremony, and he filed the minister's return.

The marriage license and the return survive.

3. *Infare, n.* A feast or entertainment given on entering a new house; esp. at the reception of a bride in her new home.
—*"The day after the wedding is the infare ... the company is less numerous, and the dinner is commonly the scraps that were left at the wedding-feast."*

The next day, Polly and Martin had their infare. It is not known who attended. Polly and Martin were country people: she, a housewife; he, a farmer and later a minister. What is known is that Polly wore a special infare dress on that Friday reception in their new home. It was dark brown muslin, with an empire waist. Richly patterned in small bright red and orange oak leaves with tan acorns, it was perfect for a heavy-harvest reception. From the high neckline down to the waist were small black, ivory buttons. At the end of the long sleeves, the same. The dress shows Polly to have been tall, full bosomed, and thin waisted.

The infare dress survives.

4. Jar, n. A vessel of earthenware, stoneware, or glass, without spout or handle (or having two handles), usually more or less cylindrical in form. Orig. used only in its eastern sense of a large earthen vessel for holding water, oil, wine, etc.
—*"At the dore there is a great iarre of water, with a... Ladle in it, and there they wash their feete."*

Also surviving is one marriage gift: a five-gallon stoneware jar, ovoid in shape, with two side "pocket" handles just below the rim. The handwritten note taped to the bottom of the jar authenticates the occasion. The jar itself also confirms the time period. Its thick, rolled rim and its cobalt-glazing are typical of such jars made between 1750 and 1820, more likely closer to 1820. The jar itself weighs twenty-seven pounds. When filled with water, it weighs seventy-five pounds.

The jar survives.

5. Civil War, n. War between the citizens or inhabitants of a single country, state, or community.
—*"The Civil War and Reconstruction represent ... an attempt on the part of the Yankee to achieve by force what he had failed to achieve by political means."*

According to the Federal Census taken on August 1, 1860, Martin Slaughter was 57; Polly, 53. They had four children living with them at home: Judith D., age 25, Martha Jane, age 16; Lavina, age 13; and Dicie Laroma, age 9. (They had six other children, no longer living at home, and thus, not enumerated on the Census: a son, John W. and five daughters: Mary Elizabeth, Lucinda Lucy, Emilia Ann "Millie", Nina, and Rosina Lee.) Their real estate was listed with a value of $1,300 (equivalent to $456,300, using today's economic status calculator) and their personal property was valued at $3,000 (equivalent to $1,053,000, again using today's economic status calculator). According to family lore, "Martin Slaughter gave each of his daughters at the time of their marriage $800 in gold and a fine horse. His wealth was in gold coins, and it was thought his coins were buried near his spring when he died." By the time of that census, Martin was a Primitive Baptist minister as well as a farmer.

The next year, 1861, the Civil War began with the Battle of Fort Sumter, April 12-14. Virginia seceded from the Union on April 17, 1861, becoming the seventh state to join the Confederate States of America. On April 19, Company D (formerly the Lafayette Guard, Petersburg) enlisted in the 12th Virginia Infantry. It reorganized on May 1, 1862, supplementing its roster with conscripts from Patrick County. John W. Slaughter (Martin and Polly's son) enlisted and became one of Virginia's 155,000 men who joined the Confederate Army. He fought in the Battle of Seven Pines (May 31 and June 1, Henrico County), and he fought in the Battle of Malvern Hill (July 1, Henrico County). On July 20, 1862, John died of pneumonia at a field hospital in Falling Creek, Chesterfield County, Virginia.

John W. Slaughter joined the ranks of 624,511 soldiers (Confederate and Union combined) who did not survive.

As the Civil War continued, it could not hit Martin and Polly Slaughter any harder than it had hit them in death, but it could hit them—and other Virginians—closer and closer to home. Because of Virginia's strategic proximity to the north and because the state housed the Confederacy's capital, Richmond, by 1864 major Union campaigns throughout the state with ongoing raids aimed at diminishing food and water supplies, left Virginians facing a level of famine they had never faced before.

Despite their economic status, Martin and Polly Slaughter were not spared from the food crisis. At one point during this period in the War, so the tale goes, Polly was at home alone, as Union soldiers approached.

Did she hear the sound of thunderous horse? A "hello" from the yard? A knock at the door? Did they enter her home?

What look was in her eyes? Fear? Confidence? Defiance? How did the soldiers see her? Old? (She was 60.) Vulnerable? Motherly?

The Union troops demanded food.

"We've no food left; we've no animals left; we've nothing left," she told them. "Look all you want—there's nothing here. All I have is a jar of honey in the spring house. You can have the honey, but please, please don't break my jar."

The troops advanced to the spring house and devoured the honey.

Did Polly watch as they went on their way? Did she rush to the spring house to check on her jar?

Poignantly, it had been spared.

The jar survives.

6. Gravestone, n. A stone placed over a grave, or at the entrance of a tomb; in later use also applied to an upright stone at the head or foot of a grave, bearing an inscription.
— "Cast the shadows of the gravestones on the silent graves."

Martin Slaughter died on May 7, 1884, age 82, and was buried in the Slaughter family cemetery in Elamsville. He had carved his own soapstone grave marker:

Dear children and companion too I leave you all in God's care. I hope we will meet in heaven above when parting and mourning is no more. Blessed are the dead that died in the Lord.

Polly died 7 years later on April 10, 1891, "Age 84Y, 7M, 24D", and was buried beside her husband.

Their stones survive.

7. Lineage, n. Lineal descent from an ancestor; ancestry, pedigree.
— "The quiet and lowly spirit of my mother's humble lineage."

One daughter born to Martin and Polly plays a pivotal role in this tale. Her name was Martha, and she married John H. Adams. Two children born to Martha and John play roles in this tale as well. One daughter, Cora Belle Martha "Sweety" Delilah Adams, married Pierce Ulysses Witt; another daughter, Jo Ann Adams, married George Harbour. To Sweety and Pierce was born Bertha Pearl and to Jo Ann and George was born Clara.

As first cousins, Clara and Pearl were close and best friends until marriage and relocation separated them. After more than fifty years they were reunited when, in 1980, I took Bertha Pearl—my mother—back home to Patrick County, Virginia, to visit Clara. Although it was the first time that I had met my second cousin, it seemed that Clara and I had known one another forever. For more than a decade thereafter, mom and I made annual pilgrimages "back home" to see Cousin Clara. Through listening to all the stories that kept the two of them up until the early hours of morning, the lineage that my mom had shared with me as a child took on a richness and a life that had been missing before.

It was during one of those visits that Clara told me the story of Mary "Polly" Conner Slaughter's encounter with the Union soldiers who took her honey but spared her honey jar. This was the moment when, in my mind, I helped Polly lift the jar filled with honey—far heavier than the 75 pounds if filled with water—and take it to the spring house.

It was during one of those visits that Clara opened up a brown paper bag and pulled out Polly Slaughter's infare dress. This was the moment when I clasped the dress, I touched the muslin, saw the vivid red and orange leaves, and rubbed each and every button. This was the moment, even if fleeting, when I took her hand—her eyes level with mine at 5' 8"—and danced around the room as I imagine she had danced with many of her guests at the feast she and Martin hosted after their marriage.

It was during one of those visits that Clara showed me the large charcoal-on-paper portrait of Polly Slaughter, still in its original frame though painted over with gold radiator paint. This was the moment when I saw Polly's penetrating eyes, saw the firm resolve in her face, and understood why the Union soldiers spared her jar.

It was during one of those visits—much later, when Clara was exceedingly ill and close to death—that I went to visit her alone and found more pieces to the tale. I did not look forward to that visit, I was not certain whether she would be up for company, and I dreaded those awkward silences that punctuate conversations with the sick and dying. But I knew that I had to go to say goodbye. So, I took along some photographs of my Christmas tree from the holidays just ended. Nearly touching the Cathedral ceiling, the tree was a gorgeous sight to behold, certain to prompt conversation. And it did.

As Clara looked at one photograph in particular, one that offered up a closer view of my living room, she raised herself up in bed, saying to her daughter, "Why, Iris, looky here. Brent's got a whole navigation of crocks just like the one Great, Great Grandma Slaughter had. You go find her crock and bring it on in here to show Brent."

Iris came back in a few minutes, proudly holding a five-gallon stoneware crock.

"Now, Brent," Clara said in a low, weak voice, hardly above a whisper, "that's the jar that Great, Great Grandma Slaughter got on her wedding day. That's the jar she always kept her honey in. That's the jar the Union soldiers spared."

I was thrilled and flabbergasted at the same time. Thrilled, knowing that the honey jar still survived. Flabbergasted, wondering why Clara had not shown me that honey jar during one of my many visits "back home" in search of relics.

8. Mantel, n. A shelf formed by the projecting surface of a mantelpiece.
—*"Above the mantle a painting by Gordon Smith... seemed full of an energy to break free."*

Clara died on November 28, 2000. Not long after, Iris called me and wanted to know what I thought Polly Slaughter's honey jar was worth and whether I was interested in buying it. I knew, of course, that it was a family relic of inestimable value, but as a collector of Virginia stoneware pottery, I knew, too, what the jar would fetch at auction. I offered Iris a more-than-fair market price, and she accepted.

The jar is ovoid in shape with "pocket" handles. Its base and rolled rim have the same diameter: 6 1/2 inches. It is 14 inches tall, and it is 10 ½ inches across the middle.

The jar is in my kitchen, resting securely on the mantel above the fireplace.

It continues to survive.

9. Portrait, n. A drawing or painting of a person, often mounted and framed for display, esp. one of the face or head and shoulders.
— *"Fixing his starting eyes upon a portrait of Dr. Enfield which hung over the chimney."*

When I bought the jar, Iris sweetened the deal by giving me the framed portrait of Polly Slaughter. It measures 15 x 30 inches. A restoration specialist removed the gold radiator paint, revealing the original ornate composition frame of plaster, wood, and gold leaf.

The charcoal-on-paper portrait is head and shoulders. Polly looks to be around 60 or so. No doubt she sat for it just after the Civil War ended. Her hair is parted in the middle. Whether it is pulled back into a bun cannot be determined because her head is covered by an indoor, ruffle-edged bonnet, tied beneath her chin. Her dress has a small plaid pattern with a high neckline and lace collar. She's wearing a solid black cape, typical of the period.

Her eyes penetrate, watch, follow all around the room wherever I go, and, I like to think, protect.

It seemed fitting that I hang Polly's portrait above the mantel, just above the jar that she owned. There, she stands guard over the jar that she so treasured from the day of her marriage, all through the Civil War, and all the way until her death.

10. Survival, n. Something that continues to exist after the cessation of something else, or of other things of the kind; a surviving remnant.
—*"What are they But names for that which has no name, Survivals of a vanished day?"*

The survival of the portrait alone does not matter. Without the tale, it's just one more family portrait that can be found in any antique shop. The survival of the infare dress alone does not matter. Without the tale, it's just a rag in a brown paper sack. The survival of the honey jar alone does not matter. Without the tale, it's like one of many that can be found throughout Virginia and the South.

What matters are the women who held in trust Polly's jar, her dress, her portrait, and her tale and passed them on for generation after generation after generation.

What matters is the woman who posed for that portrait. What matters is the woman who wore that dress. What matters is the woman who owned that jar.

What matters even more is that a Southern woman's generosity in the face of her own starvation—"You can have the honey, but please, please don't break my jar"—

ricochets through the ages together with the Union soldiers' noble act of harming neither the old woman nor her treasured wedding jar.

What matters is piecing together the pieces of a tale.

[1] Throughout this tale, the word definitions along with quotations supporting the definitions are from the *Oxford English Dictionary*.

AUGUST 29, 2022

Less Is Not Always More Until It Is

*"Yet do much less, so much less, Someone says,
(I know his name, no matter)—so much less!
Well, less is more, Lucrezia: I am judged."*

— ROBERT BROWNING
(1812-1889; English poet and playwright;
"Andrea del Sarto".)

Less is more has been around since 1855 when Robert Browning coined the phrase in his "Andrea del Sarto," a dramatic monologue inspired by the Renaissance artist having the same name as the poem's title. Nearly one hundred years later, architect Ludwig Mies van der Rohe made the phrase really popular when he adopted it as a mantra for architecture, art and design. Today, **less is more** is more popular than ever because minimalism is gaining more and more traction.

I get it. I guess. Well, actually, I guess that I don't get it. To prove that I don't get it, I had to Google some examples of **less is more** so that I could include them here at the start of this post. I can't believe that I couldn't come up with any examples on my own, but I couldn't.

Fortunately, I found a lot of examples on the Internet. However, only one or two of them found me nodding in agreement.

I really do understand that putting less focus on material things—consumerism—allows us to focus more on things that really matter and that bring us lasting happiness. Got it. Endorse it.

And I really do understand that minimalism can help the environment by reducing our carbon footprint. Got it. Got it. Endorse it twice over.

Those two concessions are about as far as I can go. Some of the other **less-is-more** examples leave me shaking my head.

Sleek, smaller design, often in a black and white scheme. Nope.

Decluttering. Nope. Nope.

Digital decluttering. Nope. Nope. Nope.

(If you desire a full understanding of why I dissed sleek design, decluttering, and digital decluttering, see "OHIO on My Mind.")

Having scoffed at those examples of **less is more**, you can rest assured that I would never consider **less is more** when it comes to gardening. That's when I draw the line in my compost heap and step across it to join sides with Robert Venturi, one of the major American architects of the twentieth century, who proclaimed that **less is a bore**.

As for me, I want my garden right now. No. I want it yesterday or the day before, and I want it to look as if I have been enjoying its lushness for years, if not forever.

Hear me and hear me well. Less is not more when it comes to the way that I garden. *I garden, I garden my way.*

I want nothing—absolutely nothing—to do with seeds. They take days to sprout, more days to grow, still more days to selectively thin, and even more days to bloom.

I want blooms, blooms, blooms. Glorious blooms. And I want them instanter.

"Those 4-inch pots are gorgeous! Look at all those blooms."

"You must like them a lot to be buying fifteen each of three different annuals."

"Oh, my. Yes. I love mass plantings."

That's a typical conversation as I make early spring pilgrimages to local garden centers, always to be reminded right after I have made my purchases:

"Keep 'em indoors until the danger of frost has passed."

No big deal. I've never minded dragging a gazillion potted plants day after day—from mid-April to mid-May—in and out of my home, kitchen to deck and back again. Hey. Like I said. I want my garden yesterday or the day before. And either way I want it looking like it's been there forever.

If you think that I have a bad attitude when it comes to seeds, I have an even worse attitude when it comes to saplings. (Think of me as a modern-day-Mae-West gardener: *"When I'm good, I'm good. When I'm bad, I'm better."*)

If I'm going to plant a tree, I certainly do not expect to sit under it from the get-go and be shaded—Hmmm, that is something for me to think about—but, at least, I want it to be big enough and bold enough to cast a shadow.

When it comes to how many plants and trees I consider to be enough, it's really simple.

For specimen plants and trees, I'm fine with one of each.

For all others, if one is good, then three, five, seven, or nine have to be better, especially since I garden in odd numbers when it comes to layout and design.

In fact, my odd-number planting rule struck me as perfect when I decided to plant bamboo. Nine clumps. Not to worry. Non-running.

That rule seemed equally perfect for my hardy bananas. Three groves. They were so small when I first planted them, that I hoped my neighbors would not notice. Trust me. They didn't. Bigger is better even when it comes to bananas. But these days my neighbors get whiplash as they drive past, and it's not because of our well-rutted road. Groves of big banana plants on a Virginia mountaintop make heads turn and make cars turn around.

Let's see whether I have anything else to prove that less is not more when it comes to my gardening. Goodness! How on earth could I forget English ivy. Well, I nearly forgot it, no doubt because for once I broke my cardinal rule of planting in odd numbers. I planted the ivy in twosies. I needed ivy to hide not only a humongous and hideous stump just below my driveway but also to hide the rock wall that I built to hide the stump.

It worked so well there that I decided some ivy would soften the stone wall surrounding three sides of my Koi Pond. The fourth side, lest you think that I slighted it, is a dramatic waterfall, cascading from a height of five or seven or nine feet or so.

I wouldn't want the world at large to know this—and I know that I can trust you, **Dear Reader**, to keep what I am about to say to yourself—but in my insistence on having my gardens look as if they have been around forever from day one, I confess that I may have made a mistake or five.

Mistake #1. Planting things too close together. Let's face it. Too close is too close.

Mistake #2. See Mistake #3. My mistakes come in odd numbers only.

Mistake #3. Not paying close enough attention to how big things will grow. Double disaster. Too close and too large.

Mistake #4. See Mistake #5. My mistakes come in odd numbers only.

Mistake #5. Not fully understanding that gardeners like me who nurture and care for their gardens end up with plants and trees that are much larger than expected. Miracle Grow grows miracles.

In case you're wondering how my less-is-not-more approach to gardening played out over time, let me share with you.

Year One. Oh, joy. This is gorgeous. This is proof. My garden looks as if it's been here for a while. It almost has that old-garden look. So there! I knew from the get-go that less is not more.

Year Two. See Year Three. I garden in odd numbers only.

Year Three. Oh, joy of joys. Everything is so lush. The garden really does look elegant and established.

Year Four. See Year Five. I garden in odd numbers only.

Year Five. Joy to the fifth. Cheers! This is an English garden at its best. Blooms, blooms, blooms. Glorious blooms everywhere. Everything in the garden is touching. I can't even see weeds between the plants. Maybe there are no weeds. Better still, even if the deer have been in the gardens, I can't tell what they've eaten.

Year Six. See Year Seven. I garden in odd numbers only.

Year Seven. Well, if I must say so myself, the stone walls really do look mysterious hidden beneath the English ivy. Here and there the sunlight bounces off a stone. For all that

I know, what I'm walking past might be the foundations of ancient Roman ruins awaiting an archaeological dig. And I am rather glad that the manicured borders around the garden beds have disappeared. Too formal was a tad too much for a mountain man like me.

Year Eight. See Year Nine. I garden in odd numbers only.

Year Nine. The season of the slow awakening finally came. I looked out my windows one day, and I realized that it was gone. All gone. To be certain, it's all there, but now it's all so overgrown and all so close together that it looks like an Impressionistic study in shades of emerald green.

From afar, it's rather dramatic. But let's face it. Gardening cannot be done from afar. Gardening requires down and dirty.

Recovery from my initial Impressionistic shock was slow, and I confess to having been in denial for a year or three. It was a downer. I felt overwhelmed by the "muchness" of it all, just as Frost's farmer felt in "After Apple-Picking":

> For I have had too much
> Of apple picking: I am overtired
> Of the great harvest I myself desired.

But I started to take heart when I started ripping out enough English ivy to fill five, seven, or maybe nine forty-five-gallon yard bags.

I got really hyped when I discovered the stone wall surrounding the red-leaf Japanese maple. Now, though, the maple has overgrown its stone wall boundaries. Joy!

"Mr. Gardener, tear down that wall."

I did, and I rebuilt it sufficiently far away from the mature maple—exactly where I should have built it to begin with.

Then I repeated the ivy demolition on the three sides of the Koi Pond. Wow! What rocks I have! I can't believe that I dug those stones out of the ground using just my pick and then managed to position them so expertly. They are stunning. Simply stunning. And with all that ivy gone, the pond is every bit as big as I recall it.

In case you're wondering about the bamboo, let me just say this. Those nine clumps have an impressive diameter of six feet. Each. Non-running? Right. This bamboo is leaping! I have renamed it ***Bamboozle Leptomorph***! (Patent pending.) I'm still trying to remove as much of it as I can from my gardens, while leaving the original clumps intact. They are gorgeous. Nonetheless, **Dear Reader**, if you would like to gift your best enemies with some of my bamboo, please leap out to me. You can assure them, if they ask: Clumping. Non-running. ***Caveat inter vivos.***

No doubt you're wondering about my bananas. Of all my less-is-not-more gardening ventures, the bananas might be my greatest success. A recent visitor commented that they reminded him of Peru! Imagine that! My own piece of Peru right here in the Shenandoah Valley. Rest assured: I'll keep the bananas. Even though they are hardy, I have to work hard at wintering them over. When they start to outgrove their allotted space, I simply overwinter smaller sections of the groves. Or I dig up perimeter pups and give them to friends. (Enemies get the ***Bamboozle Leptomorph, sine caveat.***)

The annuals? Never a problem because at the end of the season, Voila! They're gone. If I want more, I'll plant them again next year.

No doubt you know exactly where I am. That's right. I am ripping out lots of my gardens that have exceeded by far my wildest ~~dreams~~ nightmares.

This fall, just as an example, I'll be lifting and replanting 55 or so peonies that have been anchored in their spots since 1998 when I planted them with fierce determination to make them look as if they had been there forever. Trust me. These days they look as if they have been there forever and a day.

The same can be said for all of my gardens.

As I move forward with these gardening ~~challenges~~ opportunities, I will be gardener enough to own up to the fact that "Less is not more until it is."

What worked great for me for so many years is now simply too much. And too much is just too much.

But, as I own up to the shortfalls, I am seeing wide open ~~expanses~~ opportunities that I have not seen in decades. At the same time, I am seeing metaphorical steel and copper plant markers nudging their way up through the soil here and there and everywhere: **"Gardening Opportunity." "Plant Tomorrow, Today." "Just Plant It."**

Yep. I will savor the landscape's openness through fall's brilliant blaze and through winter's snowy silence.

Come spring thaw, however, my unrepentant self and I will be right back at all the local garden centers. In all likelihood, I will do it all over again unless I somehow discover that sweet spot, somewhere between ***less is a bore*** and ***less is more***.

SEPTEMBER 12, 2022

Writers: Our Forever-Friends

*"Day by day and night by night we were together—
all else has long been forgotten by me…"*

— WALT WHITMAN
(1819-1892; poet, essayist, and journalist; one of the most
influential poets in the American canon; "Once I Pass'd
through a Popular City," *Leaves of Grass*, 1855.)

Whenever I teach a literature course, I tell my students that aside from celebrating their achievements as they master the course content, I have one special hope for each of them. I want them to find one writer who will be their friend. One writer who will never unfriend them as other friends sometimes do. One writer who will be with them through all the storms of life, for a lifetime. A writer who will be a forever-friend.

What I have in mind is similar to the handful of real-life, forever-friends whom we might have, if we are lucky. It's never many. At least it has never been many for me. I have perhaps one handful of such friends. All right. Perhaps two handfuls who are in the friends-forever category. With us, we've shared so many past experiences that even if we have not seen one another in years, when we reconnect, we pick up magically on the same conversation that we were having when we last met, and we do so without missing a beat. Friends. Forever-friends.

Writers can be our forever-friends, too, with an added bonus. We can have lots and lots of them. As we read more and more, we discover more and more writers who might end up as our friends. We like them. We like what they have to say to us. We like how they inspire us. We like how they make us believe. We like how they make us feel…unalone. We like how they heal our…brokenness. Before long, we want to hang out with them. We can. Whenever we want. For as long as we want.

The great thing about writers who are our forever-friends is that when they pop up unannounced and uninvited, it's never a problem. We don't have to clean for them. We don't have to cook for them. And we don't have to clear our calendars for them. They can tag along with us just as we are. And they will do just that if we let them.

All that we have to do is be attentive, smile when they arrive, and even smile when they leave, knowing that they will come back to visit us again and again and again.

Their arrival coincides with something that we are experiencing that makes us think of something else. It's the power of association. Robert Frost captures it best:

"All thought is a feat of association; having what's in front of you bring up something in your mind that you almost didn't know you knew."

That's the beauty of having writers who are forever-friends. Their arrival is based exclusively on what's right in front of you or something that you're thinking about. Something that you almost didn't know you knew.

No doubt, you have your own writers who are your forever-friends, just as I do.

Obviously, I don't know about yours, but mine visit me multiple times throughout the day, every day without fail. I never know which writers will visit or when. But I go forth daily, confident of being strengthened and girded up by their company.

For example, Walt Whitman shook his silvery locks right in front of me as I was writing this post. I was thinking about the fact that only a snippet of a writer's work comes to my mind during an association, while all the other details of the work are seemingly long forgotten. Instantly, the lines from Whitman's "Once I Pass'd through a Popular City" flashed across my mind:

"Day by day and night by night we were together—all else has long been forgotten by me…"

Here's another example.

When I met with my Creative Writing class for the first time this semester, I had a slap-stick time promoting this blog. It was nothing more than nonsensical banter aimed at entertaining my students, but they picked up on it.

Not long after I managed to restore myself to a modicum of seriousness, one student raised her hand as if to ask a serious question.

"Professor Kendrick, did you say that you have a blog?"

I started laughing, as did the rest of the class.

A little later on, her hand went up again. I was on to her by then, but I was having far too much fun, so I acknowledged her.

"Professor Kendrick, did you give us the name of your blog?"

(When our laughter died down, my forever-friend Edward Albee paid me a momentary visit. He has chummed me since the 1960s when I was in college and he was a controversial Broadway playwright.)

"Very funny! You know, Caitlin, my hell-bent banter to promote my blog to a brand-new group of students, reminds me of the first line from Edward Albee's *The Zoo Story*."

In the play, Jerry approaches Peter, a total stranger, sitting on a bench in Central Park.

> **I've been to the zoo.** [PETER doesn't notice.]
> **I said, I've been to the zoo. MISTER, I'VE BEEN TO THE ZOO!**

I was thrilled by Albee's visit, especially since I was able to share it with my class. He came as he did and when he did because of my dogged determination to tell my students—a group of strangers, if you will—all about my blog. In the process, I remembered Jerry's insistence on telling Peter, a total stranger, that he had been to the zoo.

My students got it. They saw the association with great clarity.

On another occasion, something similar happened at the start of the same class.

As I drove on campus. I was aware—painfully so—that the grassy, undeveloped acreage all around the college was being gobbled up by townhouses.

At the start of class, one of my students shared the same observation.

In that nanosecond, former United States Poet Laureate Phillip Levine appeared. Immediately, I walked to my teacher station, googled his poem "A Story" and flashed it on the screen for students to see as I read it aloud.

It captures perfectly what my students and I had witnessed with pain that morning.

Levine chronicles the life and death of the woods that once surrounded us and ends with a chilling doomsday prophecy:

> where are the woods? They had to have been
> because the continent was clothed in trees.
> We all read that in school and knew it to be true.
> Yet all we see are houses, rows and rows
> of houses as far as sight, and where sight vanishes
> into nothing, into the new world no one has seen,
> there has to be more than dust, wind-borne particles
> of burning earth, the earth we lost, and nothing else.

And right now as I typed the above quotation, Canadian singer-songwriter Joni Mitchell popped into my head, chanting a few lines from her "Big Yellow Taxi":

> Don't it always seem to go
> That you don't know what you've got
> Till it's gone
> They paved paradise
> And put up a parking lot.

My writers—my forever-friends—visit me far more in my alone times than they do when I am teaching or, for that matter, when I am socializing.

Maybe they appear then because they know that in my alone times friends can add a richness to any moment, even ordinary ones.

Ordinary moments like weed whacking. Somehow, I end up doing that chore on Sunday instead of going to church. That's no big deal to me. I consider myself **S**piritual **B**ut **N**ot **R**eligious (**SBNR**). Emily Dickinson must be SBNR, too, because she is always with me on my Sunday morns. Her "Some keep the Sabbath going to Church" overpowers the Stihl noise through all the stanzas, rising triumphantly in the final one:

> God preaches, a noted Clergyman —
> And the sermon is never long,
> So instead of getting to Heaven, at last —
> I'm going, all along.

Or sometimes it's as simple as visitorial moments that occur when reading emails from regular friends who aren't writers. Recently, a friend who is my age wrote that his hands had grown old. I sensed his sadness and immediately thought of a poem about aging by former United States Poet Laureate Stanley Kunitz: "Touch Me." It includes the poignant lines:

> What makes the engine go?
> Desire, desire, desire.
> The longing for the dance
> stirs in the buried life.
> One season only,
> and it's done.
> [...]
> Darling, do you remember
> the man you married? Touch me,
> remind me who I am.

And then I immediately thought of Ben Speer singing "Time Has Made a Change in Me." The title alone was touchstone sufficient. And that led me to W. S. Merwin reading his "Yesterday" with the ever-chilling line:

> oh I say
> feeling again the cold
> of my father's hand the last time

It's amazing: the rich literary company that embraced me, all because of one single solitary email sent my way!

Sometimes, though, my forever-friends arrive as I try to make sense of all that's going on in our world. The ongoing COVID-19 pandemic. The invasion of Ukraine. Recent SCOTUS decisions. The January 6 Hearings. Global Warming. Poverty. Food scarcity. Gender inequality. Homophobia. Transphobia. Growing humanitarian conflicts and crises. The 21st anniversary of the 9/11 terror attacks on America.

Need I go on? Sadly, I could. Gladly, I won't. It's far too sobering.

But in those dark moments when I find myself spiritually staggering under the weight of it all, I take strength from William Faulkner's Nobel Acceptance Speech, delivered in 1950 when the world was staggering under the burden of the Cold War:

> Our tragedy today is a general and universal physical fear so long sustained by now that we can even bear it. There are no longer problems of the spirit. There is only the question: When will I be blown up? [...] I decline to accept the end of man. [...] I believe that man will not merely endure: he will prevail. He is immortal, not because he alone among creatures has an inexhaustible voice, but because

he has a soul, a spirit capable of compassion and sacrifice and endurance.

Maybe, just maybe, the need to have writers who are our forever-friends, boils down to nothing more than this. They come regardless of what we are facing. They reassure us that goodness and mercy shall prevail. They remind us to grapple with our soul, to grapple with our spirit.

They come, as Robert Browning came to me just this second, to calm us and anchor us in the full and steadfast belief that despite all the injustices, all the wrongdoings, all the travail, and all the sorrows,

>God's in His Heaven,
>All's right with the world.

— "Pippa Passes," *Song I (1841)*

SEPTEMBER 20, 2022

Foolin' Around with Time

"I wish it need not have happened in my time," said Frodo. "So do I," said Gandalf, "and so do all who live to see such times. But that is not for them to decide. All we have to decide is what to do with the time that is given us."

—J. R. R. TOLKIEN
(1892-1973; English writer and scholar;
The Fellowship of the Ring, 1954.)

Hopefully, you paid close attention to the title of this post. I don't want anyone jumping to the wishful conclusion that I'm fooling around. Well, I guess I am, but it's not with someone. I'm fooling around with time which surely makes fooling around permissible albeit boring!

But let me share with you what made me start fooling around with time in the first place. When I look around me, I seem to see lots of folks who have time on their hands. Sometimes I even hear them saying to one another, "Oh, I'm just killing time."

Thankfully, I'm not one of those folks. Instead of time on my hands, I seem to have time on my mind. I think about time a lot of the time. And I never have time to kill. I'm not even sure that I know how to kill time.

Both expressions—time on my hands and killing time—strike me as rather lame, but not lame enough to keep me from looking up their origins in the *Oxford English Dictionary* (*OED*).

"Time on your hands" goes back to 1668 with Flavell's *Saint Indeed* Ep. Ded. sig. A7: "Leave trifling studies to such as have time lying on their hands, and know not how to imploy it."

Of course, I am intrigued by the reference to "trifling studies," but I don't have time right now to look it up.

"Killing time" dates to 1751, when it appeared in Richardson's *Clarissa* (ed. 3) VIII. Concl. 266: "The more active and lively amusements and Kill-times."

In the next century, Coleridge used it in a way that intrigues me. In his *Lect. Shakespeare* (1856) 3, he writes: "Where the reading of novels prevails as a habit…it is not so much to be called pass-time as kill-time." As an English professor, I am stunned that a poet would speak so unkindly of novels!

Sometimes folks killing time or with time on their hands look at me and ask, "How do you find time to do all the things that you do? You must have all the time in the world."

I want to come back with, "Find time? How could I do that? You have 24 hours in your day, just as I do."

But, instead, I count to ten, smile, and bide my time.

Even so, those questions set me to thinking, "How do I find time to do all that I do when I'm not foolin' around with time?"

The answer is not as straightforward as it might seem. In reality, it's not about finding time. It's about managing time.

It's about realizing that when work is to be done—when goals are to be accomplished—time is not on my side. I have to worry not only about how much time I have to do the needful but also about how much time I will set aside to do the needful.

When it comes to managing time for goals and projects—both long- and short-term—I am downright **SMART**. I know how to get things accomplished on time or ahead of time.

S—Specific.
M—Measurable.
A—Achievable.
R—Relative.
T—Time-based.

In my head, I know that **SMART** can be applied successfully to daily time management, too.

But I don't always practice what's in my head. As a result, time and time again, I discover that I am not the best time manager, even of my own time. Nonetheless, I always develop some kind of plan for my time every day. Usually, I do that planning the night before, while lying in bed, right after I finish taking time to work on my blog post.

The way that I develop those plans has everything to do with how productive my time will be the next day.

Over time, I've picked up on patterns—what works and what doesn't work.

Let me start with the latter. What doesn't work for me is when I make sketchy notes of what I hope to accomplish for the day. I approach the plan so cavalierly that in no time, I'm done.

Here's a perfect example of my sketchy planning for one day, a week or two ago. Let me share without any further loss of time.

Morning Goals
- Meditate
- Bike
- Student Engagement Hours at Laurel Ridge CC

By the end of such a day, I might well have accomplished those goals and more, but I know that they did not require the entire day. I'm left somewhat satisfied, but not entirely. I have the sinking feeling that time slipped through my fingers into soft, billowy expanses of nothingness.

We all need downtime like that from time to time. In fact, some of my best ideas appear in moments when seemingly I am doing nothing.

But, as a rule, I am no fonder of nothingness than I am of stillness. I like my days to be chock-full of activities so that at day's end I can look back knowing that I had a whale of a productive time.

Here's an example of what works best for me when I'm planning a typical day. For the time being, one example should suffice because time's a-wastin'.

Morning Goals
- 5:00-5:30am | Meditate
- 5:30-6:30am | Bike 20 miles
- 6:30-7:30am | Shower, dress, and have breakfast
- 7:50am | Leave for Laurel Ridge CC. Stop for coffee

and pastry at Flour and Water. Take the leisurely and scenic Valley Pike route to the college.
- 9:30am-12:30pm | Student Engagement Hours at Laurel Ridge CC

Hopefully, you get my point. When I anchor my goals to time allotted to each task, I have a specific plan for how I will spend my time.

The beauty of this approach—aside from being more productive—is that I escape to a once-upon-a-time world simply by setting aside time to motor to the college via Valley Pike—past cornfields and the meandering Shenandoah River—rather than whirring to the college mindlessly at 70 miles an hour on the interstate.

No doubt even Benjamin Franklin would have been proud of me on my days when I use time management effectively. Franklin, of course, was ahead of his time in so many ways. Aside from realizing that time is money, his way of scheduling his own days became the prototype of the American day planner.

Sadly, I am not ahead of my time, and, most assuredly, I am not a legend in my own time. But I am fully confident that my way of planning a fully productive day—of making time for the goals that I want to accomplish—will withstand the test of time.

Painfully, too, I know that time and tide wait for no man, least of all for me. For now, then, the time has come for me to stop foolin' around with time, yours and mine.

SEPTEMBER 26, 2022

Two, Together

"I want to realize brotherhood or identity not merely with the beings called human, but I want to realize identity with all life, even with such things as crawl upon earth."

— MAHATMA GANDHI
(1869-1948; Indian lawyer, politician, social activist, and writer; embraced nonviolent resistance; inspired movements for civil rights and freedom around the world.)

The blacksnake and I friended the moment we first laid eyes on one another.

The early, dew-pearled spring morning remains as fresh in my memory as if it were yesterday. I had gone to my towering compost heap, bucket in hand, to retrieve some black gold. As I knelt at the base of its old, sweet-smelling richness, I suddenly sensed eyes. Someone or something was scrutinizing me. I was being watched. I could feel it deep in my bones. I looked all around me and saw no one. Then I lifted my eyes, and there on top of the compost heap was an incredibly beautiful, brilliantly glossy blacksnake, leaning over, looking down at me with its small eyes, its tongue darting, in red contrast to its white under chin, mellowing into soft yellow. I felt neither chill nor threat. I continued my task, all the while the two of us kept returning glances as if to make certain that we did not snap our nanosecond bond, perhaps never to connect again.

Surprisingly, the bond stretched and sunned itself over the summer. Even though I was always hoping to see my blacksnake—so much so that I often went looking for him—our encounters were sudden, unexpected ones.

Not long after our initial meeting, I was hard at work, planting a new specimen tree in the upper yard. The curly, contorted willow was already a large tree with a root ball that seemed far more immense when delivered than when purchased. By the time I dug the hole and positioned the tree, I was exhausted, but I still faced watering, backfilling, watering again, and mulching. Edging near tiredom, I walked a few steps to the nearby water hose. Reaching down, I lifted with an intent to pull. In an instant, I realized that what I had in hand had no drag. I looked. There I stood holding in midair my blacksnake friend whom I had mistaken for my black water hose. It was my second one-on-one experience. Once again our eyes locked. But this meeting was more special than the first. Now we knew one another's touch—warmth against cold, cold against warmth. I put the blacksnake down as casually as I had picked him up, and we each continued what we were doing. I could not see him, but I sensed that he watched from somewhere nearby as I finished planting the willow.

On another occasion, I had spent the better part of my day laying stone pavers for a short walkway through the garden bed outside my kitchen and building a low stone wall along the walkway's meandering edge. The sunny day bordered on scorch. I sat on the walkway, leaned back into the flower garden, admiring my handiwork. As I gloated, a cold black stream soft-bellied itself across my sweaty outstretched arm. I looked back and my eyes met the eyes of my friend, the blacksnake. I remained motionless, holding my breath, hoping that the snake would stop, linger, and perhaps even explore. Instead he slithered on his way, calmly and unhurriedly.

My next visitation was perhaps my most unexpected and the most short-lived. One summer evening, I had gone for a walk in the yard. When I went out, I didn't consider turning on the outdoor lights. But darkness had fallen by the time I started back. I could see my way easily enough because the indoor lights were on, including those in the foyer. Even if the lights had not been on, I could have footed along without really looking. And that's exactly what I did, that is until my hand clutched for the storm door and instead of an iron handle I felt a cold, smooth, muscular surface, pulsing to my touch. Only then did I look. The foyer light dimly illuminated my blacksnake friend, partially coiled around the door handle, upper body stretching toward the door top and lower body draping downward. I opened the door and went inside. My friend remained outside, leaving me to wonder whether he had hoped, for once, to be visitor in my world as I had been so often in his.

That rendezvous was the most fleeting. My fifth was the most lasting. As autumn started, my late partner Allen and I grew weary of removing fallen leaves from our Koi pond and cascading waterfalls. To make our task easier, we covered both with invisible black netting.

Our solution was perfect. The leaves floated on top of the netting instead of on top of the water. But the day came when our hearts sank as we discovered a scarlet red, black-faced cardinal struggling to escape the black netting's grab.

We lifted the netting to winged flight.

"So much for that brilliant solution," we sighed simultaneously.

I rolled the netting into a ball, left it on the small patio beside the pond, and went back indoors to help Allen with dinner.

After dinner, I went back out to throw the netting away. Reaching down, I saw my blacksnake inextricably intertwined in the ball.

Allen came out to see what I was doing.

"Look at what we've done. This is all our fault," I lamented. "We have to get the snake out of the netting."

"And just how do you plan to do that without getting bitten?"

"Go get some scissors, and I'll show you what I have in mind."

Allen came back out with a pair of surgical scissors that he was so skilled in using.

"I'll get a hold of the snake just behind his head so that he can't bite me, and you cut away and remove the netting."

Ever so cautiously, I knelt and took gentle hold of the blacksnake behind his head. Allen starting cutting away at the netting, gradually freeing the snake's tail.

As he snipped away more and more netting, the blacksnake began coiling his emerging body ever so slowly and calmly around my arm.

As Allen snipped, I gently rubbed my other hand against the snake's skin, making certain that no black netting had been left behind.

Finally, the moment came when Allen finished. I remained kneeling on the patio with my blacksnake friend coiled entirely around my arm.

What was I to do now? I had not planned for this moment of release, this moment of letting go.

I stood up slowly, all the while watching my blacksnake friend watching me. It was as if he knew that Allen and I had rescued him. It was as if I knew that my friend would do me no harm.

I walked up to the bank beside the waterfalls, gently lowered my snake-coiled arm to the ground, and let go my grasp around the snake's head.

Two, together, frozen in spirit and frozen in time, just for one second and one second only. In the next, our eternity melted. My blacksnake friend started uncoiling himself from around my arm, pausing to look back. Our eyes locked one last time before he slithered his way back into our world.

OCTOBER 3, 2022

In Bed with Famous (and Not-So-Famous) Writers

"I'm going to bed," really means,
"I'm going to lie in bed and ... write."

— Brent L. Kendrick
(b. 1947; aka "The Wired Researcher.")

Chances are good that you did a double take when you saw the title of today's post. You may have exclaimed, "No way! I've read this already."

Nope. You haven't. If the title seems familiar, you're probably thinking of "Spaces and Habits of Famous (and Not-So-Famous) Writers." But don't worry. I've changed things up: this post has a brand-new set of linen sheets.

And if you aren't thinking that you've read this post before, you are probably asking yourself, "What's going on with the Good Professor's seeming propensity for being in bed?"

Excellent question! I won't try to pull the sheets over your eyes. It's simple. **"In Bed"** makes the title catchy. It certainly makes me lie down and take notice. You'll take notice, too, when I tell you that, on average, we spend 33 years of our life in bed: 26 years, sleeping; 7 years, trying to doze off.

If the **"In Bed"** part didn't grab your attention, **"with writers"** surely did!

And I'll bet I know what you're thinking right now. Come on. Fess up. You're wondering what they're doing in bed. And now you've got me wondering, too. I'll be right back.

Thanks for your patience. I had to do a little research. If you were wondering whether they were ***having…you know…***sex, you won't be impressed by the answer that I just discovered. On average, ***having…you know***…takes up only about one third of a year (117 days) in the course of our entire life. Ironically, people think about ***having…you know***…nearly 19 times a day. I guess we spend far more time thinking about ***having…you know***…than we do enjoying… ***having you know***.

Sadly, I suspect that the 117 days of romance is substantially lower with writers, particularly those who write in bed. I doubt that they would want to be interrupted with their word play. Maybe that's why William Byrd II (Colonial Virginia aristocrat and man of letters; member of the Governor's Council; and founder of Richmond, VA) had a fondness for romantic interludes on the billiard table. "He what?" someone gasped in disbelief. Yep. I tease you not. For your own in-bed reading, check out *The Secret Diary of William Byrd of Westover (1709-1712)*. The content of his diary remained a secret until the 1940s when it was decoded. Now I know that I have whetted your literary appetite. Here, let me tease you more with an excerpt from his diary:

> in the afternoon my wife and I had a little quarrel which I reconciled with a flourish. It is to be observed that the flourish was on the billiard table.

Now you know why he wrote his diary in code. Check it out, but not now. Or, if you must, please come back and finish this post.

But let's get our writers back in bed where we found them to begin with.

For what it's worth, I was in bed already, and I intend to stay there, smackdab in the middle. After all, it's my bed, and in bed is where I write my blog posts. But I'm the not-so-famous writer mentioned in the title, so enough about me. Let's snuggle up with some famous writers who wrote in bed, and, for the time being they can join me in mine.

Surprisingly, not many writers actually write in bed. That suits me just fine. Although my bed is big—fit for a queen—I still need to be able to pull up the sheets and get comfy.

Little chance of my doing that any time soon. Long-legged Mark Twain has jumped in already. What a bed hog: writing and smoking at the same time. He's got some nerve! *"Just try it in bed sometime. I sit up with a pipe in my mouth and a board on my knees, and I scribble away. Thinking is easy work, and there isn't much labor in moving your fingers sufficiently to get the words down"* (*New York Times*, "How Mark Twain Writes in Bed," April 12, 1902).

Joining Twain is Edith Wharton, author of *The Age of Innocence*. (Well, maybe, *innocent*, but, after all, she is in bed with Twain even if I am the one who put the two side by side.) Wharton liked to write in bed because it freed her from wearing her corset, thereby liberating her thoughts. Now, at least, we all know where she kept her mind.

And I suppose we have to invite Truman Capote to hop in. He's often quoted as saying: *"I am a completely horizontal author. I can't think unless I'm lying down, either in bed or stretched on a couch and with a cigarette and coffee handy."*

On the other side of the bed—to my right—let's put some European writers. For bed-balance, we'll add three only, arranged in the same gender order as the Americans: Boy. Girl. Boy.

To my right, William Wordsworth. He wrote his poems in bed in complete darkness, and, if he lost a sheet of paper in bed, he started over. It was easier than rummaging around under the sheets. Thank God for small mercies.

On his right is Dame Edith Sitwell who slept in a coffin from time to time. Without a doubt, she'll enjoy being in bed for a change, especially since she once commented, *"All women should have a day a week in bed."* That's all fine and dandy as long as they're not in my bed.

To Sitwell's right is Marcel Proust, right on the edge of the bed. Writing in bed was not a quirk for him. It was a requirement. Age and illness forced him to stay in bed, and it was in bed where he completed *Remembrance of Things Past* as well as *In Search of Lost Time*. On the edge of the bed seemed perfect so that he could get in and out with greater ease.

OMG! I just heard a loud thud. Did you? Let me take a look. Sure enough. The not-so-famous American writer who thought up these shenanigans in the first place is at it again. He has pushed the European writers right out of the bed onto the floor.

Oh, no. I just heard another thud, though not quite as loud. Let me lean across the bed and have a look-see. As I live and breathe! Capote, Wharton, and Twain are all piled up on the Oriental rug. Twain is still smoking his pipe. Wharton is suddenly looking for her corset. And Capote is leaning back, still smoking his cigarette. Maybe he and Twain can blow smoke at one another while Wharton laces up her corset.

Well, at least the Americans landed softly. I really meant no harm, but I had no choice other than to kick the three of them out, too. Seven in my bed was six too many.

I don't know about you, but it's perfectly clear to me that writers—whether famous or not-so-famous—make strange bedfellows.

OCTOBER 10, 2022

A Wardrobe of My Own

"Love sacrifices all things to bless the thing it loves."

— Edward George Earle Lytton Bulwer-Lytton,
1st Baron Lytton (1803–1873; English writer and politician.)

Somehow, as my 75th birthday gets closer and closer, I rarely think about myself as the baby of the family.

But I am. And trust me: the youngest in the family—at least in mine—is always the baby.

Aside from the dubious distinction of being the baby, I'm not sure that the status ever included many other benefits.

Well, maybe one. When I was born, my oldest brother and sister became rocking rivals:

"It's my turn to rock Brentford Lee tonight."

"No, it's not. You rocked him last night."

I was rocked a lot. My oldest sister still reminds me.

And, on reflection, maybe being the baby came with a second benefit. My middle sister pretended that she was my mother. I had double doses of motherly affection. She still reminds me.

What sweetened my baby-of-the-family deal, though,

was the simple fact that I was born smiling. "Little Mister Sunshine" became my nickname.

Naturally, the twofer combination—baby and smile—came to mean one thing and one thing only: Brentford Lee could do no wrong.

I am certain that I was capable of doing lots of wrong. More, I could have done so and gotten away with it easily. But, by and large, during my childhood—and continuing thereafter—I tried my best to do no wrong. When I did, I tried my best to right the wrong as soon as I could, especially if the wrong had been prompted by anger. My mother taught me and my siblings to not let the sun go down on our wrath.

Once as a teenager, however, my anger caused a great hurt—to others and to me—and I did not make amends before the sun went down.

I remember that fall day as vividly as if it were yesterday.

It was at the start of my freshman year, and something happened in school that ticked me off. Whatever it was had to have been of no real consequence. I can't remember the details at all, not even one.

But I do remember that the short walk from the bus stop to my home was not long enough to soften the sharp edge of my anger.

As I approached the house, I saw on the front porch a brand new, light brown, faux-wood, metal cabinet. It had two doors that opened out from the middle, and it was about four feet wide and six feet or so tall.

I went right past it, deliberately banging the screen door against the wooden frame as I walked inside. My mother was standing at the kitchen stove with a big smile on her face, not to be undone as I slammed my books on the kitchen table.

"What is that ugly thing on the porch?"

My mother looked at me and started to respond, but my ongoing rant gave her no chance. She kept on cooking dinner.

"It's hideous, just hideous."

My mother remained silent, as I marched back out to have a second look, banging the screen door, going out and coming back in again.

"Who's it for?" I asked, showing an unbecoming attitude that still makes me cringe.

My mother's *"It's for you"* hung in the air, echoing against itself over and over in my mind. *"It's for you. It's for you. It's …"*

She smiled softly as she kept on cooking.

"Your dad and I thought that you might like to have a wardrobe of your own to keep all your new school clothes in."

I had always loved clothes, and now that I was in high school, I loved them even more. Sweaters. Slacks. Socks. Always matching. Always the best that my summer yard mowing jobs could buy. Always bought on lay-away at the best men's store in a small city nearby. My mother took great pride in how I dressed, and she took even greater pride in knowing that I was known as the best dressed kid in school.

"For me? I don't want it. That wardrobe is so ugly. I'll never use it. Never."

My mother looked away and didn't say another word about the wardrobe. Her face was still. Her smile, broken. Her joy, gone.

And that ended it. My dad put the wardrobe downstairs. I don't remember who used it. It didn't matter to me that it was a wardrobe of my own. What mattered to me was that I thought it was ugly. What mattered to me was that I vowed to never use it. What mattered to me was that I never did.

The wardrobe was still downstairs when I graduated from high school with honors and went away to college.

It was still downstairs when I graduated from college with honors and moved to our Nation's Capital.

The wardrobe was still downstairs when I started working at the Library of Congress.

When I came back home for visits during those late teenage and early adult years, neither my mother, my father, nor I ever mentioned my wardrobe. It was as if it had never entered our home. Yet it had entered, and it remained.

And then the day came when the wardrobe of my own rose up from afar, right in front of me, right before my very eyes.

I was struggling with my monthly budget. My handsome salary as an editor at the Library of Congress had an equally handsome competitor: the high cost of living in D.C., combined with paying off student loans. As I did my math, I suddenly realized that I just couldn't have everything that I wanted. I had to make hard choices. I had to make painful sacrifices just to make ends meet.

In a flash, I realized that when my parents chose to buy me a wardrobe of my own, they chose to make sacrifices. My mom chose to do without her new dress. My dad chose to do without his new shoes. My siblings who were still at home had no choice. This time my parents chose to sacrifice for me as they had chosen to sacrifice for all of us, all down through the years.

Immediately, I picked up the phone and called my mom and dad. We had a long, long conversation about a wardrobe of my own.

I don't know when *"I'm sorry"* brought forth such joyful tears.

The tears could not undo that teenage day when I was so lacking in gratitude. But my mom and dad let me unburden my sorrow, and across the miles and across the great expanse of time, they washed it away with their unconditional love.

Seven years had passed, but, finally, the evening sun went down on a wardrobe of my own.

OCTOBER 18, 2022

It's Not a Corset. Don't Force It.

*Is it a corset
or primal wave?
Don't try to force it.*

— FROM ELAINE MITCHELL'S "FORM"

Lately, I've been thinking a lot about writing. I have no doubt that it's because I've been writing these posts faithfully every week for nearly an entire year. And I have no doubt that it's also because I'm teaching Creative Writing this semester. Naturally, I spend lots of my time talking with aspiring writers about writing.

In fact, when I met with my students last week, we did two, one-minute reflections.

For the first, we reflected on the **joy of writing**. Let me share some of their responses:

- Creating my own world.
- Finding words that describe my own feelings.
- Gaining an understanding of my own life.
- Discovering something about my own identity.

- Daydreaming.
- Letting my thoughts spew out.

Getting it done—the rhythm, the music, the wish, the dream, and the fear.

For the second reflection, we tackled the **challenges of writing**. Again, let me share:

- Getting started.
- Finding an interesting topic.
- Putting myself into my writing.
- Encouraging my paragraphs to talk to one another.
- Choosing which idea to explore.
- Connecting the beginning, the middle, and the end.
- Accepting my writing as it is.

I had planned a third reflection, but we ran out of time. Here's what it would have been: **discoveries about writing**.

For this one, I'll take the lead, sharing my own ideas, based largely on what I've discovered about writing as I wrote my weekly blog posts this year.

By and large, what I've discovered has been by way of reminders. **To start, writing isn't easy. It isn't spontaneous. And it isn't magical.**

Here's something else that I have rediscovered. Writing is work. It's hard work. It's lots of hard work.

Work. Hard work. Lots of hard work. That's my mantra these days when I'm working with other aspiring writers. I front-load the conversation: get ready for rich, robust, and heavy mental lifting.

At the same time, over the last year I've reminded myself—and others—that even though the hard art of writing isn't magical, it is filled with magical moments.

Let me share some of mine.

Magical Moment. Getting hooked on an idea that makes my world fade away.

Magical Moment. Letting an idea explode in my mind as magically as Pop Rocks explode in my mouth.

Magical Moment. Focusing on old-soul insights that have come back to me from far, far away and from long, long ago.

Magical Moment. Fooling around with organizing what I'm writing until I get comfy with one structure that pulls me in close and whispers, "Yes. Let's do it."

Don't get too excited by these moments. They are magical. But let me remind you: they are not magic.

And trust me. The next part—the actual writing—has no magic at all. Sometimes, it might not even have magical moments. The actual writing can be grueling, if not downright defeating, especially since first drafts never hit the mark. Never. Mine don't, at any rate. Sometimes, even my 13th draft doesn't seem quite right. How's this for a confession? Sometimes, I've gone as high as 22 drafts. Admittedly, the differences between any two drafts are sometimes majorly minor, and the changes will be unknown forever to all except me. Nonetheless, the work of writing—of revising—goes on and on and on.

And writers keep at it. I keep at it, knowing that what I write will never be perfect, but knowing, too, that at some point it's as good as it's going to get.

What I have discovered as well is the simple fact that my scholarly writing is in many ways far easier than writing my personal essays like today's post. My own scholarly work on The Humourist as well as on Mary E. Wilkins Freeman, for example, has singleness of purpose and focus. Easy-peasy, lemon-squeezy.

On the other hand, writing my weekly blog is more challenging, mainly because I don't focus on the same topic every week. My topics change. As reluctant as I am to admit it, I'll admit it anyway: I'm never sure from one week to the next exactly what topic will bubble up.

That's not to say that I don't have lots of ideas for my posts. I do. I have plenty. In fact, whenever I have an idea for a post, I immediately start a WordPress draft. I give it a working title, and I include as many notes as possible so that when I return, I can glide back into my thinking and writing groove.

Right now, for example, I have 25 drafts in various stages of completion, ranging from *"The Power of Showing Up"* to *"Dating after Twenty-Two"* to *"Mishaps Make Memories."* I suppose I could also mention *"Working Out a Plan"* or *"A **Horror**scopic Week"* or *"What My Father Saw."* Or I could mention that I might have *"My Gardening Attire"* finished by next week. I might. But, on the other hand, I might not.

I'm not trying to generate future blog traffic by teasing you with alluring and inviting titles that may or may not morph into posts. Simply put, I have come to the realization that my ideas must germinate in the dark caverns of mindfulness and mindlessness. They must sprout and pop up whenever they are ready for the light of day. No sooner. No later.

All of my tentative topics and all of their accompanying draft notes are simply placeholders. Nothing more.

Yet it occurs to me that maybe they are far more than mere placeholders.

They are talismans. Not to bring me power. Not to bring me luck. But rather to bring me back to the illuminated intensity of the split second when an idea sought refuge within me and pleaded for a some-day home.

What I have discovered, then, is that I need lots and lots of talismans. They are my antidote to the numbness and paralysis that I know fully well will set in if I have no writing options. I don't write well when my storehouse of options is empty. When that happens, I feel that I have forced myself into the all-too-tight corset of being compelled to write on one topic and one topic only.

On the other hand, when I have many, many topics, one of them might be precisely the one that captures my fancy precisely when my fancy needs to be captured.

It won't have anything to do with talismanic luck. And it won't have anything to do with magic.

It will have everything to do with my willingness to let my ideas take their own shape, whatever those shapes might be, without being corseted, without being laced up, and without being forced.

I want my ideas:

- to leave themselves ample space to move around in.
- to do what they want to do.
- to be what they want to be.

It's really straightforward. My greatest discovery about my own writing is my everlasting need to unlace the corset that constricts my thoughts. It's my everlasting need to let my ideas breathe and expand freely, whenever and however they wish.

OCTOBER 24, 2022

My Gardening Attire

"Anyone can get dressed up and glamorous, but it is how people dress on their days off [that's] the most intriguing."

— ALEXANDER WANG
(b. 1983; American fashion designer known for his
urban designs and his use of black.)

It's no secret. I love to garden. Actually, I talk about gardening a lot in my posts. Three focused exclusively on gardening. You may recall "Two, Together" and "Less Is Not More Until It Is." And if you don't recall those posts, you may remember The Joy of Weeding.

But unless you are a gardener yourself, you may be wondering why on earth I'm writing about gardening when we're reaching the end of October.

Of course, you're wondering. I understand. Spring, which ushered in the end, is so far behind us that it's nothing more than memories of sudden and energetic growth spurts, filled with verdant hope and promise, poised on the threshold of new life.

Then came summer ushering in such fulsome lushness that it transformed the world into a landscape of sensational, razzle-dazzle impressions, but its memory, too, is on the wane.

Now, fall. Here we are midst October mist, with decadent decay exposing bony branches beneath blooms and leaves still clinging, sighing the song of letting go, rustling ghostly memories right before our eyes.

Soon and very soon, winter will bring freezings, earth-heavings, and dead stillness, with roots connecting underground, communing in generative darkness.

The seasons come. The seasons go. And then they start all over again. (But only when publishers see fit to send out new gardening catalogs.)

But my goodness! Here I've gone and let me and you get snowed by reveries of the gardening seasons.

Sadly, putting in the seed is not the thrust of this post.

Instead, it's all about putting on my gardening ... ?

Threads? As in the slang word going all the way back to 1926? Let me unearth its origins and see what I can find. *Threads* was first recorded in *Wise-Crack Dictionary: More than 1,000 Phrases and Words in Every-Day Use Collected from 10,000 Communications Received during a Newspaper Prize Contest and Other Sources* (eds. George H. Maines and Bruce Grant, vol. 1).

Well, it's doubtful that I will don any gardening *threads*, although it was fun trying the word on for size today.

Maybe, instead, I will put on my gardening **costume**. Sometimes—and this really is true—sometimes I think about what I happen to be wearing—whether in the garden or out of the garden—as my *costume*. I'm chuckling to myself right now because that usage puts me in the good company of Samuel Johnson who used it in his *A Journey to the Western Island of Scotland*: "Dr. Johnson in his Hebridean Costume" (1775).

But for this post it's a Greenthumb down for costume and another Greenthumb down for threads.

How about **Clothes**? It has an interesting origin as well, going all the way back to *c*888 when it appeared in Ælfred's translation of Boethius' *De Consol. Philos.*: "Wæpnu, and mete, and ealo, and claþas" (xvii).

I had to dig really deep for that Old English origin. But come on: I can't even pronounce the words in the sentence where *clothes* appeared. Let me edge up to the surface a bit to 1484 Middle English when *clothes* as we know them appeared in Caxton's translation of G. de la Tour-Landry's *Book of the Knight of the Tower*: "She … arayed her with clothes of gold, and flouryshynge of ryche ermyns."

There. That's much better. I like being able to pronounce the names of whatever it is that I might be wearing when I garden.

Since I seem to be tilling in the right direction, perhaps I will narrow my definition of *clothes*, especially since mine are certainly not of gold and furs. I would look perfectly silly in clothes like that, and, besides, I couldn't afford them anyway since I teach at a c-mm—ity college.

Let's see. Ah, yes. **Dress clothes** might work since I have a few. *Dress clothes* goes all the way back to 1838 when it first appeared in Lady Charlotte Maria Bury's *Diary*: "All the gentlemen … looked beautiful in their dress clothes."

For my *dress clothes* I have things like suits and sports jackets. But I rarely wear them when I'm teaching, unless it's a special event. On normal days, I wear Oxford dress shirts—usually blue or purple (Those are the only colors, right?)—with button-down collars; Windsor double-knotted ties; double-pleated, cuffed pants; and wingtip, lace-up shoes with real leather soles. (Please tell me that they do not make dress shoes that do not have leather soles. If you must tell me otherwise, break it to me gently and have some smelling salts handy.)

Ironically, my colleagues and my students think that I wear my *dress clothes* when I garden. They even think that I wear my *dress clothes* when I split wood.

Sure. Right. Dress shoes. Dress pants. Dress Shirt. Windsor double-knotted tie. Genuine leather shoes. Imagine. They really think that's how I dress when I garden. They have even told me so. Right to my face. The nerve.

But let's move on. Someone's trying to tell me something.

"*Say what? I object vehemently. They do NOT call me a* **stick-in-the-mud**."

Well, I don't think they would call me that, but let me see what my trusted friend Mx Oxford has to say. "Look at the old stick-in-the-mud!" (*Satirist, or, Censor of the Times*, 1832) (I was hoping, with great verdancy, that *mud* in *stick-in-the mud* would have something to do with garden soil. Was I ever wrong!)

Now I'm hearing someone else whispering in my ear.

"*Stop goading me! They don't call me a* **dandy**, *either.*"

Hmmm…*dandy* might actually be better than *stick-in-the-mud*. Mx Oxford will know. "A Dandy is a Clothes-wearing Man, a Man whose trade, office, and existence consists in the wearing of Clothes" (Thomas Carlyle, *Sarto Resartus*, 1834).

Isn't that just *dandy*? I admit, though, that the usage of *dandy* in the quoted sentence seems as contorted as a willow.

Now that I think of it, however, twelfth Librarian of Congress Daniel Boorstin was sometimes seen as a **DAN***dy*. Well. Yes. Of course. He always wore his signature bow tie. *Bow tie Dan.*

While I'm not sure that I like having people perceive me as a *dandy*, I don't mind it at all if it puts me in Dr. Boorstin's company. Who knows. His bow tie made him stand out in the world of learning and librarianship. Maybe my clothes will make me stand out in the world of education, and, when it comes to gardening, maybe my clothes will make me outstanding in the field.

But let me get back to the word **attire** that's part of this post's title. I struggled with that word choice. I've never thought of using *attire* to refer to what I wear, on any occasion. "And do you now put on your best attyre?" (Shakespeare, *Julius Caesar*, 1623).

However, since I do put on my best *attire* for my students and my colleagues, it seems appropriate to include the word in the title. All of my protestations notwithstanding, they are certain that's what I wear when I garden.

Maybe this post will convince them otherwise. I have taken off my **threads**. I have taken off my **costume**. I have taken off my **clothes**. And I have taken off my **attire** which I never had on in the first place.

Now look at me. Well, on the other hand, don't.

Give me time, at least, to get dressed in the sad clothes that I actually wear when I garden. As will be evident, even a *wordster* like me lacks the ability to gussy up clothes like mine that are pitifully mundane.

When I garden on my days off, *I wear an old, tattered baseball cap—faded burgundy—brim forward.*

When I garden on my days off, *I wear the oldest, grungiest t-shirt that I own. I own several. I like grunge options.*

When I garden on my days off, *I wear blue jeans so faded, so wholly holey, so fringed, and worn so bare in all the right places that they would fetch a fortune on all the wrong fashion racks.*

When I garden on my days off, *I wear steel-toed, unstylish, waterproof work boots that allow me to be comfortable and confident in all the tough places where I tend to go.*

That's it. That's what I wear when I garden on my days off.

It goes without saying that I am thrilled beyond thrills that my students and my colleagues see my **attire**, my **clothes**, my **costume**, and my **threads** through a lens that commands such respect.

If they could only see me on my days off—especially on my gardening days—they would be intrigued by my ability to reinvent not only myself but also my attire.

OCTOBER 31, 2022

A Halloween Obsession

*"The roldengod and the soneyhuckle
the sack eyed blusan and the wistle theed
are all tangled with the oison pivy
the fallen nine peedles and the wumbleteed."*

— May Swenson
(1919-1989; American poet and playwright; "A Nosty Fright".)

I know. I know. It's Halloween. **BOO!** That's as far as I'm going to go. Don't expect any tricks in this post. You won't find any. With a little luck, though, you might find a treat. Perhaps two. I found a big one, and I was not even expecting it.

But before I tell you about my big treat, I must tell you that I am **spooked**. Truly and positively *spooked*. Yep. I am.

I cannot believe the batty thing that I have done.

Somehow, I have allowed myself to be spirited into the notion that just because October 31 this year happens to fall on a Monday—the day that I publish my blog—I somehow have to make this post fit the hobgoblin occasion.

To *spooked*, let me now add **phooey**. So, *phooey*. It's all a bunch of **hocus pocus.**

Since when have I ever written anything for an occasion? Sure, I write from time to time, as in occasionally. But an **occasional writer** is one who writes for specific occasions, with or without the benefit of a patron who supports the arts.

Two Colonial Americans known for writing on specific occasions come to mind when I think of occasional writers.

One is Anne Bradstreet, the first writer in our Colonies to be published. Her volume of poetry *The Tenth Muse Lately Sprung Up in America* (1650) sounds rather sprightly. Indeed, Bradstreet knew fully well how to cast occasional poetic spells, especially on her husband and on the Royal Family. Here's a perfect example, with the occasion revealed by the poem's title: "A Letter to her Husband, absent upon Publick employment." And here's another where the occasion that prompted the poem is equally evident in the title: "In Honor of that High and Mighty Princess Queen Elizabeth of Happy Memory." Parts of the poem no doubt left Colonial men feeling jittery and unbalanced:

> Nay Masculines, you have thus taxt us long,
> But she, though dead, will vindicate our wrong,
> Let such as say our Sex is void of Reason,
> Know tis a Slander now, but once was Treason.

Into the mix we must add Phillis Wheatley (1753-1784), the Sable Muse of the American Revolution and author of *Poems on Various Subjects, Religious and Moral* (1773). Her poem "His Excellency General Washington," written in 1775 during the American Revolution, is a perfect example of occasional poetry. Far better, though, is her poem "On Being Brought from Africa to America":

> 'Twas mercy brought me from my *Pagan* land,
> Taught my benighted soul to understand
> That there's a God, that there's a *Saviour* too:
> Once I redemption neither sought nor knew.
> Some view our sable race with scornful eye,
> "Their colour is a diabolic die."
> Remember, *Christians*, *Negros*, black as *Cain*,
> May be refin'd, and join th' angelic train.

No doubt the ending of her poem left Colonial Christians feeling jittery and unbalanced. If they didn't feel that way, they should have. Wheatley saw the truth that they may have been too blind to see.

But since Wheatley and Bradstreet were both poets, I started wondering whether occasional writers are always poets.

A quick google search chilled me to the bone because I had to read what I uncovered several times. Even then I was not certain that I could break the spell of what it really meant.

Read an excerpt for yourself and then we can compare our fright notes.

> [...] the key concept of occasional literature and its specific position between writer and patron, fiction and reality. The latter is defined in terms of two kinds of referentiality: on the one hand, the text's connection to the occasion (pretext/performance); on the other, its (literary/potentially fictive) representation of a 'reality' that is relevant to that occasion.

All right. I get it, but only because I bring to the reading of the paragraph prior knowledge of occasional literature.

Without that prior knowledge, would I get it? I don't think so.

I suppose that I could rewrite the passage in plain English, but since the original was written in academic English, it might lose something in translation. And what if the author heard about my translation and decided to translate it back to academic English. That version might be even more frightful.

Wouldn't that be a hoot!

I had not thought of it until now, but that scenario is incredibly similar to what happened to Mark Twain and his "Jumping Frog of Calaveras County." Twain wrote the story in English with lots of dialect. Then it was pirated and translated into French—literally, word for word— with no attempt to capture the many colorful nuances of dialect. Twain found out about the French version and translated it back into English. The intriguing literary *menage de trois* was exposed to the entire world in 1903 as *The Jumping Frog : In English, Then in French, Then Clawed Back into a Civilized Language Once More by Patient, Unremunerated Toil.*

While my google search for occasional writers thrilled me because it prompted me to conjure up how Mark Twain clawed his famed story back into civilized English, it spooked me away from digging further into the catacombs of occasional writers.

Nonetheless, my goblinesque spell was not broken.

Somehow, I remained cauldron-bent that this post would ride along on some sort of literary broom.

I soon came up with what I thought was a perfect slant: **famous writers who died on Halloween.** Wouldn't that be fun! Indeed, a number of famous people died on Halloween, including Henri Houdini (1874-1926) who made a career out of defying all odds, but in the end could not out-magician the Grim Reaper. However, I found only one writer who died on Halloween: Natalie Babbitt (1932-2016), writer and illustrator of children's books. In her best-known work, *Tuck Everlasting*, a family discovers life everlasting.

Obviously, that angle handed me no real treats. How about the flip side: **writers who were born on Halloween?**

Lest I be accused of being a trickster, let me tell you up front that I know already of one writer whose birthday is October 31. (But I will swear on a stack of pumpkins that I had forgotten all about it until I started writing this part of the post.) She, however, will follow John Keats (1795-1821), English Romantic poet, whose poem "'Tis the Witching Time of Night" is fitting, perhaps, for Halloween:

> 'Tis " the witching time of night",
> Orbed is the moon and bright,
> And the stars they glisten, glisten,
> Seeming with bright eyes to listen —
> For what listen they?

The opening line of Keat's poem is, of course, a play on the "Soliloquy" in Shakespeare's *Hamlet*.

With that out of the way, let's move on to the woman writer who shares her birthday with Halloween. She is none other than my lady, Mary E. Wilkins Freeman (1852-1930). I say "my lady" because she has bewitched me into spending five decades digging up her life and letters, and I am still not finished. At the turn of the twentieth century, she and Mark Twain were America's most beloved writers. And when Twain was celebrated with lavish abandon on the occasion of his 70th birthday, Freeman was his guest, and he escorted her into Delmonico's where she dined at his table. Anyway, I just perused my *The Infant Sphinx: Collected Letters of Mary E. Wilkins Freeman* to see whether she had written any letters on any of her birthdays. I found two, but neither mentioned her birthday or Halloween.

But in one letter written late in her life, she reflects on the October 4, 1869, flood, which was among the most disastrous floods in the history of Brattleboro (VT) where she lived at the time:

> I remember the Flood with a capital F, when Whetstone brook went on a rampage, and Brattleboro was cut in twain by a raging torrent, in which lives were lost, and—a minor tragedy, savoring of comedy to all save the chief actor—a rooster went sailing past on a rolling pumpkin into the furious Connecticut river. [Letter 461]

Maybe Freeman was always out trick-or-treating. I doubt it. More likely than not she was at home, working on one of her own spooky supernatural stories for which she is well known, most notably her *The Wind in the Rose-Bush and Other Stories of the Supernatural* (1903). If you like stories about body-snatchers—of sorts—you might enjoy her "Luella Miller," one of her most critically acclaimed supernatural stories with Luella cast as a New England vampire:

> Weak heart; weak fiddlesticks! There ain't nothin' weak about that woman. She's got strength enough to hang onto other folks till she kills 'em.

Actually, talking about Freeman's stories of the supernatural requires a brief nod to two of her literary ancestors.

If you're thinking Edgar Allan Poe, you're right. Although Freeman claimed that she read nothing which she thought might influence her, in the same letter she acknowledges that she read Poe. [Letter 441] Without doubt, the madness in Poe's "The Fall of the House of Usher" and Freeman's "The Hall Bedroom" are kin, with both stories calling into question the sanity of their respective narrators.

And if you are thinking of Nathaniel Hawthorne in addition to Poe, good for you. Freeman read him as well. Just as Hawthorne was heir to a Puritan tradition, think of Freeman as heiress to the same Puritan tradition but with a far greater emphasis on psychological probing and on characters with such warped wills they border on the grotesque. Sir Arthur Conan Doyle called Freeman's novel *Pembroke* "the greatest piece of fiction in America since [Hawthorne's] *The Scarlet Letter*" (*The Infant Sphinx*, 2-3). A good Hawthorne story to read on Halloween might be his "Young Goodman Brown":

> "Welcome, my children," said the dark figure, "to the communion of your race! Ye have found, thus young, your nature and your destiny. My children, look behind you!" They turned; and flashing forth, as it were, in a sheet of flame, the fiend-worshippers were seen; the smile of welcome gleamed darkly on every visage.

And we can't look back at Freeman's literary ancestors without noting several of her literary offspring. Freeman's exploration of grotesque characters—village types with strong-wills, walking blindly the warped paths of their own existence—made heads turn in her own time and paved the way for future writers who were equally fixated on unearthing their own grotesque characters.

It's not too great a stretch of the imaginative web of literary influence to say that without Freeman, we wouldn't have Sherwood Anderson's tales of grotesque village types memorialized in his *Winesburg, Ohio*. Don't be fearful. Open the book and read "The Book of the Grotesque" or "Hands." Or go beyond *Winesburg* and read one of Anderson's later stories "The Man Who Became a Woman."

The web grows larger with another writer known for his Southern Gothicism. Who does not recall the macabre ending to William Faulkner's "A Rose for Emily"?

> For a long while we just stood there, looking down at the profound and fleshless grin. The body had apparently once lain in the attitude of an embrace, but now the long sleep that outlasts love, that conquers even the grimace of love, had cuckolded him. What was left of him, rotted beneath what was left of the nightshirt, had become inextricable from the bed in which he lay; and upon him and upon the pillow beside him lay that even coating of the patient and biding dust.
>
> Then we noticed that in the second pillow was the indentation of a head. One of us lifted something from it, and leaning forward, that faint and invisible dust dry and acrid in the nostrils, we saw a long strand of iron-gray hair.

And somewhere in the web we might even find Toni Morrison. Though she denied it, she was heavily influenced by Faulkner. (She had to have been influenced by him. After all, she did her master's thesis on Faulkner.) Therefore, Morrison could have been indirectly influenced by Freeman as well, at least by Freeman's significant role in the American Gothic literary tradition. In fact, in Freeman's "Old Woman Magoun," the grandmother's decision to murder her granddaughter Lily to save her from a fate worse than death is not too unlike Sethe's decision in Morrison's *Beloved* to murder her daughter rather than have her face the horrors of slavery.

Well, one thing is not up for conjecture. This post has taken twists and turns that I never expected. Go figure.

Now the challenge is how to bring the post to its logical conclusion. Initially, I had every intention to end with the last few lines of "A Nosty Fright":

> Will it ever be morning, Nofember virst,
> skue bly and the sappy hun, our friend?
> With light breaves of wall by the fayside?
> I sope ho, so that this oem can pend.

But now another ending is required.

I am shrieking with laughter. To think that I started this post by protesting that I was not an occasional writer—one who writes on special occasions. Yet look at what I've gone and done. I've managed to dig up a lot of literary supernatural greats and, without any original intent whatsoever, I've managed to explain how they're all connected in one way or another to my lady, Mary E. Wilkins Freeman, known to her closest friends (and to me) as Dolly.

How twisted is that? And just think. **I did it all quite by accident on the occasion of her Halloween birthday!** That makes it even more bizarre!

I believe fully that I am bewitched! No, I believe fully that I am possessed. Either way, I have a solid defense: **the goblins made me do it.**

Bewitched and possessed, let me mount my broom, summit my mountain, and screech in a voice sufficiently loud to wake the living and the dead:

Happy 150th Halloween Birthday, Dear Dolly!

NOVEMBER 7, 2022

The Other Side

"Dogs have a way of finding the people who need them, and filling an emptiness we didn't ever know we had."

— Thom Jones
(1945-2016; American writer primarily of short stories.)

What can I say about the dogs in my life? Well, for starters, I've had quite a few. Now, stop it already. I'm not talking about those dogs. I'm talking about real dogs, the four-legged ones. You know. Our pets. Our best friends. Our confidantes.

The first dog in my life was **Brownie**. All that I remember about him—tapping into nothing more than my own memory—is his curly brown hair and his wonderfully large, black, wet nose. I was hardly more than a toddler, and he was my mother's dog. Anything else that I might know about Brownie, I learned from my mother. Dog memories run deep. **My mother saw Brownie through**.

My dad brought the next dog into my life. **Spotty** was a coal-mine foundling. All mine. He had the spotted coat of a brown-and-white Beagle, but his stocky frame, unusually large ears, large paws, and short-but-wavy hair barked

Collie. Spotty lived outdoors and slept in a doghouse that my dad and I built, outfitted with a bed that my mother made. Since I was a grade-schooler, he spent more time with my mother than with me. He followed her around all day, especially when she was outdoors, hanging laundry on the clothesline. My mother taught Spotty to sing, and she enjoyed mimicking his operatic accomplishments. I never heard Spotty sing, but I learned that love is not diminished when shared. **My mother saw Spotty through.**

My next dog, **Lassie**, leaped into my life right out of the popular television series *Lassie*. Both Lassies were Collies. Somewhere I have a Polaroid of me, summer-sun-bleached hair, holding my prize-winning sunflower. Lassie was surely nearby, but she's not in the photo. I discovered quickly after one short season that she would be far happier running the wide open farm fields that became her new home. Sometimes love means letting go. **I wonder who saw Lassie through.**

After that summer of 1959, I didn't have another dog in my life for many, many years. Actually, I was a graduate student, and the name **Brecca** caught my fancy as I studied *Beowulf*. I decided to buy myself a dog associated with water and swimming. A Saddleback English Springer Spaniel seemed perfect. Brecca was my first pedigree dog, and he was the first dog in my life to live with me indoors. Brecca watched over me through thousands of hours of graduate work—the endless cycle: Reading. Research. Writing. Repeat.—and never grew weary. When I completed my doctoral work and returned to DC, I was the winter caregiver for my mom and dad for a decade. Brecca followed my dad up and down the hall as he walked to regain strength after a stroke left him partially paralyzed. And when my niece/goddaughter, Janet, came along, Brecca followed her as she crawled all around the house and up and down the stairs, always positioning himself to ensure her safety. When his ear cancer proved untreatable after a first surgery, he would patiently lie on his side as I applied homeopathic compresses. His follower-trust triumphed to the end. **I saw Brecca through.**

Sparky—a Dalmatian—came next, followed by **Maggie**—a Blue Tick Coonhound. Grief can be sudden as I came to learn and as the speaker in Robert Frost's "One More Brevity" had learned long before:

> *I was to taste in little the grief*
> *That comes of dogs' lives being so brief,*
> *Only a fraction of ours at most.*

My family veterinarian saw Sparky through.
I saw Maggie through.

After those two doors closed, **Hazel** entered through an open one. My late partner, Allen, and I decided to adopt a dog. Since we both worked and were away from home during the day, we planned to adopt two dogs so that they would be company for one another.

As we started the adoption process, "Must play well with other dogs" topped our list of requirements. The animal shelter assured us that Hazel loved other dogs, so we brought her home. She was a mature, nine-months-old puppy. She was house trained within a week. She jogged right past her chewing stage. She never jumped up on chairs, sofas, or beds. She was well behaved, even off leash. Then came the day when she ventured to a neighbor's house and started a fight with a dog twice her size.

At that point, we knew that we would not adopt another dog to keep Hazel company. She adjusted beautifully to our mountain home and to our professional schedules. We found ourselves molding our lives around hers, taking more and more vacations at dog-friendly VRBO destinations. Though calm and serene, Hazel always looked like the reddish blonde Husky-Lab puppy that we first fell in love with. She played the part flawlessly right up until the night of her last day. **Allen and I saw Hazel through.**

We both knew that we would bring another dog into our life. But we were both quiet. For some reason—inexplicable to me, even now—I wanted Allen to take the lead in finding our new best friend, so I waited for him to initiate the conversation. When he did, he agreed to do the solo search, even agreeing to my single stipulation: no black dog. He understood why after I explained that one of my sisters had a black dog that died tragically.

After a week or two, Allen came home and gave me his angelic, twinkly-eyed smile.

"I've found the perfect puppy for us!"

"What kind?"

"I'm not sure. She's a mix, about seven months old, and she's been spayed."

"Photo?"

"No. But I met her today. You'll really like her."

As I found out, "Perfect Puppy" belonged to one of the hospital surgeons with whom Allen worked. Allen had arranged a visit for both of us the next afternoon.

When Dr. Stevens opened the door to greet us, a black puppy—yes, black, all black except for a small, white brushstroke on her chest that an artist might have forgotten to color over—made her escape and raced down the walkway. I sat down on the stoop and watched. The puppy turned, saw me sitting there, and came charging back—a whirlwind of short-haired, shiny waves—and sat down, smack dab on my feet.

The black puppy won my heart then and there.

I beamed Allen my widest smile. "She's going home with us."

We worked out the details with Dr. Stevens. Allen wanted to bring our new best friend home in his Toyota Tacoma. I headed on home in my Jeep.

When they arrived, I was sitting in my reading chair in the living room. As if she knew exactly where to find me, the black puppy ran to where I was and sat down, smack dab on my feet, just as she had done at Dr. Stevens.

Allen sat across from us on the sofa, and the three of us stayed in position for the next several hours.

Finally, Allen got up. Without invitation, the black puppy jumped on the dark brown, leather sofa and put her head on a ruby-colored throw. The color contrast was striking, and, in an instant, I knew.

"Husband, I've got a name for our puppy."

"Yeah? What do you have in mind?"

"Ruby."

He came back into the living room, looked at her, then at the throw, and, finally, at the sofa. He knew, too. **Ruby** became our Valentine's Day gift, one to the other, each to the other two.

Ruby has the general build and gentleness of a Labrador Retriever; the face and solo-bonding bent of a Boxer, and the strong-willed temperament of a Beagle.

Whatever she is—and she's all of those things and more—she's the perfect dog that Allen sized her up to be when she was just a perfect puppy.

From the start, she knew how to show each of us equal love. She was always with Allen while he sipped his morning coffee and perused his various digital newspapers. She was always with me while I pondered evening academics online. She was always with both of us when we watched *Star Trek* or, her favorite, the *Great British Bake Off*. When Allen and I cooked, she always watched from the dining room door where she stayed until we finished our meal and Allen put his last bite in her dish. When we gardened, she ran back and forth between the two of us.

To Allen, the joy of feeding Ruby. To me, the joy of having Ruby smack dab on top of my feet whenever I sat down, or, as time went on, on my lap. To me, the joy of brushing her.

I usually brushed her in my office after finishing my evening academics, the two of us sprawled out on an Oriental rug. As I brushed, she would give me knowing looks from a far-off, far-away land. Invariably I felt the need to talk with her.

"I don't know who you are, Ruby, but I know that you are an old, old soul come back to see me through. Who are you?"

Ruby never seemed to mind my one-sided conversation. In fact, she seemed to nod in knowing affirmation. And I became more and more convinced of what I felt from the start. How can it be that I don't know who she is? And, yet, I have known her. And, yet, I know her.

The three of us continued our daily routines and rituals from February 14, 2018—when Ruby entered our lives—until January 28, 2021, when Allen lost his life, after a short, three-month, lung-cancer battle. **I saw Allen through.**

The rituals and routines, though not the same, go on and on and on. Ruby still likes to sit on the deck of an afternoon around 4:00, fully confident that once more she will see her other "daddy" driving up our mountain road in his Toyota Tacoma. Some days, I wait and watch with her.

What the three of us once did together, Ruby and I now do as the inseparable Dynamic Duo that we have become. She is always at my side, always by my feet, always within earshot. Listening. Watching. Waiting.

I hope that the rest of our journey—Ruby's and mine—lasts for a long, long time. With every passing day, I am more and more convinced: **Ruby is an old, old soul come back to see me through to the other side.**

NOVEMBER 14, 2022

Celebrating the Gateway to Who I Am

"I'm Mad as Hell, and I'm Not Going to Take This Anymore"

— (Rallying cry shouted by anchorman Howard Beale in the 1976 movie *Network*.)

For decades, I have gifted myself with special birthday gifts. I always buy the gifts months in advance. I always enclose a special note, reminding myself of how special I am. I always wrap the gifts in extravagant, over-the-top gift wrap. And, then, I hide them. With any luck, when my birthday rolls around, I'll remember not only the gifts that I bought myself but also where I hid them.

This year, though, I decided that one gift to myself would come a few days before my birthday and that I would share it with the world, right here in my blog.

Actually, on November 20, I will celebrate my 75th birthday. (Cards. Chocolates. A Viking Cruise. Any or all of those gifts are welcome. I used to include a 4-door Jeep as an option after the Chocolates, but these days I feel like a gladiator in the Jeep Gladiator that I drive. So I tossed in a Viking Cruise as a gift option. Just saying.)

So let me tell you about my birthday gift. I mean, after all, my life in general is so public that talking about one of this year's gifts shouldn't be a big deal. Right? Wrong. I had to think long and hard before deciding whether to go public.

Now, I'm betting that you're scorching to know what my gift is. I certainly hope so. I promise you that the big reveal shall come in just another candle or two. After all, 75 candles make quite a virtual glow, and I hate to blow them out too quickly. Oh, what the hell. I'll go ahead and blow them out. No doubt, they'll all light up again.

All right. The candles are out, so let me get glowing with my gift before they flame up again and distract me.

Simply put, I've had one too many: "How are you, **Sweetie**?"

Simply put, I've had one too many: "Can I help you, **Dearie**?"

Simply put, I've had one too many: "Did you find what you were looking for, **Honey**?"

Let me pause to reassure you. I do not think, not even for one nanosecond, that the people who greet me with those terms of endearment are being mean-spirited or rude. They have good intentions.

And let me pause to give you another reassurance. Greetings such as those often have strong regional ties, especially in the South. I grew up there. It's my home. I know.

Others who grew up in the South know, too. For example, one of my students in the Virginia community college where I teach had this to say when my class and I had a rich and robust conversation recently about **Sweetie**, **Dearie**, and **Honey**:

"I work in a grocery store, and I greet everyone that way."
"Even customers in their twenties or thirties?" I queried.
"Hmmm. No."
"How about forties or fifties?" I pursued.
"Fifties, maybe. It depends on how old they look."

So there. We have it. "Depends on how **old** they look."

As for me, I was born **old**, and I've always looked **old**. But it wasn't until my sixties and seventies that others started calling me **Sweetie**, **Dearie**, and **Honey**.

And, quite frankly, it doesn't matter whether the greeting is a regional, hard-to-break custom or not.

And, quite frankly, it doesn't matter whether the greeting is well-intentioned or not.

Such greetings fall into a category of their own—side by side with **Racism** and **Sexism**. The category has a name. **Ageism**.

All three—**Racism**, **Sexism**, and **Ageism**—diminish our humanity and push us toward being "lesser-thans."

Sweetie, **Dearie**, and **Honey** are especially diminishing in settings where the name is right there in front of the person who isn't calling you by your name.

Here's a perfect example. A few years ago, I had to have a CT scan at a nearby medical center. Obviously, I was feeling more than a little anxious. I needed to feel that regardless of the outcome, the person I was when I walked in would be the same person when I walked out. I needed to feel that regardless of the diagnosis, I would still be me. I needed to feel that I would still have my identity.

The diagnosis was a good one. But, sadly, during the short time that it took for the CT scan, I was called **"Sweetie"** two times, all the while that I was asked each time to verify my date of birth and my full name. Duh. I have a name, dammit. Why not use it? The check-in specialist as well as the radiographer were looking right at it while requiring me to verify it. By not using my name, I felt diminished and robbed of my unique identity.

More recently, the same thing happened when I went to my local pharmacy for my annual flu shot, the same pharmacy where I've been vaccinated for the last 24 years. I know everyone who works there. They know me, too. I've had many of them in one or more of my classes. The pharmacy technician approached me with the syringe and band-aid, midair.

"Name and birth date, please" was followed with, "Which arm **Sweetie**?"

Duh. I have a name, dammit. Why not use it? The technician was looking right at it while requiring me to verify it. By not using my name, I felt diminished and robbed of my unique identity.

Quite frankly, I've been identity-diminished and identity-robbed one time too many. And like anchorman Howard Beale in *Network* (1976), "I'm mad as hell, and I'm not going to take this anymore."

Here's why I'm mad as hell. And here's why I'm not going to take this anymore.

At this point in my life—as I approach my 75th birthday—my father is dead, my mother is dead, my oldest brother is dead, many of my closest friends and colleagues are dead, and my partner is dead.

One of the few things that I have left to remind me of my humanity is my name. My name is the gateway to my identity. My name is the gateway to who I am.

Without my name, I'm just another **Sweetie**.

Without my name, I'm just another **Dearie**.

Without my name, I'm just another **Honey**.

So here's my birthday gift to myself this year.

I will no longer allow others to call me **Sweetie**, **Dearie**, or **Honey**. I will no longer allow others to diminish my identity.

Whenever those well-intentioned terms of endearment grate my ears and pierce my being, I will rise up to the full height of my politest best, and I will do my utmost to turn those ageist moments into learning moments.

My come-back might be as simple as:

"Why, thank you, Elliot. I'd love it if you called me by my name: Brent."

Or maybe I'll try something like this:

"Thanks, Skyler. Do you know the most beautiful word in any language?"

"In any language? No idea. What is it?"

"A person's name."

"Really."

"Yep. Isn't that amazing. By the way. I'm Brent. Next time we meet, feel free to call me by my name."

Now that I've unwrapped my gift in this blog—right here in public—I'm thinking that this might just be the best birthday gift that I've given myself in a long, long time. I can't think of anything better than celebrating the gateway to who I am. Who knows. It might just be a gift that keeps on giving.

NOVEMBER 21, 2022

Hor(r)o(r)scopic Contemplations

"Frankly, anything I say to you is useless and probably more deceiving than revealing. I tell so much truth in my poetry that I'm a fool if I say more. To really get at the truth of something is the poem, not the poet."

— Anne Sexton
(1928-1974; American poet known for her confessional verse. "Interview with Patricia Marx, *The Hudson Review*, Winter, 1965-66, vol. 18, no. 4.)

Ask my siblings what they think of first when they think of me, and they will probably say, "Turkey." Mind you: they don't think that I'm a *turkey* as in *inept, stupid,* or *naïve*. In fact, they are proud of their baby brother. (When you're the youngest in any family, you're always the baby, even when you are a Septuagenarian.) And my oldest sister Audrey, an Octogenarian, is especially proud of my blog. She's patient enough to let me read my post to her by phone each week, the night before I publish. It's become part of our cherished routine.

But here's why my five siblings think of *turkey* first when they think of me.

They were born at home. I, on the other hand, was born in a hospital on November 20. By the time my mother and I made the trip back home—via an ambulance, no less! What an auspicious beginning, especially for a coal-camp baby!—she was not up to preparing the usual dinner for the occasion. It's a Thanksgiving they will never forget. I won't either. They won't let me. The horror of it all.

Obviously, since I celebrated my 75th birthday yesterday and since Thanksgiving is this coming Thursday, the connection between the two events is nearly as strong as it was the year that I was born and knocked my family out of a turkey.

Somehow that connection has set me to thinking about **other major** world, national, state or local events that took place the year that I was born. Maybe everything was majorly horrific.

Indeed, some say that things are rather horrific these days. Just last week I heard someone talking about how high grocery prices are and that it's getting harder and harder to bring home the bacon and eggs.

I don't eat a lot of bacon, so I haven't paid close attention to those prices, rising or otherwise.

But I'm always interested in what things cost. So I did some quick-and-dirty research. Right now, bacon costs about $7.22 per pound.

I know more about eggs than I do bacon. I bake a lot, and I buy lots and lots of eggs. Believe me: they are pricey at $3.95 a dozen.

Just for the sake of comparison, when I was born in 1947, bacon was 64 cents per pound. But don't start salivating for the olden days. Adjusted for inflation, that pound of bacon comes to $7.76. As for the eggs, in 1947, you'd pay 70 cents for a dozen. Adjusted for inflation $8.16.

But since it's Thanksgiving week, what about the turkey dinner? This year, it seems that a traditional, classic Thanksgiving feast is more expensive not only because of inflation but also because of supply chain interruptions and the avian flu. But just how horrific is it? The average cost of this year's holiday meal for 10 is $64.05.

In 1947, the same meal for a family of ten cost $5.68. Again, don't start drooling over the olden days. Adjusted for inflation, it would be $48.16.

Viewed from those inflation-adjusted perspectives, maybe it's not that much harder to bring home the Thanksgiving dinner, the bacon, and the eggs than it was 75 years ago.

But I have to share something else with you. (Thanksgiving, after all, is all about sharing.) While I was researching my birth-year food prices, I stumbled upon my horroroscope for 1947. Oops! I meant horoscope. Somehow mine always seem so horrible that the misspelling comes naturally.

Yet let me share something utterly amazing. Even when they seem horrible—and sometimes downright insulting—I still enjoy reading them. But, hey. Don't worry. I'm a savvy horrorscope reader. Here's the trick that I use to always end up with the best scopes! I keep browsing until I find the one that I like. Then I grab hold and refuse to let go. Be forewarned. I am Scorpio. I never let go. Proceed at your own risk.

Still with me? You are a Brave Soul, Dear Reader! Read on.

When I stumbled upon my 1947 horrorscope, I was so intrigued that I saved it in my virtual Horrorscope Folder, along with the thousands upon thousands of others that I have saved. Do the math. Start with the age of accountability. (For me, that was four; I was remarkably precocious and precociously remarkable. And, let me assure you: I was as modest then as I am now.) Continue from that age forward with daily, weekly, monthly, and yearly horrorscopes. I am appalled not by the numbers—I just did my own math—but by the fact that I just revealed so much to the entire world. Trying to cover it up now, though, will do no good whatsoever.

So I'll just keep right on with my reveal, picking right up with my 1947 horrorscope.

"Fierce, Intense, Ambitious, and Loyal. Scorpios question everything, and work hard to understand all things. Are very intense, loyal and kind. Jovial, Honest, Perfectionist, Protective, Inventive."

OMG! That is so me. I'll put this one in my Virtual Folder. **KEEP.**

On the other hand, maybe I'll **UNKEEP** it, especially the next part that I just now saw:

~~*"But do not take their easy going attitude for weakness. This element is known to be one of the most ferocious and powerful of them all. Be extensively cautious when they're in an off mood and don't force them into an unfavorable situation they don't want to be in."*~~

Hmpff. I don't like that at all. It's not me. Well, I have an easy fix. **UNKEEP.** Better still, I'll just redact it. There. I did it. You'll probably forget the horrific assassination upon my character. I hope so. Sadly, I won't. The insult will linger, long. And I will hang on to it, long. And I will get even.

Well, that ended up being an unexpected downer. Maybe I will recover by reviewing what my horoscope happened to be at the start of this year. I kept it, so it must have captured my fancy in one way or three:

"A brand-new Scorpio is emerging! Welcome reinvention vibes. The year ahead evokes an important process

that only happens a few times in your life. But first, you must shed layers of yourself that are no longer 'you,' parts of your identity that were constructed from pain or past experiences rather than forged from an authentic sense of 'This is who I am.' [...] A heart-fluttering new romance to artistic projects to buzzworthy fame [...] drawn to someone wildly different than your usual 'type' [...] Take charge of your erotic desires, even if that exploration takes you off the beaten path."

OMG. This is so good. Now I remember why I kept it. Thirst. **KEEP.** Yes. **KEEP.**

And what about November 19, the last day of my 74th year?

"You've experienced a tragic ending or two, and it's made you distrustful of the world. But, the truth is, things are happening for and not to you. [...] Embrace the transformation process [...] You're going to meet a new version of you on the other side of this storm!"

Bring it on! I am ready! **KEEP.**

Better still, what about my horoscope yesterday when I turned 75?

"You've breathed new life into romance today [...] You [...] get into an esteemed institution. [...] You'll be starting a daily connection with a new romantic interest who may actually live far away from you. Despite the practical difficulties, you are curious as to what this might develop into."

Damms. Romance? Far away? Be still, my beating heart. That's so good that I'm tempted to call it quits right here and now. And I'm about to wrap things up, but first things first. **KEEP.**

Since I started this post with food—turkey and Thanksgiving and such—I suppose it would be fitting and seemly for me to stuff a little more food into the post. Horrorscopic food, that is.

"Scorpios tend to love extremes, and they can get bored with some of the typical tastes of the Thanksgiving table, since it's the same year after year. But with its bright flavor and candy-colored appearance, cranberry sauce keeps things interesting. From its blood-red color to its intensely sweet and tangy flavor, it adds a complex yet satisfying zing to a Thanksgiving meal. No canned cranberry sauce on Scorpio's Thanksgiving menu, please!"

KEEP. UNKEEP.

UNKEEP because my good friend Fr—k and his good wife B—b and their good friend J—s are joining me for Thanksgiving dinner, and Fr—k specifically requested canned, jellied cranberry sauce. And he shall have it. ~~(And he shall never know that when I reached for the canned, jellied cranberry sauce, I had to use my smelling salts to keep from passing out right there in the grocery store.)~~

But to be faithful to my wild and exotic Scorpionic side, I will also offer up a second cranberry sauce, with fresh cranberries popping in Grand Marnier, along with orange zest, and ground ginger. I will add candied ginger after it's cooked, just to take it over the top. When I'm complex, I'm complex. When I take it up a notch or five, I'm better. (Thank you, Mae West.)

Maybe our hor(r)o(r)scopic contemplations aren't so horrible after all. Maybe we can control our narratives by making inflationary adjustments, literally and metaphorically. Maybe we can make judicious decisions about our narratives: what to put in ~~(and what to leave out)~~. Then, with a little luck and a smidgen of stardust, maybe our narratives—our self-fulfilling prophecies—won't be horrific after all.

NOVEMBER 28, 2022

The Joy of Baking

"Sharing baked goods with your friends and neighbors is a great way to feel connected or make new connections."

— Pamela Honsberger
(A family doctor and director of Physician Engagement and Leadership Development at Kaiser Permanente in Orange County, CA)

Thankfully, Thanksgiving is past. Don't get me wrong. Dinner was awesome. Turkey. Gravy. Buttered Green Beans. Creamed Spinach. Candied Sweet Potatoes. Jellied Cranberry Sauce. Cranberry Sauce in Grand Marnier with Ground Ginger and Candied Ginger. Homemade Dinner Rolls. Pecan Pie. Pumpkin Pie. Cherry Pie.

Far more important than the dinner, though, were my guests. Friends chose to give up Thanksgiving in their own home to spend the day with me in my mountain home. And they brought a new friend who also chose to spend the day with us rather than in his own home. I was truly honored by their company. (Thank you, Frank, Barb, and James!) And isn't that what Thanksgiving is all about? Being with friends and loved ones in a communal celebration not only of good food but also of life's beyond-measure blessings. How incredibly important it is to slow down on at least one day of the year to give heartfelt thanks.

But now that it's past, I'll return to my regular baking once again. The Jamaican Black Cake that I've been working on for weeks will take center-stage. The dried fruits—prunes, dark raisins, golden raisins and cherries—have been soaking in 140 proof rum and port (equal amounts of each) for several weeks now. I may very well undertake the bake this weekend. I have never baked a Jamaican Black Cake before, but last year my Strasburg (Virginia, not Austria) correspondent shared a *New York Times* article with me about Jamaican Black Cakes. This year, I am filled with joyful anticipation of the soon-to-happen bake.

I have been an incredibly busy baker this entire year. Muffins. Scones. Bread. Fruitcakes.

What prompted my baking frenzy was simple. I resurrected my love of sourdough, and I created a culture of my own using nothing more than flour, well water, mountain spores, time, and patience. No doubt you remember my "Oh, No! Sourdough!" (If not, this would be the perfect time to read it, right after you finish reading this post.)

I've had lots of fun with the sourdough muffins. I like big ones, and mine are bakery-style jumbo muffins. The Morning Glory Muffins proved, perhaps, the most popular, followed by the Triple Chocolate Muffins. But the White Chocolate Macadamia Nut Muffins were favored by many people. So were the Lemon Blueberry Muffins and the Banana Blueberry Muffins. Several muffin aficionados even claimed that my Banana Blueberry Muffins were the best they had ever had during their extensive world travels. (Being a suck-up will get you more muffins every time!)

Most recently the Pumpkin Muffins have been winners, only to be outdistanced by the Triple Ginger Gingerbread Muffins.

I've baked about **43 dozen or so** of those jumbo jewels, and I've shared them with students, colleagues, and neighbors.

The Sourdough Scones were a huge success, too: Banana. Banana Blueberry. Apple.

I baked about **7 dozen or so** in small batches, shared exclusively with friends and neighbors.

Sourdough Bread is up next! You just can't go wrong with regular Sourdough Bread, that is until you try Multi-Grain Sourdough. But, then, Parmesan Black Pepper Sourdough is a fierce flavor contender.

I baked about **34 loaves** of Sourdough Bread, and I shared them with colleagues, friends, neighbors, and even strangers who became fast friends.

As for sourdough cakes, I baked one: a Chocolate Orange Bundt Cake.

It was so delicious that I ate the whole cake all by myself without sharing. I suppose, however, that I am sharing simply by mentioning it here and by declaring its deliciousness.

But I baked lots and lots of fruitcakes. No, not Sourdough Fruitcakes. I'll be foolin' around with them next year. I've found a few recipes.

This year I stuck with my mom's fruitcake recipe that she perfected during 70 years or so of baking. Her fruitcakes were legendary and the best, ever. You may remember my "In Praise of Fruitcake." (If not, this might be the perfect time to read it, but not until you finish reading this post.)

One year my mother baked 34 fruitcakes and shipped them to her friends all across America.

I didn't bake that many, but I am super proud of the **16 fruitcakes** that I baked this year.

Let me tell you a little bit about them. I know—and you do, too—that I teach English. But when it comes to math, I know all the numbers (plus the secret ingredient) for the 16 fruitcakes that I baked this year.

This is when I need a drum roll. (Great! Someone heard my plea and reached out. That might very well have been the most melodious drum roll that I have never heard. Thank you!)

So, with no further ado, here's the moment you've been salivating for. Here's what went into those 16 fruitcakes: 24 pounds of candied cherries; 16 pounds of candied pineapple; 16 pounds of golden raisins; 16 pounds of pecans; 16 pounds of butter; 16 pounds of flour; 9 pounds of sugar; 98 eggs; and 1 gallon of peach brandy.

All right. That's as much as I am willing to divulge. The special proprietary blend of spices is staying right here with me in my kitchen.

I will tell you, though, that most of the 16 cakes are bespoke. Most of them are gifts. However, I have set aside a few to share with people who don't even know they need a fruitcake yet. Won't they be surprised!

I imagine that you're thinking that I must be exhausted from all this baking. I'm not. The various joys of my bakes far outweigh the weight of their ingredients.

Here's why. So many other things go into baking. **<u>Planning</u>**. (I sometimes plan my bakes weeks and months in advance.) **<u>Research</u>**. (I love the research angle and find myself running culinary reference just as my mother ran Biblical reference. Right now, I am researching Sourdough Stollen and running reference on all the various recipes.)

Anticipation. (As I pitted cherries last week for a pie that one of my Thanksgiving guests requested—halfing one half of the cherries; quartering the other half; that was not his request; that was simply part of my perfect-cherry-pie recipe—I stood at the kitchen counter joyed beyond the tedium, simply anticipating Frank's first-sight and first-bite reactions.) **Performance against Plan**. (Do the bakes measure up? Most times, thumbs up. Sometimes, thumbs down. Sometimes, a trash can is a baker's best friend: it accepts and never tells. Trust me. I know.)

But at the end of the day and at the end of the bake, the greatest joy of all the many joys of baking—the joy that always rises to the top, for me—is simple. I can share it with you in four words:

The joy of sharing.

Actually, I can share it with you in one word:

Sharing.

DECEMBER 5, 2022

My Literary Fruitcakes

"It's always the same: a morning arrives in November, and my friend, as though officially inaugurating the Christmas time of year that exhilarates her imagination and fuels the blaze of her heart, announces: 'It's fruitcake weather! Fetch our buggy. Help me find my hat.'"

— Truman Capote,
(1924-1984; American novelist, playwright, screenwriter, and actor. "A Christmas Memory.")

It's no secret. I love food. I love to cook. I love to bake. And, when it's fruitcake weather, I love to lose myself in baking fruitcakes.

Yes. Fruitcakes. MAHvelous fruitcakes! Say what? You don't like fruitcake? No way! I'll bet that you've never had a really good fruitcake. Not to worry. I'm not going to try to turn you into a fruitcake or into a fruitcake lover.

But, hey. Come on. Show me a little respect, too, won't you? Just stop it right there. Right now. I've heard them all, heard them all already, all the fruitcake jokes.

What baffles me is how the ancient, noble, beloved fruitcake became the loathed butt end of some of the worst jokes in the world.

I'm tempted to blame Johnny Carson for them all. Every last one of them. I'm sure, though, that fruitcake jokes didn't start with him, but his fruitcake joke is, without any doubt in the world, the worst in the annals of baking. Maybe that's why it's the most well-known. I'm sure you know it. On his *Tonight Show* during the 1960s, Carson quipped:

"The worst Christmas gift is fruitcake. There is only one fruitcake in the entire world, and people keep sending it to each other, year after year."

People keep sending Carson's fruitcake joke to each other, year after year, too. Look. I just sent it to you.

And, no doubt, you've heard others like this one:

"Why does fruitcake make the perfect gift?

"Because the U.S. Postal Service hasn't found a way to damage it."

And who hasn't heard this one?

"If you don't like it, use it as a doorstop."

But it gets worse than any of those dried and false jokes that couldn't come to life if they were soaked in all the finest brandies in the world! There's one fruitcake joke that is truly alive and lives year after year in Manitou Springs, Colorado. It comes to life annually during its Great Fruitcake Toss, celebrated since 1996. People pitch fruitcakes. People launch fruitcakes. People toss fruitcakes. And if my post makes you want to pack up your cake and join the people, you still have plenty of time to make arrangements. The next Toss will be on January 28, 2023. No fruitcake? No problem. (Don't you dare ask for one of mine! You've got your nerve.) Rent one at the festival. You can, for one dollar. Go. Go on. Let your fruitcake fly.

That's quite enough about fruitcake jokes. I'm not certain how I got pulled down that rabbit hole anyway.

My intent was simple and straightforward. It occurred to me that it might be fun to explore fruitcakes in literature. No. No. I don't mean writers who are fruitcakes. They all are. (Trust me: I know firsthand.) I simply mean literary works about fruitcakes. You don't even have to like fruitcake to be intrigued by such a hefty intellectual pursuit, especially if you like literature—as I do—and even more especially if you like fruitcake, too, and I do (but only the ones that I bake using my mother's legendary recipe).

The first literary work involving fruitcake that popped into my mind was Truman Capote's 1956 autobiographical short story "A Christmas Memory" featured in the pull quote to this post. Even if you haven't read the short story, I'm betting that you've seen a movie version. I've seen several, but my favorite is from 1966, featuring Geraldine Page, one of my favorite actresses. (No actress can evoke heartfelt longing and nostalgia with a scrunched face better than she, and she did it at my tearful best in her *Trip to Bountiful*.)

What popped into my mind next wasn't a literary work at all. Instead, it was a writer—one of my favorite poets: Emily Dickinson. Though famous and acclaimed today, she was an obscure poet in her lifetime—with only 10 of her poems known to have been published while she was alive—but she was highly regarded as a baker. Her father would only eat bread that she had baked. Recluse though she was, children in Amherst (MA), where she lived from 1830 to 1886 and only left on three occasions, would stand in the yard beneath her bedroom window as she lowered baskets of her freshly baked gingerbread. She was especially known for her black Caribbean Christmas cake. Houghton Library at Harvard University owns Dickinson's handwritten recipe and the tradition of baking her cake continues today. It is so important that Canadian poet M. NourbeSe Philip wrote an essay, "Making Black Cake in Combustible Spaces." She will read it as part of a moderated conversation from Dickinson's home on December 12, 2022: "The Emily Dickinson Birthday Tribute."

I've never made Dickinson's black cake, but just this past weekend, I baked a Jamaican Black Cake that's close to hers. My home is still redolent from more than four cups of rum and port that I soaked all the dried fruits in for several weeks before my bake. The cake is a beauty! I will let it age probably until Valentine's Day 2023. After I taste sweet success, I may reach out to Houghton Library and invite myself to join Team Cake, a group of Houghton bakers who recreate Dickinson's cake, rigorously adhering to her recipe, and share it with colleagues and friends on Dickinson's December 10 birthday. Wouldn't that be a grand culinary adventure. Look out Houghton. Here I come.

The next writer with a fruitcake recipe is none other than Eudora Welty—American short story writer, novelist, and photographer. Her fruitcake is on the opposite end of the spectrum. It's a White Fruitcake that sounds similar to mine. (For mine, I use brandy to soak the fruits before baking and to preserve the cakes after baking. If a little brandy is good, a little more is better, especially when it comes to fruitcakes.) Welty redeems herself, though, by adding a cup of bourbon to the batter. She redeems herself further with the note at the end of her recipe:

"From time to time before Christmas you may improve it with a little more bourbon, dribbled over the top to be absorbed and so ripen the cake before cutting. This cake will keep for a good white, in or out of the refrigerator."

Her fruitcake recipe—given to her by a friend, Mrs. Mosal—was immortalized in the 1971 Symphony League of Jackson cookbook for which Welty wrote the "Foreword," commenting:

"*I often think to make a friend's fine recipe is to celebrate her once more, and in that cheeriest, most aromatic of places to celebrate in — the home's kitchen.*"

See there. Books give life everlasting to everything, even fruitcakes.

Dare I confess that those three literary fruitcake associations—Welty, Dickinson, and Capote—were the only ones that I knew readily.

I suppose that I could end the post now, but I can't. Not just yet. If I did, I wouldn't get to share the fruits of my research.

So let me start by sharing when the word *fruitcake* was first used as a reference to a type of cake. 1687 is a long time ago, but, candidly, I expected the word to have been coined far earlier. I was a little disappointed. But, anyway, it appeared that year in a heading in J. Shirley's *Accomplished Ladies Rich Closet of Rarities*:

"*Instructions for a gentlewoman in making of marmalade, paste of fruit ... fruit-cakes, honey*" (vi. 38).

Since I was perusing the OED already, I decided to see when *fruitcake* was first used to suggest extreme eccentricity or insanity, as in **nutty as a fruitcake**.

It was first used in that context on March 5, 1911, in the *Chicago Sunday Examiner*:

"*Isn't Ethel a sweet girl, as sweet as a piece of cake?*"

"*Why, I think that she is as nutty as fruit cake*" (v. 5/2).

At this point, my research into fruitcakes in literature took a turn that surprised me. Really surprised me.

I browsed "famous short stories about fruitcakes." No famous ones.

Then I tried "famous poems about fruitcakes." No famous ones.

In a search of desperation, I tried "famous novels about fruitcakes." Again, no famous ones.

At last, I tried something straight forward: literary fruitcakes.

O. M. G. What I found left me trembling in my virtual research tracks.

I landed on an article with nearly that exact title: "The Literary Fruitcake" written by Don Webb. It chronicles the literary travels of one specific fruitcake, from its first gifting in 1843 all the way up to its being stolen on Christmas Eve, 1993.

The story line alone is powerful. Imagine. A fruitcake—whether beloved or maligned— deemed important enough to have survived for 150 years, without having been eaten; to have been passed on from one writer to the next; and to have been documented meticulously with every gifting. It is nothing short of amazing. I doubt whether most of us could document our own family lineage that far back with the precision that Webb achieves in his first-person narrative.

Aside from being a story of surviving against all odds, it's made all the more fascinating simply by the famous writers associated with the cake. They are beyond belief, but they are the very reason I kept reading the narrative. How could I not be aware of the fruitcake associated with so many famous writers?

Well, I was not. So I kept reading. In fact, once I started, I could not stop.

Queen Victoria, it seems, gave the fruitcake to **Charles Dickens** in 1843 after the first dramatic reading of his *A Christmas Carol*.

Some years later—in 1865—**Bram Stoker** stole the cake at a publication party for Dickens' *Our Mutual Friend*. For years afterwards he showed the cake to friends every now and then. But eventually the spell of the fruitcake novelty wore off.

When Stoker published his *Dracula* in 1897, he passed the cake on to **Arthur Machen** (*The Great God Pan*) who passed it on to **Algernon Blackwood** (*The Willows*).

Wouldn't you agree that this is deliciously fascinating? Yes, indeed. It is captivating. And to think that I still have to share how the cake was passed on through more literary hands for another hundred years.

Not to worry. I'll speed it up. This fruitcake was old to begin with and it's getting older by the word. But before speeding things up, let me state—just for the official record—that my interest in this narrative lies not with the fruitcake but rather with its famous literary owners.

After Algernon Blackwood, the fruitcake ended up with **Gertrude Stein** (*The Autobiography of Alice B. Toklas*) who didn't really want it, but her partner **Alice Toklas** persuaded her to keep it. It might amuse you to know that it was around this same time that Alice came up with her famous recipe for hashish fudge. It might amuse you even more to know that the "recipe" wasn't hers after all. When her *The Alice B. Toklas Cookbook* was about to be published in 1954, the book had empty pages. The publisher added filler recipes, including one for Hashish Fudge submitted by avant-garde artist Brion Gysin. Alice was clueless and had never tested the recipe! Read all about it in the *Scientific*

American. Yes. *Scientific American*. Whoever says that the humanities don't matter needs to read "Go Ask Alice: The History of Toklas' Legendary Hashish Fudge."

But let's get back to our famous, traveling literary fruitcake.

Stein gave the cake to **Ernest Hemingway** (*The Old Man and the Sea*) who then passed it on to **James Joyce** (*Ulysses*).

When Joyce died, the fruitcake went to **Samuel Beckett**, prior to the publication of his *Waiting for Godot*.

Then in 1959, **William Burroughs** went to Paris to finalize publication plans for his *Naked Lunch*. While there, he managed to meet with Beckett—his literary hero—for 30 minutes or so. When he left, he wanted a memento and took what he believed to be a brick in the bottom of Beckett's closet.

As you might have guessed, it wasn't a brick at all. It was the famed fruitcake. Burroughs gave the cake to **Allen Ginsberg** (*Howl*) who gifted **Jack Kerouac** (*On the Road*) who passed it on to **Thomas Pynchon** (*Gravity's Rainbow*) who traded it to **Mary Denning** in exchange for her knowledge of Pre-WW II chemistry.

(Dayum! I didn't know that I could go so fast. **Note to myself:** Leave out all the nitty, gritty details and hasten the pace every time.)

Don Webb—the narrator of "The Literary Fruitcake"—bought the cake for $150 dollars, took it home to Austin, Texas, and eventually decided to eat it on Christmas Eve, 1993.

Sadly, when he and his wife came home that evening, they discovered that their home had been robbed. The thieves had taken the fruitcake along with other valuables.

The police never located the fruitcake. Over the next few months, though, graffiti began to appear on wall after wall throughout Austin.

And then I read:

"... *the driven thief released the intensity of his soul. ... We never sought out the writer, for we feared our presence might interfere with his process, but we grew fiercely proud of the words that covered our walls. Soon all of Austin was obscured by the words by the words of perfection:*

"'*We, who dwell in the holy shrines, will preserve this treasure unto the ends of time.*'"

It was not until then—not until the very end—that I realized: I had been had. I had been had big time.

I could not believe it: I, the English professor who knows fully well—and even warns his students—not to trust first person narrators, especially in first person accounts of fruitcakes passing through the hands of royalty and an incredible number of auspicious British and American writers.

If it seems too good to be true, it probably is too good to be true.

But it's okay. It's really quite okay. I've been had many, many times down through the years. Sweet Scorpionic revenge is always mine.

I just made reservations to fly to Manitou Springs, Colorado, so that I can participate in their January 28, 2023, Great Fruitcake Toss. I have reached out to Collin Street Bakery to see whether they will sponsor me.

Here's what I'm going to do for my Fruitcake Toss Extraordinaire that will make world-wide headlines. I'm going to wrap Duper Don Webb up real tight in all the printed and virtual copies that I can find of his "The Literary Fruitcake." And then I'm going to give a celebratory "Heave-Ho" as I catapult the nuttiest fruitcake of them all—the author who pulled off the biggest fruitcake heist ever and told the biggest fruitcake joke ever—as far into the thin air as possible.

For once, I'll let a fruitcake fly with glee.

DECEMBER 12, 2022

Turning Towards

"Respond to every call that excites your spirit."

— RUMI
(1207-1273; Persian poet whose work focuses
largely on love and mysticism.)

Are you wondering whether I omitted something accidentally from the title? I didn't. I left the title open-ended, deliberately. I'm hoping that it prompted you to ask, "Turning towards **what**?" Yes. Precisely. Towards **what**?

Towards this. Towards that. Towards everything. Towards everything that matters in our lives. Towards the truth that's right in front of us, the truth that's teetering on the brink of all.

As simplistic as it might seem, sometimes the greatest truths are the ones right in front of us, staring at us, bidding our attention, asking that we turn towards … the truth.

What got me to thinking about this truth—the importance of turning towards—is an article that I read a few weeks ago. Dr. John Gottman and Dr. Julie Schwartz Gottman, happily married for 35 years, have spent 50 years studying successful relationships. In one study, they were able to predict with 94% accuracy whether a marriage would last, after observing the couples for just 15 minutes.

"One of the biggest determining factors was how often a couple 'turned toward' their partner instead of 'turning away.' When a couple turns toward each other they make what we call 'bids for connection.'

"Bids can range from little things like trying to catch your attention by calling out your name, to big things like asking for deeper needs to be met.

"The happiest couples are savvy enough to notice when their partner is making a bid, and drop what they're doing, if necessary, to engage." (**"Here's the No. 1 Thing that Makes Relationships Successful,"** *Make It*, November 21, 2022).

When one partner makes a bid, the other partner can respond in one of three ways.

1. Turn towards—engage with the attempt to connect.

2. Turn away—ignore or not notice the attempt to connect.

3. Turn against—shut down the attempt to connect.

As I read the article, I swayed and nodded in total agreement. Of course. Turning towards—engaging with the intent to connect—is the truth that can make or break a relationship.

After my moments of affirmation, I had an epiphany. If turning towards our partner is the number one thing that makes our love relationship successful, why wouldn't "turning towards" other types of interpersonal relationships bring equal success? Family relationships? Pet relationships? Friendships? Acquaintanceships? Professional/work relationships?

And what about straightforward, simple things in our lives that place bids for our attention, bids for connection. Maybe they're so routine and so mundane that they've lost their curb appeal. Maybe we've turned against the bids. Maybe we've turned away from the bids.

But what would happen, for example, if we turned towards the bed to be made? The dishes to be washed, dried, and put away? The furniture to be dusted? The floors to be vacuumed? The windows to be polished? The trash to be taken out? The grass to be cut. The list is endless and never ending. Yet I wonder: what would happen if we turned towards—leaned in, faced, and engaged—those mundane bids for attention as soon as they called to us?

And what about bids that call to us from other life ventures?

What about work? What would happen if we turned towards our careers? The noble work that we are called to do? The opportunities that seem to fall in our laps? The opportunities that we can create because we have a vision, because we have a dream? I wonder: what would happen if we turned towards—leaned in, faced, and engaged—those work bids for attention as soon as they called to us?

What about our physical well-being? What would happen if we turned towards those pounds to drop? The muscle mass to gain or regain? The bike to pedal? The weights to lift? The marathon to run? The mountain to climb? The walk to the mailbox? The 10,000 steps a day? The healthy dietary choices? I wonder: what would happen if we turned towards—leaned in, faced, and engaged—those physical bids for attention as soon as they called to us?

What about our financial security, short-term and long-range? Our assets? Debts? Income? Expenses? I wonder what would happen if we turned towards—leaned in, faced, and engaged—those financial bids for attention as soon as they called to us?

What about our psychological well-being? What would happen if we turned towards accepting ourselves as we have been, as we are, and as we are yet to become? Towards the things that add meaning, give us purpose, fill us with hope? Towards all that brings us joy, contentment and delight? Towards our worst fears and greatest expectations? I wonder what would happen if we turned towards—leaned in, faced, and engaged—those psychological bids for attention as soon as they called to us?

What about our spiritual well-being? Interestingly enough, many world religions reinforce the importance of turning towards. Buddhists often turn towards the East. Christians turn towards the Cross. Jews turn towards the Wailing Wall. And Muslims turn towards Mecca. I wonder what would happen, regardless of our belief or our unbelief, if we turned towards—leaned in, faced, and engaged—that spiritual bid for attention as soon as it called to us?

And, then, ponder this. If we spent our lives turning towards—leaning in, facing, and engaging—all the things that really matter, what do you suppose would happen when the time comes that we must turn towards death itself? I cannot help but believe that we would be ready to lean in, face, and even embrace that most unknown of all the Holy Unknowns, fully confident that the truths we turned towards throughout our life's journey will see us safely through to the Great Beyond.

DECEMBER 19, 2022

Growing Up More than Once

"When I let go of what I am, I become what I might be."

— Lao Tzu
(Ancient Chinese Philosopher and Writer;
Founder of Taoism)

The idea for today's post exploded magically in my head one Friday morning last spring as I drove to campus for a Creative Writing class. I started thinking about the fact that Fall 2022 would be my last semester as a full-time Professor of English at Laurel Ridge Community College. In the midst of my reverie, I had an insight. I've been blessed with the luxury of growing up more than once.

Now I'm writing about that epiphany of many months ago. Candidly, until I started working on this post, I hadn't given a lot of thought to the meanings that the expression "growing up" can have.

The most common, of course, relates to the challenges that we all face as we progress from childhood through puberty into early adulthood.

That meaning goes all the way back to the Coverdale Bible of 1535:

> *"The childe Samuel wente and grewe up, & was accepted of the Lorde & of men"* (1 Samuel ii. 26).

Sometimes, however, the expression can be used to criticize someone who is being silly or unreasonable. I'm thinking of that memorable line in J. D. Salinger's 1951 novel, *Catcher in the Rye*:

> **"For Chrissake, grow up."**

I'm not certain that anyone has ever told me to "grow up." When I was young, people told me that I was old for my age. Now that I am older, people tell me that I am young for my age.

Be that as it may, I've never considered "growing up" as a once-in-a-lifetime rite of passage where we make it to adulthood. One day, we arrive. One day, we've grown up. Voila!

For me, "growing up" has been an ongoing journey from Point A to Point B, where Point B is never the end. Instead, it becomes the starting point of another journey.

Let me explain.

Many people might assume that since I was born in the coalfields of Southern West Virginia my Point A of "growing up" was related directly to "getting out." Even today, West Virginia is the fifth poorest state in the nation. Without doubt, I remember vividly and well the hardships of poverty—the challenges of living from paycheck to paycheck.

What I remember far more are the values and hard work ethic that my dad (a coal miner) and my mother (a fundamentalist minister) instilled in me. What I remember far more is that they taught me to appreciate, value, and celebrate diversity. What I remember far more is that they taught me to embrace and accept everyone.

What I remember far more are the educators who knew the subjects that they taught and who taught those subjects with passion. What I remember far more are the educators who loved their students and took personal interest in us. They were living witnesses to everyone in the coal camp: we could transform our lives through education just as education had transformed their lives.

For me, my first "growing up" had nothing to do with "getting out." It had everything to do with getting educated. It had everything to do with going to college.

By the third grade, I was telling everyone that I was going to be an English Professor. Looking back, I wonder what planted that idea in my head. I had never met a professor. None lived in my coal camp or in the slightly larger town where we moved when I started the third grade. I had no idea whatsoever what an English Professor did. I had no idea what I would have to do to become one. But I minced no words about it. I was going to become an English Professor. Yet, how could that ever happen? I would have to go to college and that would cost big bucks that my parents didn't have. Where would the money come from? My teachers and my parents had answers for me. "Work hard. Do your best. Get good grades." After a few years of seeing my commitment to academic success, they expanded their answer: "Keep it up. You'll get scholarships. You'll see."

And that's exactly what I did. I went forward with faith, and, as a rising high-school senior, I started the college-application process. Acceptance letters came one by one but without any scholarship offers. I felt good—really good—

about being accepted. Sure. Feeling good would pay tuition. Sure. Feeling good would pay for textbooks. Sure. Feeling good would pay for room and board. Yep. I felt good.

Doors were opening for me to get educated, but, ironically, I couldn't pay to cross the threshold.

Then, just a month or two before graduating third in my class, I received a letter from Alderson-Broaddus University that changed my life forever. I had been accepted with a comprehensive financial aid package—scholarships, Work Study, and student loans—that covered all expenses.

Can you imagine. Me. A hard-working, coal-camp kid with a dream, going off to college. Me. The first in my family to go to college. I pinched myself, and off I went to college.

As part of my studies at Alderson-Broaddus, I had two academic internships in Washington, D.C. One was with Senator Robert Byrd, doing administrative tasks in his office and delivering mail to United States Senators. The second was with the former Department of Health, Education, and Welfare—Division of Two-Year Colleges.

When I graduated cum laude from Alderson-Broaddus in 1969 with a Bachelor's Degree in the Humanities, I landed a position at the Library of Congress, as an editor in its MARC Project. After a year, I moved up and became an editor in the National Union Catalog, Pre-1956 Imprints, hailed as the bibliographic wonder of the world.

Can you imagine? Me. The hard-working, coal-camp kid with a dream and three books in his early childhood home—the King James Bible; Webster's Dictionary; and Sears Roebuck Catalog—working as an editor in the world's largest library, the place with all the books.

I pinched myself over and over again. I was living in my own apartment in the shadow of the Nation's Capitol. I was working in the world's premier library. I was a federal employee with a handsome salary and first-rate benefits.

I had grown up. Or so I thought.

Three years into my federal career, I got hooked on research. The yearning for more learning descended upon me, and I realized that I needed to grow up again.

Off I went to the University of South Carolina where I earned my Ph.D. in American Literature, where I became a Mary E. Wilkins Freeman scholar, and where I experienced, for the first time, the joy of teaching.

I was armed with credentials, but I had only one college professorship offer, with a salary so low that I could not afford to accept the position.

I went back home to the Library of Congress where I remained for a total of twenty-five years. I continued my Freeman research and published *The Infant Sphinx: The Collected Letters of Mary E. Wilkins Freeman* (Scarecrow Press, 1985). I worked with the best professionals in the federal sector. I continued my earlier work as an editor in the *NUCPP-Pre-1955 Imprints*. I became the Training Coordinator for the United States Copyright Office and then Director of the Library's Internship Program and after that Special Assistant for Human Resources, giving HR advice to department heads as well as to two Librarians of Congress.

I spent a total of twenty-five years as a federal employee, as a researcher, and as a scholar.

Surely, I had grown up. Or so I thought.

But when I turned fifty, I started feeling antsy about that childhood dream of becoming a Professor of English. I started feeling antsy about that childhood dream of long, long ago. I started fussing with myself every day and throughout the days:

"If not now, when."

On a leap of faith that I would find a college home, I took advantage of a 1998 early retirement from the Library of Congress. I sold my Capitol Hill home, bought myself a Jeep, and relocated to my weekend home in Virginia's Shenandoah Valley.

In August 1999, Lord Fairfax Community College (now Laurel Ridge Community College), opened its doors to me, first as an Adjunct Professor of English and then as a full-time Professor of English.

Some might say that my childhood dream was deferred for a long, long time.

Others might say that I had to grow up twice before I was ready to grow into the professor that I would become.

I tend to agree with the latter group. My education, my research, my scholarship, and my federal service positioned me to move into academe at the perfect moment. I was prepared for my teaching journey. I was ready for my teaching journey.

Now I have come full circle to where this post began. After twenty-three years, this semester was my last one as a full-time professor at Laurel Ridge Community College. On Friday, December 9, I taught my last class there as a full-time professor.

What an incredible journey it has been! I am so grateful to my Laurel Ridge family who have journeyed with me. And I'm even more grateful to more than 7,000 students, who believe —no, more than 7,000 students who know— that an education will transform their lives just as my life was transformed by education. I am pleased beyond measure that they let me be their learning coach. Every day, they gave me one more chance to do it better. Every day, they gave me one more chance to get it right. Every day, they let me be, me. Every day, they let me be a part of the magic.

Surely, I am grown up now.

I daresay that you have guessed it already. I'm not. In fact, I just heard someone say:

"The good professor is going to grow up again."

Yes. That's exactly what I'm going to do, for the fourth time in my life. I just did some quick and dirty math. It seems to me that each time I grow up takes nearly twenty-five years. With a little luck, the next growing up will take about the same number of years and will be filled with lots of scholarly research, writing and publishing; lots of teaching; and lots of service. Who knows. Only time will tell.

But here's how I see things right now. By the time I reach 100, I might have grown up. And, if I haven't, I'll keep right on with the important work of becoming what I might be.

DECEMBER 25, 2022

Fruitcake Magic

"From time to time, I savor a slice, but I'm parceling it out ever so rarely and ever so thinly. I want the magic of this fruitcake to last forever."

Let me tell you about the magic of fruitcake. I know. You probably think that's a ridiculous claim. Most folks hate fruitcakes because they're hard and dry and filled with citron and raisins and Lord knows what all. Most are so bad that jokesters rightfully disparage them as next year's paperweights or doorstops.

Obviously, those naysayers never tasted one of my Mom's fruitcakes. Obviously, those naysayers never experienced the magic of my Mom's fruitcakes. For time immemorial—seventy years, perhaps longer—she perfected her fruitcake recipe, recording her adjustments religiously. For one single, seven-pound fruitcake, she uses four pounds of cherries, golden raisins, pineapple, and pecans. For her batter, she mixes just enough to hold the fruit and nuts together, and it's rich with a half dozen jumbo eggs, a pound of butter, and a magical blend of lemon juice, vanilla, freshly grated nutmeg, cinnamon, and allspice. And when it comes to fruitcakes, Mom's no tee-totaler. Her fruitcakes are redolent with booze. She soaks the fruit in brandy before baking, and, once her baked cakes have cooled, she nestles them in thick layers of brandied cheesecloth, replenished weekly—starting in August when she bakes her cakes and continuing through Christmas when she gives them away.

Mom shared her treasured, secret recipe with me, right after two strokes in quick succession left her paralyzed in both legs and one arm. She was 92 then. It was the last year that she made her fruitcakes, from start to finish.

For the next few years, I made the fruitcakes. Everyone raved, even Mom. To me, however, something magical seemed missing.

Then, one year, my oldest sister called, claiming the ritual as hers. Mom had given her the recipe, too.

My sister followed it with precision, but as she started spooning the batter into the tube pan, she broke down in tears. She phoned Mom, who lived just two houses away.

"It's all mixed," she sobbed, "but it's not going in the pan right."

"Audrey, bring it on down here and prop me up in bed. I'll show you how to do it."

My sister went down and propped Mom up. With her one good arm and all the love and courage that she could muster, Mom packed the batter into the pan, pressing it down with the back of a wooden spoon, as only Mom knows how to do. Then she adorned the top with a ring of brandied, candied fruit flowers, just like always. Undoubtedly, that fruitcake was her most beautiful, ever, and it tasted just as first-rate as any Mom ever made all by herself.

My sister gave me a huge hunk of that love-laden fruitcake—undoubtedly, the best in the world and, sadly,

Mom's last. I have it wrapped in brandied cheesecloth, and I keep it in the freezer, the same way that Mom always kept one or more fruitcakes, from one year to the next. From time to time, I savor a slice, but I'm parceling it out ever so rarely and ever so thinly. I want the magic of this fruitcake to last forever.

DECEMBER 26, 2022

Finding Far More than My Fitbit

"When you bring the light into your dark house, that is when you see the cobwebs and spiders."

— RAJNEESH
(1931-1990; Indian spiritual leader who preached an eclectic doctrine of Eastern mysticism, individual devotion, and sexual freedom.)

Those who know me well know how much I live by my Fitbit. Those who read my blog posts regularly know it, too, and no doubt remember my "Fit as a Fiddle: The Inefficient Way."

I swear by my Fitbit so much mainly because I consider it to be my Doc-in-a-Watch, not that I need a doc in my watch or anywhere else, for that matter. My once-a-year doctor doesn't like it too much when I tell her all about my Fitbit. Her skepticism always prompts me to give her an accelerated show-and-tell Fitbit Continuing Medical Education session, explaining everything that my Fitbit monitors and tracks:

- *Steps per hour and per day.*
- *Sleep score—duration, deep sleep and REM sleep, and restoration.*
- *Exercise readiness score.*
- *Skin temperature.*
- *Resting heart rate.*
- *Breaths per minute.*
- *Heart rate variability.*
- *Blood oxygenation.*
- *Atrial fibrillation.*

My Fitbit and I are so connected that it leaves my bod for two reasons and two reasons only.

The first is when it needs to be recharged. I time ~~my~~ its rechargings precisely so that my Fitbit doesn't lose track of my steps and other vitals. The charger is on my kitchen counter, right next to my other life force—the coffee pot.

The second occasion that my Fitbit leaves my bod is just before I step into the shower. Then I put it on the shelf right below my toiletry cabinet. As soon as I step out of the shower and dry off, I put my Fitbit back on my wrist and go about my day.

My method of living a Fitbit life was foolproof until Friday, December 16. I knew in advance that the day would be charged emotionally. I had to attend my college's end-of-year celebration, where some colleagues who were retiring would be recognized. I fell into that category, too, but I am not **ret—ing**, even if I would be recognized as such. There's a really negative word embedded in re**TIRED**. Yep. You guessed it. **TIRED**. And to pick up a title from one of my favorite James Cleveland spirituals,

"I Don't Feel No Ways Tired."

Here's the second reason that December 16 became charged emotionally. The day before, an Arctic blast hit our region, iced over my mountain world, and iced me indoors. Dang. How could I be recognized if I couldn't make it to the celebration?

On the morning of the event, it looked as if my icy world had melted a little, but I wasn't quite sure since it was nowhere near daylight. I started fretting.

I continued to fret when I took my shower. I continued to fret when I dried off. I continued to fret when I went upstairs to dress for the day.

By then it was daybreak, and I could tell that my mountain road was clear enough for me to Jeep off.

I kept on readying myself, and just as I put on my bracelet, I realized that I had not put on my Fitbit.

I raced back downstairs to get it, and to my horror, it was not on the shelf where I knew that I had left it.

Maybe I left it on my desk? Nope.

Maybe on the charger? Nope.

On my dresser? Nope.

Maybe it came unclasped and fell on the floor? I walked all through the house. Nope.

I repeated the trek. Nope. The Fitbit was not to be found.

I couldn't continue looking. I had to head off to the college celebration. All the way there, I played and replayed every move that I had made earlier in the morning. I couldn't put it out of my mind.

When I arrived and met up with one of my best friends, I blurted out:

You won't believe what I did this morning. I lost my Fitbit, right in my own home.

Jenni knows me all too well:
How do you know whether you're alive?
I'm not. Without my Fitbit, I'm not alive! I have no stats whatsoever! I'm not even sure that my heart is beating.

I managed to distract myself from time to time during our three-hour celebration, but as soon as I started my drive back home I replayed, once again, every move that I had made.

As soon as I walked in the front door, I decided to get out my brightest flashlight and shine it systematically everywhere throughout the house. The damned Fitbit had to be there, somewhere. I looked all over the floors. I looked on top of every piece of furniture. I looked behind every piece of furniture. I wanted my damn Fitbit, dammit, and I wanted it right then and there. I hope that you are sensing my desperation.

What I did not want were the cobwebs that I found. Yes. Cobwebs. Now I was doubly horrified! For real. I was appalled. In fact, my heart sank, even if I didn't have my Fitbit to log and record the sinking. How could this be? I mean. I know that I tease a lot about housecleaning. Who does not remember my riveting and memorable post "My Imaginary Guests"? More important, I had cleaned house thoroughly for my Thanksgiving guests. And the month before I had cleaned house thoroughly for Veteran's Day guests. And I could keep rolling the calendar back, and I could keep talking about how I cleaned house for this occasion or that occasion or for this guest or for that guest.

But what good would that do me? I had shined a light, and I had seen those cobwebs. The horror or it all. Cobwebs. I thought that I was doing a near spic-and-span job with my cleaning.

My first impulse was to have at the damned cobwebs that had taken me unawares. But how could I? I wanted them gone. All gone. Right now. That would require tackling my entire home, room-by-room.

My second thought was simple:

This is no big deal. Sit down and work out a plan.

That's just what I did. But alas! As I worked out my plan, I became even more horrified.

The cobwebs that I had found—the cobwebs that I didn't even know were lurking in unseen and unvisited spots—were real ones. Their little filament lines looked like fluffy dust streamers. And from time to time I could even see anchor points attaching the web to the walls.

But somehow I started thinking about metaphorical cobwebs. What cobwebs would I find if I shined a light into the nooks and crannies, the corners and crevices, and all of out-of-the-way places in all the other areas of my life. Dare I look? What would I find? Would you be brave enough to look at your metaphorical cobwebs in the areas of your life? What would you find?

I started thinking about my grieving for my late partner Allen. Am I as healed and whole as I sometimes think? Or if I shined a bright light, what unexpected cobwebs might I find?

What about my prayers? Am I as celebratory in prayer as I have reason to be? Or if I shined a bright light, would I find myself on my knees only when I have needs?

And, bringing in something seemingly trivial, what about my refusal to talk about that **ret—ment** thing that other people do all the while that I'm **reinventing** myself? I wonder what cobwebs I would find if I shined a bright light on that area of my life?

To be certain, we all have areas of our lives where, from time to time, we might benefit by bringing in the light so that we might discover the hidden cobwebs impacting:

- *Our physical health.*
- *Our emotional health.*
- *Our spiritual well-being.*
- *Our financial health.*
- *Our relationships with others—at home, at work, and in our communities.*
- *Our intellectual growth.*
- *Our career growth.*
- *Our downtime and our playtime.*

Follow me? Of course, you do. You've got your own cobwebs lurking around in your life just as I have them lurking around in mine. Bright light. Bright light.

And what about me and my Fitbit fixation? Dare I shine a bright light on that area of my life? Oops! I think that I just did that in this post.

Oh. By the way. I found my Fitbit, but not with my bright light. When my bright light efforts failed, I broke down and bought the **Find My Fitbit** app for $5.89. You bet. It's a real app, and it really works. It led me right to where my Fitbit had fallen down between the bathroom wall and the back of the toilet tank.

I was thrilled that I found it. I was thrilled that I was whole once more. But I was even more thrilled that I had found far more than my Fitbit.

About the Author

DR. BRENT L. KENDRICK taught more than 7,000 students at Laurel Ridge Community College (Middletown, VA) over a twenty-three-year career. They applaud his enthusiastic, passionate, and energetic teaching style. One student commented, "Dr. Kendrick could excite a stone to write."

He is widely known for his scholarly work on Mary E. Wilkins Freeman and is the editor of her collected letters, *The Infant Sphinx*, praised by *The Journal of Modern Literature* as "the most complete record to date of Freeman's life as writer and woman." He is currently working on a new, two-volume update—*Dolly: Life and Letters of Mary E. Wilkins Freeman. Vol I: The New England Years (1852-1901). Vol II: The New Jersey Years (1902-1930).*

He earned his Ph.D. in American Literature from the University of South Carolina. After a twenty-five-year career at the Library of Congress–where he received the institution's Distinguished Service Award–he relocated to the Shenandoah Valley of Virginia and taught at Laurel Ridge Community College from 1999-2022. The State

Council of Higher Education in Virginia (SCHEV) named him one of the top twelve educators in the Commonwealth (2008). He received the Chancellor's Award for Teaching Excellence (Virginia Community College System, 2010). He was a Chancellor's Professor (2012-2014). He was the first recipient of the Susan S. Wood Professorship for Teaching Excellence (2016).

www.ingramcontent.com/pod-product-compliance
Lightning Source LLC
LaVergne TN
LVHW091549070526
838199LV00030B/614/J